A Suspect Quartet

Four Aphasic Novelettes

Book 4: The Suspect Speaker Series

James Stephens

Published by DMS Publishing, 2025

A Suspect Quartet

This is a work of fiction.
Similarities to real people, places, or events are entirely coincidental.
Mostly.

First edition: April 2025

Epub ISBN: 978-1-0670747-0-8
Kindle ISBN: 978-1-0670747-3-9
Amazon Paperback ISBN: 978-1-0670747-4-6
IngramSpark Paperback ISBN: 978-1-0670747-2-2
Draft2Digital Paperback ISBN: 978-1-0670747-1-5

Internet link: books2read.com/suspect4

Written by James Stephens
email: james.stephens.dms@gmail.com
facebook: https://bit.ly/3bH6kZr

Books by James Stephens:

The Suspect Series Series:

Suspect Speaking

Epub ISBN: 978-0-473-56625-8
Kindle ISBN: 978-0-473-56626-5
Paperback ISBN: 978-0-473-56624-1
Internet link: books2read.com/suspectspeaker

More Suspect Speaking

Epub ISBN: 978-0-473-62486-6
Kindle ISBN: 978-0-473-62487-3
Paperback ISBN: 978-0-473-65881-6
Internet link: books2read.com/moresuspectspeaking

Even More Suspect Speaking

Epub ISBN: 978-0-473-71238-9
Kindle ISBN: 978-0-473-71239-6
Paperback ISBN: 978-0-473-71237-2
Draft2Digital Paperback ISBN: 979-8-224-09106-5
Internet link: books2read.com/evenmoress

A Suspect Quartet

Epub ISBN: 978-1-0670747-0-8
Kindle ISBN: 978-1-0670747-3-9
Amazon Paperback ISBN: 978-1-0670747-4-6
IngramSpark Paperback ISBN: 978-1-0670747-2-2
Draft2Digital Paperback ISBN: 978-1-0670747-1-5
Internet link: books2read.com/suspect4

The Suspect Speaking Series

Aphasia is the loss of a previously held ability to speak or understand spoken or written language, due to disease or brain injury. *The Suspect Speaking Series* features stories and poems and novelettes about people who have difficulty in verbal communication. People with aphasia.

People with aphasia have individual communication difficulties:

- some can't read very well, or their attention span is limited
- some have impaired vision so reading text is difficult
- some can't find the sense in the syntax
- some lack contextual understanding, or comprehension of ideas
- some understand the words, but they can't pronounce them
- some insert other words or phrases instead of the ones they actually mean.

The vocabulary of these stories is deliberately adult because aphasia doesn't diminish intellect.

The stories and poems give a taste of what aphasiacs go through.
More of the frustrations and blessings of life with aphasia.
Every day.
Every conversation.

The Suspect Speaker Series is ideal for:

- People with aphasia
- The carers, families and supporters of people with aphasia
- People who have no idea about aphasia but want to know more about the condition and, coincidentally…
- People whose main language is not English. The progressive versions are useful for English vocabulary.

Books 1 and 2 of the Series, *The Suspect Speaker* and *More Suspect Speaking*, have 15 short stories. Each have an A, B, and C versions.

- The A version is for people who have difficulty reading. The sentences are compact, the layout is spacious, and descriptions are sparse – perfect for people recovering from the effects of aphasia.
- The C versions are for people with aphasia who enjoy being *read* to – by carers, family members, and supporters.
- The B versions are in-between.

Book 3, *Even More Suspect Speaking* has seven short stories and poems plus a set of five interrelated short stories called *The Kumanu Group*. Each of the short stories has two versions: A and B.

A Suspect Quartet is the fourth book in *The Suspect Speaker Series*. It has four novelettes (well, three longer short stories and one novelette) about people with aphasia. The other three books had shorter and longer versions for each story. This is not the case for *A Suspect Quartet* but each one has short chapters, easier to deal with if your reading (or listening) stamina is limited.

The subjects are various: A celebrated but depressed artist and his protege, a Sci-Fi tale about a survivor of an explosion, a hunky adrenalin junky looking for meaning, and a fantasy involving an apprentice magician and his friends.

The stories are gritty, tragic, funny, and romantic.

Enjoy.
James Stephens

Acknowledgements

AphasiaNZ (http://www.aphasia.org.nz/)

and all their CAA's and management

Wellington, Hutt and Kāpiti Aphasia Community

Naomi Bondi: Speech Language Therapist

and an amazing rock climber

Cecilia McNeil: editor – a scrupulous but patient superintendent

And my whānau:

- my forebears – for genetics and opportunity
- my siblings for encouragement
- my wife – with a half of a century of care, tolerance and love
- my children who were immensely supportive, even if they don't know it yet
- and my seven…no, eight…no, NINE grandchildren who kept me grounded – sometimes literally.

A Suspect Quartet

1: Provocateur

2: Cypher

3: SKIDADDLE

4: The Muddled Mage

Provocateur

Preface :

I am part of an Aphasia Group that meets every fortnight with a Community Aphasia Advisor (CAA) under the auspices of AphasiaNZ. We follow a programme that encourages us to speak to each other in a 'safe and non-threatening environment'. It is a place where people with aphasia can say, comment, react with other people who know the difficulties of aphasic communication. Nothing is rushed. People can take the time to say what they want to say without others butting in.

One of the programme ideas is a *Word Of The Day.* I was looking up a word for one meeting and I came across 'SONDER'. John Koenig coined this term in his *Dictionary of Obscure Sorrows*.

Sonder is the realisation that each random passerby is living a life as vivid and complex as your own.

I looked at the 'aphasiacs' in our group. Over time, I had learned the biographies of these people and I was always amazed at the variety of their previous careers: top-level corporate management, big bank lawyers, truck mechanics, Post Office engineers in remote places around the country, business consultants, university lecturers, opera singers... But, you wouldn't know it when you met them. They had the huge variety of the communication difficulties that aphasia presents.

I wanted to explore this idea, this concept of 'sonder' in a story.

Reuben, Petro Pavliuk, Sue and the Aphasia Group were part of the story, but when I got into the details, the back story and the character's motivation – especially that of Reuben and Petro – it grew, and grew. I realised it was more than just a 'short' story. Their story was more compelling.

So, I removed this story, *Provocateur,* and wrote another short story about a journalist who discovers the meaning of 'sonder'.
Sonder is part of the *Even More Suspect Speaking* collection, book three of *The Suspect Speaker Series*.

Provocateur has the same group of characters as *Sonder,* the short story, but with a different slant in this 'novelette' edition. A prequel, if you like.

Provocateur

Chapter 1: A sentence

Reuben was the undisputed 'Magnum Graffiti Artiste'.

Well, that's what he called himself. He maintained that he was an artist. *Not one of those bloody tagging tossers. My art has meaning and fuckin' political significance. Yeah!*

His 'art' and its 'political significance' was a moot point, and somewhat controversial: skulls and skeletons; dismembered animals in pornographic poses; political and business celebrities in the form of chimeras; guillotine scaffolds; guns and explosions; carnage and murder… And where it would make the most impact: public walls, buses, train carriages, highway advertising signs, and bridges.
Yep. Controversial.

Caught by the police ten times with spray-paint-can-in-his-hand, he didn't admit that he had 'graffitied' at least ten times that number. *The secret was not explicitly signing my frickin' name. I signed my creations cryptically – my shit hidden in the subject. Ha ha ha! The fuckin'-pigs can't cope with that.*

But ten misdemeanours were enough for the police and the courts.

'I read your file and the statements from your social workers,' commented the presiding judge at the District Court hearing. 'I see you as an intelligent and able youth and clearly you have considerable talent. But this anti-social, this reprehensible blight on the public landscape cannot be tolerated. The public are outraged. Your images are not appropriate, especially for children.

'I see you are unemployed and collecting the Jobseeker benefit[1]. I sentence you to six months community service, with at least twelve hours served each week. You will report to the Johnsonville Community Centre, Thursday, next week. Your manager will report to me after that time and if your work is not satisfactory your Jobseeker support will be terminated. Dismissed.'

Huh? the sullen Reuben thought. *Aw shit! Twelve hours a week over six months. And my dole*[2] *could be fucked. Bugger! I guess judgie didn't get laid last night.*

Actually, Reuben didn't really need the dole handouts. His parents were rich. But divorced.

His business-man father remarried his secretary, a sultry, twenty-four-year-old college graduate. *Cradle-snatching*, was Reuben's indictment and he didn't get along with this young step-mother. *Gold-digging ho*[3] *with a shitty attitude.* Reuben moved into an apartment above the garage to avoid them, but *my old man and the bimbo were seldom there anyway. Always away – livin'it up somefuckin' where.*

Julie, Reuben's mother, remarried too. With her best friend Kirsten. They were somewhere overseas having a wild and footloose time – *Lesbian-shit in Singapore or Hong Kong or Timbuktu. Yay! Another new stepfuckin' mother. Whatever…*

Reuben was angry.

---

1 Jobseeker Support is a weekly payment from the Aotearoa New Zealand's Government that helps people while they are looking for work or can't work right now.

2 dole = benefit, the Jobseeker Support

3 ho = whore

As a way to be *semi-independent from my loser parentals,* he applied for the Jobseeker Support. The means test of his father meant he didn't get much money, but it was enough for him to get his graffiti equipment – the spray paint, brushes and solvents.

Now, it was all under threat.

Chapter 2: The Community Centre

He reluctantly reported to the Johnsonville Community Centre the following Thursday. The manager read his body language fluently: head bent, shoulders downcast, arms crossed, with a surly, resentful face. She had seen it all before – rebellious, disrespectful, sulky, ungracious youths. This attitude didn't fly with her.

'You will work at the Community Centre – six hours on Tuesday and six on Thursday. Okay?' she said with a no-nonsense tone. 'Sweeping and vacuuming the floors, cleaning the bathrooms, dumping the rubbish-bins, miscellaneous office work, and… ' – she hesitated and grudgingly Reuben's eyes met hers – '…volunteering for any groups that need you. Each month you will report to me about your progress. That will be the basis of my report to the courts after your six months is up. Okay?'

Reuben reluctantly nodded.
He knew that the 'Okay' was code for 'I-own-your-arse-for-twelve-hours-a-week-for-six-months-and-don't-forget-it!'

The manager smiled joylessly and showed him the cleaning cupboard and the layout of the community centre. Then, left him to it.

Twelve hours. Tuesday and Thursday. Cleaning the shitter, sweepin' trash… Bugger.

Despite his surliness, Reuben was a good worker and conscientious. He vacuumed and swept and emptied the bins and cleaned the bathrooms. He went to the staff room for lunch. The other staff and regular clients at the Community Centre seemed to be old, fusty, opinionated and gossipy.

Three of the older women bailed him up in separate incidents, and questioned him about his reason for being there. Reuben didn't expect this interrogation and he was fudging for an answer but they didn't wait for an explanation. Instead, barely waiting to take a breath, they carried on talking to themselves about whatever interested **them**.

Self-involved plebs with their own agenda, buttering their aggrandising karma before they kark[4] *it!* He escaped to the courtyard outside and ate his lunch in solitude.

After two and half hours there was nothing to tidy or clean up, so he swept the clean floors again and emptied the almost empty bins again for the rest of his Thursday sentence. He knocked on the manager's door so he could clock off. She gave him an impassive look. 'See you next Tuesday.'

Reuben was almost, **almost** tempted to graffiti the entrance to the Community Centre that night – *maybe, ancient rats eating their own and each others limbs, with a queen rat sitting at a desk in front of a computer…* – but the thought of his terminated dole made him bide his time.

Next Tuesday he arrived at eight-thirty nine. The manager glared at him, dramatically looked at her watch and tapped the dial ominously. 'Eight-thirty,' she mouthed. He stalked down the corridor to the cleaning cupboard. *What a bitch,* he thought. *Complete and utter bitch.*

After lunch the monotony started to get to him – cleaning, vacuuming, sweeping, trash collection, bathroom cleaning. Reuben was a creatively active soul – he couldn't stomach these tedious chores.

Shit! I can't do this gig. It will make me spare! Maybe I should look at volunteering?

---

[4] kark = die

He looked at the board in the foyer and studied the classes that the Community Centre was offering on a Tuesday or Thursday.

Kāpiti Coast ESOL
Gray OnLine – Internet for Seniors
Donald Trump Bridge Club
Twinkle Toes Ballroom Dancing
Kidz-Musik Bugz
Justice of the Peace service
Kāpiti Coast Aphasia Group.

Fuck! No gaming or Art classes.

Most of the groups were self-explanatory but he was not sure about ESOL on a Tuesday or the Aphasia Group on Thursday.
He googled them both on his phone. 'ESOL' was an acronym for:

`English as a Second or Other Language.`

Errgh. Not for me.

He typed in '`aphasia`' and discovered it was:

> `'a language disorder caused by damage in a specific area of the brain that controls language expression and comprehension. Aphasia leaves a person unable to communicate effectively with others.'`

He cleaned and vacuumed and swept and took out the trash, mulling over the possibilities.

That could be interesting. Better than bridge club or ballroom dancing. And Kidz-Musik Bugz – shit no, no, no! Yelling kids.

So…Aphasia? Maybe my art stuff could be useful? And no talking. And at least they will not talk me to death like most gerries[5].

---

[5] 'gerries' = a derogative term for 'geriatrics'

Chapter 3: Aphasia: research

On Thursday, Reuben dawdled in the corridors in the Community Centre and missed his usual lunchtime to make sure he could speak to the coordinator of the Aphasia Group. At last Room 3 opened and a collection of elderly and/or disabled people emerged. Aghast, he backed away to the wall of the corridor.
Human detritus! Gerries, spazzes[6]. How can you do anything with this lot…?

Before he could renege his decision, a bald man came out of the room. The man seemed to be paralysed in the arm and leg on his right side. He was stooped and his head was tilted like a tree that had seen too many southerly gales. He turned his intense gaze on Reuben. His smile was disarming, his intelligent eyes sparkled and, with a cheery smile and a sing-song voice, he trumpeted 'Goot maahning! Goot maahning! Goot maahning!'. Without stopping for Reuben's response he carried on down the corridor to the exit. His gait was an easy rocking motion like a wooden-wheeled toy with eccentric axles.

Actually, it's afternoon…? was Reuben's cerebral response but the sanguine greeting charmed him and he smiled unconsciously. Then he collected his thoughts and his negative decision.
Nah, nah, nah. Maybe not! I can't deal with these spazzies. Maybe Ballroom Dancing would be better…

As he turned to go down the corridor the door of Room 3 swung violently open and smashed Reuben's nose. Despite the tears that sprang into his eyes, he could vaguely see a young woman racing down the corridor waving a leather hat in her hand and calling 'Geoff! Geoff!' In the distance, the bald man turned slowly as the woman reached him and accepted the hat.

---

[6] 'spazzes' = a derogative term for 'spastics'

Reuben watched the exchange distractedly – he was more concerned about his nasal passages and the threat of getting blood on his tee shirt. When the woman returned to Room 3, Reuben straightened up and studied her.

She was Asian, about thirty, with jet-black hair in a ponytail. She had a nose piercing and several rings in each earlobe. Her slim body was clad in an apricot-coloured blouse, skin-tight jeans and stylish sandals. He stared at her appreciatively. She was suddenly aware of him, loitering at the door.

'Yes?' she questioned as she reached for the door handle and opened the door.
'Yes?' Reuben said dazedly, and confused.
'Are you coming to see me?'
'Ah…um…' Reuben thought quickly.
She's hot… Better than the other staff plebs. Maybe the Aphasia Group would not be bad. And better than sweeping and cleaning loos[7]*…*
'Ah…I am looking for volunteer work,' Reuben half-lied 'and maybe I could help with the Aphasia Group? I could help to…' He looked into the room and saw the morning tea paraphernalia and the board games gear. 'I could make morning tea or set up with the games or…'

'Oh! Well…I guess…? It would be good to have some help. Um…I am Sue. Sue Lee.' She indicated her name tag, braced the door with her foot, then held out her hand. Reuben dived in to shake it.

'I'm the CAA for this area,' she explained. Reuben's puzzlement was obvious and she explained. 'The Community Aphasia Advisor. For Aphasia New Zealand. Do you know about aphasia?'

'Sort off. A communication disorder?' he replied, his recent Google search saving him from embarrassment.

---

[7] 'loos' = toilets

'Well done. Most people have no idea!' She entered the room and turned to the mess on the table and rapidly gathered the spare biscuits, tea containers, coffee tins, sugar and milk and put them carefully into a bag. At the same time, over her shoulder, she remarked: 'So…you want to help? We have weekly meetings – from 10:00 to 12:30 – every Thursday.'

'Perfect,' Reuben said. 'My senten…my…I work on Thursday. So… Perfect.'

'Good. That's good.' Sue cleared the table and faced Reuben. 'Sorry…I have another appointment…I have to get these things…' She paused and looked at him intently 'Actually, can you help now? My meeting is in fifteen minutes, so… Can you get the tea and coffee cups and plates to the kitchen and put them in the dishwasher?' She smiled winningly.

Maybe, coquettishly, Reuben mused.
'Sure. No problem,' Reuben replied.

He transferred the tea and coffee things to a trolley as Sue began to gather her session material – the whiteboard markers, pens, paper, games – into her suitcase. Reuben surreptitiously studied her derrière. *Hmm. Nice arse.* Suddenly, Sue sat upright and turned, and Reuben panicked that she had guessed his salacious thoughts – but apparently not.

Sue said, with a pleading look on her face: 'Um…um…before that… can you do one other thing. I need these pages photocopied for my meeting. Can you do that? You know how to work the copier?'

He had no idea how the photocopier worked or if he could use it, but testosterone was standing in for rational thought. 'Yes. Sure. No problem-mo,' he immediately replied, and cringed.
What gives…? Problem-mo? Flirting? What a Loo-Ser.'

But Sue didn't seem to be put out. She located four pages from her folder and thrust them at Reuben. Affected by her brisk manner he raced out of the room and sped to the office.

The photocopier was warming up and Reuben slapped his thigh impatiently. *Surely, use of the copier would be idiot proof?* he prayed. At last the green light shone and Reuben placed the four pages in to the feeder, pressed the button and hoped for the best.

The photocopier clacked and whirred and grabbed the documents one at a time and inserted them in the bowels of the machine. It seemed to take forever but one by one the photocopies landed in the out tray and the originals went back into the feeder.

Reuben grabbed each one in turn, absently perusing the writing. Apparently it was a list of the participants in the Aphasia Group and the topics and subjects they were discussing.

Suddenly, his eyes focussed on one name in particular.
Peter Pavliuk.

Surely? It can't be? Impossible! Is it…possible? Surely not?

Dazed, he turned around and almost ran in to Sue, who was leaving the manager's office. 'Thanks! Thanks so much!' as she grabbed the photocopies and the originals from him and whirled off to the exit.
She turned before going through the door and shouted at him: 'The dishes? And can you meet me in Room 3 about 9:30 next Thursday and I will give you the programme? Okay?'

Without waiting for an answer she turned and left, the doors swinging shut behind her.

Chapter 4: Petro Pavliuk: remembered

Admiring her retreating body, Reuben thought back to the photocopied information.

Pete Pavliuk. Surely not? But 'Pete' is…is quite like 'Petro'. Maybe an Anglicised form. And 'Pavliuk' is not a very common surname. Could it….? I thought he was dead… If he is alive he would be…75? 80 years old? Could it be…Petro Pavliuk!

At high school, Reuben studied the works of Petro Pavliuk in his art class. By the time he graduated high school, he had come to revere Petro Pavliuk. Idolise him.
He is a legend. A god! I ***love*** *his art.*

Pavliuk became an inspiration for the young painter – then and now. The old man's technique and subject matter were often reflected in Reuben's – illegally – created graffiti works.

Reuben searched his memory.

Petro Pavliuk, born in 1943, was a Ukrainian immigrant, arriving in Aotearoa New Zealand as a six-year-old. He grew to be an avant-garde, radical painter and sculptor and influential performance artist.

He painted murals on walls, underpasses, pavements, bridges, vans, buses and ships that advocated a green environmental message. He painted them on these backgrounds because they could be seen from the houses, apartments and penthouses that surrounded them by their owners, these 'aristocratic fuckin' fat-cats', as he called them.

Usually the subject matter was controversial and challenging.

For example:

- A stylised world globe shaded by a nuclear mushroom cloud and cockroaches with military armour and helmets riding space rockets to the stars.
- A polar bear, seals and penguins with plastic bags on their heads lounging on an ice floe as if in a luxury spa.
- A coiled hydra, each one with a caricature of a contemporary politician, biting off birds' and animals' heads.

He signed his works as: PePuk.

He was amazing. Legend. A great painter and activist. And maybe, he's here?

'Are you zombified? Or just vacant?' his manager abruptly shouted from her office.

'No, no. Just cleaning Room 3,' he replied. He turned but spun back and poked his head through the manager's doorway. The manager had a frustrating but enquiring look on her face.

'Actually,' he said, 'I just spoke to the Aphasia Advisor. Sue Lee. I want to volunteer for that group. Help set out the morning tea and the games and what not…'

The manager nodded abruptly. 'Sure. That's okay. It will count on your hours, but make sure that the other tidying up, sweeping and cleaning is kept up to scratch.'

She turned back to the work on her desk. In his haste to get away, Reuben didn't see her smile. Sue had already told her about Reuben's offer.

Reuben cleaned up the remaining morning tea equipment, stacked the dish-washer in the kitchen and returned to vacuum out Room 3. But his mind was elsewhere.

Petro Pavliuk. Really? Here? I can't believe it? ***Here?*** *He is in the Aphasia Group? Coincidence? Or maybe it is a sign?* he thought.

It seemed to Reuben that a divine providence was manifest.

Hopefully.

Chapter 5: Petro Pavliuk: research

The next week limped along like a recalcitrant donkey. He couldn't wait for Thursday. In the interim Reuben used the internet and the local library to check if Petro Pavliuk was:

a) still alive
   and…
b) still active
   and…
c) possibly in this area.

He could not see any reference to a 'date of death' in the encyclopaedias. No obituaries.
Thank goodness. I guess he is still alive at least.

He rediscovered most of the art works and murals of Pavliuk that he had studied at high school. His younger exploits were well-documented. Reuben studied the photos of his red hair, straggly beard and muscular body. The artist was a live wire.

And there was more. Film works, cartoons, sculptures, mosaics and performance pieces – some a bit controversial.
Okay, a **lot** controversial.

For example:
Once, he painted a zoological and marine-, land- and water-scape on a plaza. In the middle he erected a four-metre pole with a platform at the top. He sat on the platform for two weeks while his acolytes ferried food and drink up to him using pulleys. He defecated and mixed his urine into the paints he flung down on the plaza below him, blotting out the painted creatures and plants. The title of this art work was: *Humans – deal with your own shit!*

With a contentious political election looming, he had himself suspended with a bungy cord, naked, alongside a warehouse wall for forty-five minutes, seesawing and bouncing, painting red, blue, green and black abstract forms, while his fans applauded. He called the work *Swinging vote.*

In the 1990s, Pavliuk was nominated for an MBE, a Queen's Honour Award for Art, but he refused to accept it. The newspapers made a thing about it, stating that it was an 'outrage' and 'an insult', a 'communist plot denigrating the Commonwealth honour'.
But that was water under the bridge, thought Reuben.

And he discovered that it was not the first time the media had vilified the artist.

In the 1980's Pavliuk had made international headlines with a controversial mural in the centre of Wellington. On the wall of a car park, facing the entrance to the Independent Mutual Insurance (IMI) National Headquarters building, Pavliuk created a mural highlighting IMI's investing in all sorts of ecologically unsafe projects – fracking, open-cast mining, off-shore palm-oil plantations, et cetera.

In the daylight the mural showed a contemporary bush scene with native trees, birds, geckos, weta and insects.

But at night, with the additional "glow-in-the-dark" pigments that Pavliuk had inserted, the mural displayed in – twenty-metre-high-letters – 'IMI is a F**k**g Nature Criminal'.

For people the meaning of the asterisk's was never in doubt but they made it difficult to class it as an obscene art-work. The police and the council were reluctant to intervene. It was sensation and many national newspapers featured it in their news reports.

The mural and its coded message stayed there for three weeks but 'somehow, someone' spilt litres of black paint over the wall destroying the mural.

If IMI was involved, as many presumed, this vandalism backfired.

Before it was a national incident, but after the destruction of the mural, the before and after images hit the **international** headlines. IMI were forced to go on the defensive and poured significant money into ecological and green-technology start-ups and organisations.

Brilliant. Fucking brilliant. And maybe he's here. My hero! Maybe I can meet him!

Chapter 6:
A Crash Course

On Thursday, Reuben beat the manager to the front door. He waved her on as she unlocked the door of the Community Centre but his declaration of 'Keen to work!' seemed suspect to her. Over her spectacles the manager stared at him but didn't say anything. Reuben rushed past her into the building. She grinned.

Reuben was already in Room 3 when Sue arrived at 9:30. She was wearing her skin-tight denim jeans, and a yellow t-shirt under a loose white shirt. Again, her hair was in a ponytail, and she wore a subtle gold necklace and matching earrings and her almost transparent make-up. Briefly, he looked her up and down admiringly and just met her eyes as she flashed him a sunny smile.

'Hi Reuben! You're bright and early!' She put her suitcase and bags down, and crossed to the folding tables stacked against the far wall, beckoning Reuben to help her.

Together they carried one of the tables to the opposite wall and put it down on its edge. Sue silently demonstrated how the legs folded out and a ring that locked it on the left side of the table. Reuben copied her with the legs on the right side. They turned the table right side up and Sue plonked her suitcase and bags on top.

'See? A lot of things can be achieved with no words at all. Most people with aphasia are quite aware that talking is over-rated. But, communication is important. Most people with aphasia can improve given time and patience. That's what we do for them in this session – help to improve their communication experience.'

They set out another two tables against the wall. Sue covered one with the name tags of the members and Reuben set out some of the biscuits, tea bags and coffee on the other. Then they unstacked the chairs and put them in a circle in the middle of the room. Sue sat in one chair and indicated that he should sit also.

'So – aphasia. Hmm…' Sue considered what she was going to say. With a shake of her head that sent the ponytail swinging fetchingly, she squared her shoulders and spoke.

'Aphasia: often it's a stroke-related disorder but it could be a brain injury, or brain tumour or an element of dementia. People with aphasia are not retarded – their mind and intelligence remains the same. If no other complications are present, their intelligence is okay.

'However they may find it hard to talk, write, read, and understand what is being said. The communication is …well, suspect. So – this group is for people **with** aphasia. We talk and discuss in an environment that is safe and appropriate.'

Sue studied Reuben to make sure he understood what she was saying. He nodded.

'What I mean about 'safe and appropriate',' she continued, 'is that most people with aphasia take a long time to get their sentences out. Often they are stuck on words or use the wrong word or the syntax is skew-whiff. In real-life situations, a lot of people talk over or interrupt them. Or the conversations are quick-fire, changing subjects or topics and the person with aphasia can't keep up.

'You know the concept of a 'tokotoko[8]'. A 'talking stick'?'

---

[8] tokotoko = a traditional Māori carved ceremonial walking stick. On a marae it is a symbol of authority and status for the speaker holding it.

Again Sue faced Reuben and searched his face for understanding.
'Yeah, yeah. I know the concept,' he answered quickly.

'Well – we don't actually have a 'talking-stick' but when a person is speaking, we don't interrupt them until they indicate that they want some help. Patience is the key. We persevere with them and don't interrupt them. It is very frustrating for the person with aphasia when **someone** finishes their sentence with what **they** think they were going to say.
'So – patience. And no interrupting or speaking **for** them.'

Sue studied Reuben's face with an intensity that was almost confronting. Gulping inwardly, Reuben carefully nodded and, satisfied, Sue went on.

'Okay… when I speak to them, I slow everything down.
S l o w . E v e r y t h i n g . D o w n .
'And we don't give them too many choices or options. For example, if I say to them: 'Do you want to go to the beach or the zoo or the library or a café?' – for them, all these choices make it too hard to answer. Better to give them questions with 'yes/no' answers or no more than two choices. Okay?'

Again, he nodded.

'Simplify the sentences. I don't mean 'dumb it down'. As I said, their intelligence is normal. They **know** the words. But, for them, a sentence should have one idea – not lots of 'and' and 'but' or 'also' words. No parenthetical phrases. You know what I mean?

This time, Sue caught Reuben's quizzical look.

'Um…' she looked at the ceiling for inspiration. Again, Reuben's testosterone came to the fore and he studied Sue up and down admiringly, but his higher self emerged just before she looked at him again. Clearly she had come up with another idea.

'For example,' Sue looked at him intently, 'Reuben, when you came in here, and I don't mean the other day but this time today, just ten minutes ago, I thought you were looking for another room, because you looked lost or puzzled and I thought you were looking for the ballroom dancing group also you were singing a song, like a waltz or a foxtrot, and that reminds me about another composer of dance music also it was on the radio, the breakfast show, the one with the guy who was the front person for that TV show on channel three…'

She paused for breath, and placed her hands before her, upright, in a supplicating gesture. 'See? Parenthetical. Too many phrases and ideas, all mixed up. Most people with aphasia can't cope with this number of ideas in a statement. So, we give them one sentence, one idea.'

Reuben nodded affirmatively. 'I get that.'

Sue breathed with an inaudible whistle and nodded encouragingly.
'So … Talking-stick. Patience. S l o w. D o w n . Yes/No questions. One sentence, one idea Okay?

'And another thing: not a problem with this room, but often distracting noises are difficult for people with aphasia – a TV, a radio, or too many people talking at once. That's a conversation killer for these people.'

Sue stood up and gestured a ta-da with her arms. 'I sure you'll figure it out. Just ask me if you are unsure. So – can you get the cups, saucers, mugs, spoons, plates for morning tea? There should be a trolley in the…'

'Yep!' Reuben said and got top his feet. 'I know where that is.'

He nodded and disappeared through the door.

In the communal kitchen he rapidly set up the morning tea equipment, added some cake forks and a stack of napkins and arranged them all on the trolley. On the way out he almost ran over the manager's feet as she came in for a cup of tea. 'Sorry! Sorry!' he yelled as he sped up the corridor. 'Just delivering to Room 3,' he yelled over his shoulder.

The manager stared at him. She didn't say anything but, again, a slight smile played on her lips.

Chapter 7: Reuben's First Meeting

When Reuben entered Room 3, a woman and man were speaking to Sue.

The woman was elderly. *Old. At least 80.* She had grey haired rolled into a loose bun, straggly bits like broken cobwebs. Her clothes hung loose about her frame but their colours were vibrant: orange, red, purple knitted jersey, royal blue skirt and purple leggings. Her brown shoes were misshapen blobs on her feet.

Reuben thought the man was at least 10 years older than the woman. *Old? Ancient!* His hair was a thin, ash-grey comb-over, and his face crinkled and wrinkled like a crumpled brown paper-bag. He was stooped and carried a cane in his right hand. His clothes were nondescript: khaki, brown, tan and ordinary black shoes.
Super-old and super-unfashionable.

Reuben parked the trolley on the wall beside the tea, coffee, milk, sugar and biscuits on the table. As he fussed about the things on the tray, Sue turned and announced: 'Reuben. Meet some of the team. Hannah and Norman – this is Reuben – he is going to help us with our session.'

Hannah and Norman greeted Reuben with a daunting enthusiasm. They had their name tags emblazoned on their chests. Norman had his hand out before Reuben could blink. He responded weakly. Handshakes were not part of his greeting repertoire.

'Hell...Hell...Hell-lo, Reub...Reubn...Reub-bin,' Norman spoke with a hushed voice. 'Glad for that...me...that could...out...it. Uurgh.' He wrinkled his nose and a sour and deprecating expression formed around his mouth. 'Sorry...sorry... Um...um...Good. Good.' All the while, the handshake went on and on.

Hannah interrupted that interminable-handshake by insinuating herself between Norman and Reuben and replacing his hand with her own.

'Reu-ben! A gut…good…name. Gut for …us that you ze…are…tut-ti.' Hannah had a marked accent. *German? Italian?*

The two of them stared intently at Reuben. *Like I am an interesting experiment.* 'Glad to be of…um…use,' he said lamely to the two elderly people.

Reuben returned to the morning tea table. Over his shoulder he saw other people in dribs and drabs. They all wore name tags. Every time, Reuben looked up expecting Petro to come in but he was always disappointed. Standing at the back of the room he lowered his head and surreptitiously glanced at the room full of aphasiacs.

So many decrepit gerries and spazzes, thought Reuben, wrinkling his forehead and shaking his head disconsolately. *What am I doing here? Sure, I want to meet Petro Pavliuk but where is he? And* ***what am I doing here?***

At 10:00am precisely, Sue stood up and addressed her 'audience'.

'Kia ora koutou, welcome everyone!' she said, looking around the circle and catching everyone's eye. 'Before we get on with our meeting, I want to introduce Reuben. He is going to help.' She gestured like a circus ringmaster at Reuben who ducked his head and nodded indeterminately into the space ahead of him.

There was a general hubbub of responses from the crowd: 'How-dee', 'Kya-a-aw-ra', 'Hal-low', 'Gut…gut…gut…hal-lo' and a tuneful sing-song 'Goot maahning! Goot maahning! Goot maahning!'

'Come here...come here...,' Sue called Reuben into the circle. Reluctantly, he approached from the edge of the room, sat down and glanced around at the 'clients' as Sue went on.

'Well...Norman. You are the chairperson for this meeting. Can you introduce the meeting?'

As Sue sat down Norman rose from his chair with difficulty, and, with visible effort, spoke to the group. 'Hell...Hell...Hell-lo...ever-ry-one. Ki-a-aw-ra[9]. What a beau-beauti-ful da-ay...hmm?' He glanced around the circle appreciating the affirmative nods from several members. 'Be...be...um...be-fort be-gin-ning...um... any ap-pol-pol...pop-ologees?

Sue raised her hand. 'I have some apologies for the meeting. Amina can't be here today – she has a doctor's appointment. And Steven and Klara are on holidays up north with their families. Have you heard from anyone else?' Sue looked around the group.

'Um...um...Yang has bu-zzy...bus-sy...with a birth-daa-ay it is...is... is it with famil-lee,' a Māori woman spoke.

'And...and...and...,' one of the men said, 'I thunk...thin...nk...that Abby-gal...Abby-gal...is not com...com...comm-ett...com-mingt.'

'Oh? That is a shame!' Sue replied to the man. 'She was going to talk about her trip to the Pinnacles. The Pinnacles over in Wairarapa. Beside Ngawi.' Sue looked around the circle.
'Have you seen them? The massive rock formations? They made some of the *Lord of the Rings* film there.' Sue nodded encouragingly but, apparently, no-one had been there before.

---

[9] Ki-a-aw-ra = An aphasic attempt on 'Kia ora', a Māori expression, literally translated is is 'have life' or 'be healthy'. It is used as an informal greeting or farewell equivalent to 'hi', 'hello', or 'goodbye' and can be used as an expression of thanks similar to 'cheers'.

'Ah well. Next time. So...Norman? The *Theme of the Day*?'

'Ah...ah...um...um...,' Norman faltered, but regained his composure. 'Ah...the theme...is faff...fav...fav-rite...fav-our-ritt...ca-fah...ca-fah-fah-fay-ss. Ca-fays. Mine...mine... is Darrk Horsht. Dark...Hors-suh. At the beach... in Par-ta – para – unu...u – mu...'

Darrk Horsht? C'mon! Dark Horse. Just say it. Dark. Horse.
Reuben zoned out.

He noted that Sue was slowing her speech down by a good margin. *Ah,* he thought. *It makes it easier for the oldies to hear. And – I guess – it will encourage them to do the same themselves? Maybe. Huh – as if they have something important to say.*

*Nah... **What** am I doing here!*

Dispassionately, he studied the circle of aphasiacs arcing around Sue.

Chapter 8: The 'Clients'

There were six men and three women and each had a name tag. On his left, Reuben saw Norman and Hannah, who he had already met.

Next to them was Anne, a slight, mousy woman with a navy blue track suit and purple hair. She was nervously gripping a cane in her left hand.

Then there was Mark – an elderly man with a patrician air and a full head of grey hair that curled around his ears and the nape of his neck. He was the one who mentioned that 'Abby-gal' was not coming.

Next, Geoff was completely bald. Reuben recognised him as the person he met at the door last Thursday with his sing-song voice and the missing leather hat. He had a paralysed arm and leg and his stance was stooped but his eyes were bright and observant.

Kiri was a Māori wahine[10] dressed in a shapeless black, white and red gown with a big bust, big stomach and strong legs in black leggings. *Looks like she dressed in a circus tent!* Reuben thought irreverently. Her natural curly grey hair fell over her ears and her shoulders. She had a lip and chin tattoo[11] and her green eyes matched the magnificent pounamu[12] pendant around her neck.

---

[10] wahine = woman

[11] Aotearoa/New Zealand women can have a moko kauae, a traditional Māori female chin and lip tattoo. It is considered a physical manifestation of their true identity.

[12] Pounamu is a hard, highly valued jade. It is also called greenstone. Pounamu is regarded as a taonga (treasure) by Māori and most Aotearoa New Zealander's, many of whom have a strong spiritual connection to the stone.

Wow! The pendant is a taonga[13]*. It is beautiful,* Reuben thought admiringly.

Sue was next, then the other three men. The first was ancient, thin and very stooped with legs and rigid arms that stuck out like a staple. His badge proclaimed his name as 'John'. He wore a tweed jacket over a white shirt and a floral tie. His trousers were brown corduroy. *The tie – maybe it was a joke. I bet his granddaughter dressed him. And he is soooo thin. And those arms and legs – a stick-figure.*

Next to him was a swarthy gentleman with silver hair and thick glasses. He was speaking as Reuben surveyed the group and he heard a definite accent. *Ashmud,* read Reuben from the name badge. *Indian? Paki? Hmm…so, a curry-muncher, huh?*

On his right, Reuben peered at the name of the last man. *David. David? But not from here, I suspect?* His handsome face and hands were dark-skinned, his hair was streaked black and silver, and his hooked nose was hawk-like. He dressed well – tailored sky-blue shirt under a purple cashmere jersey, tailored black trousers and shiny black hand-made shoes with tan leather mid-soles. *Yeah…not from here. Maybe middle eastern? Arabic? Terrorist!*

The 'favourite cafés' theme was still going on. Reuben half-listened to the halting and incoherent conversation around him. He understood the concept of the 'virtual talking-stick', that the person who was speaking would not be interrupted, but it was so difficult when he thought he knew what the person was trying to say. By the time the speaker finished, Reuben had sometimes forgotten the context of the dialogue. The verbal idiosyncrasies, the hesitations and repeated words or phrases, the stilted accents, complicated things a bit too.

Anne was speaking.

---

[13] taonga = a treasured item.

'Usul-lee…um…usa-usu-lee the Goost Gros-suh,' said Anne, ducking her head down like a prayerful supplicant. 'The Good Gro-sher. When I get coff-see. That knew them…um…um…me … they knew me … and what I…will… want – so that's good! Cup-chi-no and ca-rrock cake..'

Anne looked up almost defiantly for a moment. Then she recognised that her fellows were aphasic colleagues and her face relaxed. They **all** knew.

'They knew…knew…knew…um…know…me. And ca-rrock cake is delsh-ing…del-li-scious. Yum-mee!'

Sue said 'Thank you Anne. Maybe, we should sample that carrot cake!' She cast around the group. 'What about you, Geoff?' she questioned.

'Fav-rite caf-es. Fav-rite caf-es. Fav-rite caf-es. Woo-hoo,' he delightfully responded with his sing-song voice. 'Espresso Rescue. Rescue. Rescue.'
He looked at Anne intently and smiled. 'Know me. Know me. Know me.'

Anne flashed a grin at Geoff and checked: 'They knew…know you… too! Yes?'

Geoff nodded affirmatively. Then he held out a small book from his jacket pocket. 'Flashh cards. Flashh cards. Flashh cards. Woo-hoo!'

He held it out to everyone. On the cover, it explained that the owner has aphasia with a simple explanation of what the condition was. Geoff turned the pages.

Simple written instructions or picture graphs were displayed: His name, his phone number and address; 'Bus Stop'; 'Toilet'; a gradient chart with a sad face on one end and a happy face on the other.

Geoff rifled through the pages and displayed the ones he was looking for: a sample of coffee styles including Flat White, Latte, Cappuccino, Mocha, Decaf, Short black, Long black, Americano, Iced coffee; and another page including cake; sandwich; toasted sandwich; slice; donut; quiche; pie…

He pointed out his order. 'Make Easy. Easy. Easy,' he chortled. Everyone laughed.

What am I doing here? I can't stomach this mumbling, fried speech. They are so ancient, gerries, spazzes… I've nothing in common. The only one I wanted to see was Petro, but he is not here so…

As if by divine providence, the corridor door banged open. Sue got up quickly and held the door as a wizened, wrinkled man entered the room in a powered wheelchair. His name tag was clearly visible.

Peter.

Chapter 9:
Morning Tea - Coffee?

Peter's right hand was awkwardly placed and the fingers bent like the talons of a dead bird. His left hand held the joystick control and he came in with a stop-start, halting sort of movement. His crew cut hairstyle and his scrubby beard were a dirty grey with a faint tinge of ginger. On his feet, he sported worn jandals[14].

He ploughed his wheelchair into the wall and jammed the door half-open. 'Fu-fu-fu-ck!' he said loudly. His wheelchair was cast like a sheep on her back.

'Language!' said Sue in a prosaic voice that betrayed the frequency with which this admonition was used.

'Shit – sorr-ree!' Peter blared, as Sue helped him to extricate himself from the doorway.

Reuben stood up in alarm and knocked his chair over. He busied himself picking up the chair so he was facing the wall as the newcomer manoeuvred himself to a position in the circle. Sue was fussing over him, moving the chairs around to fit in his wheelchair and a chorus of aphasic welcomes came from the others.

'Hell…hellll…hell… Ohhh!', 'How-dee', 'Kya-a-aw-ra', 'Hal-low', 'Tride to…make…some…from morrr-ning tee?', 'Lo', and the inevitable sing-song 'Goot maahning! Goot maahning! Goot maahning!'

---

[14] Jandals are a type of rubber sandal with a strip of material between the big toe and the other toes and over the foot with no backs. They are called 'thongs' in Australia and 'Flip Flops' in UK and USA.

The man nodded to the others in the circle and then abruptly burst shouted: 'Bads Traf-ff-fick.' A pregnant pause. Then guffaws, giggles and laughter as they realised he was not driving his wheelchair on the road. 'Jok-ker!' Asmud said and Mark stumbled out: 'Funit! Veri veri fun-nit!'

'Okay, okay. Thank you Peter. ' Sue was keen to get the meeting back on track. Hannah – you were saying about your favourite cafés?'

'Um…um…the kaff-fee is um…o-o-okayz…,' Hannah declared hesitantly, 'but ze tor-te is bed-der. The kuch…kuch-en and tort-tez iz…iss at the Takez the Kuch-en in … Low…Low-er Huttz… and…'[15]

To Reuben, this was a non-sensical blur. He remained standing at the morning tea table, appalled. He gazed at the latecomer. No doubt about it – he was Petro Pavliuk. But – his stooped stature; the nose; the eyes; the cartoon-like grimace on his face; his pot belly and the food stains on his red jersey. *What happened? What? How can it be? Why?* The questions ran around Reuben head as he stared at the man, until…

'Reuben? Reuben?'
Startled, he directed his eyes to Sue.
'Sorry? Um…,' he questioned her question.
'I think it is time to have morning tea,' Sue nodded around the group, then looked at him again. 'Can you get the kettle from the kitchen…'

'Sure! Sure!' and he sped out the door to the corridor.

As he filled the kettle with boiling water, the questions still plagued him. *Pavliuk. What a wreck. Why? What should I do now?*

He returned to the room and placed the kettle on the table and backed away.

15 Translation: 'The coffee is okay, but the selections of torte is better. The cake and torte at the Take the Cake in Lower Hutt is …'

Maybe I should go. I don't like it here. I can't do this…

He was on the verge of leaving, but he glanced at jean-clad Sue, squatting down to talk to Ashmud and David.
Hmmm…her bum is like a peach… he thought appreciatively. *Um… okay…at least it is better to work with Sue rather than vacuuming and cleaning.*

Sue rose to the table, judiciously close to the elderly folk when they were pouring the hot water into the cups, helping those you were infirm or disabled by paralysis or arthritis.
Sue glanced at Reuben and he got the message. *Help out!*

Geoff was still sitting down and Reuben realised, with his paralysed arm, he could need some help. Reuben approached him.

'Want some tea or coffee or juice?' he asked abruptly.
'What? What? What?' Geoff's cheerful sing-song voice answered.
Again, Reuben asked: 'Would you like a cup of tea? Or coffee? Or juice or water? Or milk?'
'Um…Um…Um…' Geoff was, apparently, bamboozled. Reuben remembered that Sue had told him – that too many choices are confusing for people with aphasia.
'Do you want a cup of tea?'
'Non! Non! Non!' Geoff said, with a twinkle in his eye.
'Cup of coffee?'
'Yay! Yay! Yay!'
'Milk?'
'Yay! Yay! Yay!'
'Su-gar?' Reuben place the second syllable higher in tone. Geoff's sing-song voice was infectious. Reuben had to stop himself from breaking into a 'call and response' melody.
'Non! Non! Non!'

Reuben grinned and turned to the morning tea table and he saw Sue nodding approvingly. He blushed.

When he returned with the cup of milky coffee, Reuben turned to see if anyone else needed help. Sue was talking to Petro and beckoned Reuben over. Gingerly, he crept over.

'This is Reuben. He is a volunteer who is helping with our meeting. Reuben – Peter. Peter – Reuben. Reuben, can you get a cup of coffee for Peter?' Satisfied that her work was done, she left the two of them.

Hesitantly, Reuben approached the man in the wheelchair.
This is Pavliuk? My artistic legend? Fuck. He's a wreck!
He looked around him.
And what about the rest of them. Shit. Broken, wasted human leftovers. Remnants. I have to get out of here. Get out of...

Suddenly he felt a sharp pain in his shin. 'Peter' had driven his wheelchair into Reuben's leg. Petro's sneering look questioned the youth. Reuben shuddered and closed his eyes for a second.
The vicious old shit!

Convention demanded that he should see what the older person wanted. Not run away. He exhaled quietly and faced Petro.

'Um...cup of coffee?'
The man in the wheelchair screwed up his nose and smirked 'Yup!' The bass tone was insultingly guttural.
'And...milk?'
'Nah!'
'Sugar?'
'Nah!'
'Right-o. Get it for you.'

Reuben turned to the morning tea table again. The exchange was so different from his 'conversation' with Geoff. It was off-putting and abrasive.

Why am I here? This is not the Pavliuk I expected. Anticipated. Where is his…his… well, art? Where is his creativity? Shit – I don't know about this. Fuck! He is a wreck. Pot-bellied. His hands – useless.

And what about the rest? They can't cope with a single sentence. And Geoff – what a mess. He repeats everything he says. Norman and Hannah — frail and needy and …feeble? Broken. Ancient history. Has-beens…

Reuben almost walked out the door but he glimpsed Sue as she continued chatting up her 'clients'. Something about her manner made him hesitate.

But…Norman's eyes. There was something … vital in there. Something lively. A sparkling intelligence. And Geoff – always smiling. Optimistic – despite his lack of words. Hannah – something fierce. Potent. Hmm… Maybe it is there for all of them? Maybe it would the same with Petro.

I didn't give him a chance. Bugger. I ***should*** *give him a chance. Maybe the Pavliuk that I think I know is hidden in there. Maybe I can…work to bring him back? Okay…okay…I can stomach it for a week or two. Shit. Still better than sweeping the floors and cleaning toilets.*

The exchange of thoughts took him a couple of moments as he poured a cup of black coffee for Petro.

Okay…okay… So…I have to have a strategy. Hm…um…um…
Aha! I got it…

Grinning, he put two chocolate biscuits and half a blueberry muffin on a plate and returned with the black coffee to the cantankerous man.

‘Hmmph,’ the bass voice greeted him by way of thanks.

‘Sure. Not a problem.’ He paused for a moment and said softly: ‘PePuk’.

Reuben was rewarded by a penetrating look: a look of mixed astonishment and wariness.

‘Whad? Whad?’ Petro said grimly in a harsh whisper. He challenged Reuben with his eyes, and wagged his beard at him. His left hand was clenched, the other useless.

‘PePuk.’ Reuben didn’t back down. He turned so the others in the room couldn’t see him, and he whispered: ‘PePuk. Your name is not Peter. It’s Petro.’

‘No! Pee-ter. Pee-ter!’ His cracked voice rose and he violently gestured to his name tag. ‘Pee! Ter!’

‘Nah. Nah.’ Still whispering and shaking his head Reuben intimated: ‘You are Petro Pavliuk. You are an artist. A great artist. I know you.

‘Pe. Tro. Pav. Liuk. PePuk,’ he said, triumphantly arching his eyebrows and grinning.

Chapter 10: Discovered

Petro looked around the room suspiciously to see if anyone was listening in to this covert conversation. Another challenging look.

'Shhh, shhh.' He looked around again and stared at Reuben.
'Huh! Huh! Name? Name?' he said in a guttural whisper

'Reuben,' he said quickly.
Petro looked puzzled and Reuben remembered something that Sue had said: S l o w i t d o w n. 'Reu. Ben,' he enunciated carefully.

'Ha! Rude. Man!' Petro cackled. 'Rude. Man!' his eyes alight with mischief. He guzzled the blueberry muffin.

'Sure. Rude Man,' Reuben acknowledged, 'but I know your work. I studied it at school. I am an artist too. Your work – your politics, your activism – inspired me. I **know** your work.'

Petro eyeballed Reuben, seeking to understand what this youth really wanted. Reuben squatted down beside the wheelchair.
'I just want to know – what happened? Why you disappeared? Why you…you…'

Reuben couldn't articulate the real reason – *Why you didn't create any more art works? Why didn't you become the immortal legend I wanted you to be? Why are you…so decrepit?*

Petro looked down, digesting what Reuben was saying and the underlying message. His expression changed from suspicion to thoughtfulness to consideration. Reuben beseeched him wordlessly.

At last Petro gave Reuben a meaningful look..
Then he whispered: 'Group.' He gestured around the room. 'Group. Pe-ter. Aft-ft-tuh. Waz. Aft-tuh-war-ds – Cof-fee – Pee-tro. O-kae-ey.'

Reuben was puzzled. 'Um…what?'

Petro grimaced and frowned at him. He grabbed Reuben's jersey with his left hand and half-whispered into the youth's ear, spit spraying: 'Group. Pet-ter. Aft-tuh-warz - Pee-tro.' He stared intently for signs of comprehension.

Reuben dredged up some of the information that Sue gave before the meeting. *Say what you heard him say and confirm.*
'Um…um…I think you said that you want to be 'Peter' in this meeting, but afterwards I can call you Petro? That's right?'

Petro nodded quickly, and questioned: 'Cof-fee?'

'Sure,' Reuben affirmed. 'I have an hour off for lunch. We can go the café across the road? Okay?'
Petro nodded again.

Slyly, he said in a stage whisper: 'Rude. Man' and then he dismissively busied himself balancing the cup of coffee and the plate of biscuits.

Reuben stood up, elated, and turned around to see if anyone had noted their conversation. But they were all busy, scoffing the morning tea and making stumbling conversations with anyone who would listen.

Chapter 11: The meeting transformed

From then on, for Reuben, the rest of the meeting was transformed. Metamorphosed.

The prospect of meeting with his artistic legend was upper-most in his mind. But he realised that it could be fraught with difficulty.

Obviously Petro's aphasia was quite severe, so Reuben studied Sue's techniques and reactions as she went about her work.

He noted, again, the way she spoke s l o w e r ; the way she repeated her understanding about what she thought the person was saying; the way she patiently waited for her group to say what they wanted to say, and only prompted them if they indicated they needed help; the way she cajoled them and made sure that everyone had a chance to say what they thought, or felt; the way she used short sentences, not rambling on, parenthetically.

Phew! Sue has skills. I have to learn these techniques. And patience!

And he learned that each person in the group had an individual response for their own aphasia. Before he was shutting out the groups jigsaw conversations. Now, he listened. Between their hesitations and staccato stuttering they had much to say to each other.

Geoff, for example, triplicated every second, third or fourth word in his sing-song manner. Formerly irritating, Reuben saw this as a mechanism for him to sort out his words – get his tongue around what he wanted to say.

When Mark could get his words out or when Reuben could decipher them, he saw that Mark used big words – things like 'reprehensible' and 'commendable' and 'stupendous'. Obviously Mark's vocabulary was excellent – only the delivery was suspect.

Reuben saw the sense of humour of the 'aphasiacs'.
With his idiosyncratic accent Ashmud called himself the 'Aph-asian Asian' and in response Kiri called herself the 'Wordless Wahine'.
This time David had the 'Joke of the Day' and he got out: 'What you name…a fake…noo-dlee-ss?' After a questioning look for all the circle and David wrote the answer on the board: 'Im-pasta'.
The laughter was spontaneous from everyone.
Mark again stumbled out: 'Veri veri joc-culah!' and Geoff burst out a veritable aria of 'Haa-hee! Haa-hee! Haa-hee!'

Hannah often used foreign terms in her speech that puzzled Reuben but most of the group understood her perfectly. When she said, in her halting way: 'We…we…whent..for Wein and the Kuch…Kuch-hen was…dolce!', Norman whispered in Reuben ear: 'Wein is…um… um… Veee…Vi-e-nah. The cit-tee. Kuch-hen is…cakk…cake. And dol-ce is del-ly…del-llely…de-lly-ous…um…um…sweet.'

Reuben nodded his thanks and turned to him. He looked into Norman's eyes and the same lively intelligence was evident in their twinkle. He looked across at Sue. She lifted her chin and her right eyebrow and grinned with evident amusement and satisfaction. Her message was clear: *Ah! You understand.*

Sue closed the meeting after discussing the next week's agenda and role: the chairperson, the theme, who would have a speech, or The Word or The Joke Of The Day. The circle stood up and filed out, farewelling Sue and Reuben and each other.

Norman and Petro were the last to go. Norman was speaking to Sue so Reuben targeted Petro and whispered: 'I have to clean up. Café in twenty minutes?' Petro nodded imperceptibly and pointed his wheelchair at the door.

Norman, having finished his conversation with Sue, stood beside the door and ushered Petro out without further damage to the wainscoting and door frame. They disappeared down the corridor.

The door for Room 3 closed and Sue turned to Reuben. 'What about that?' A casual interrogation.

'I thought it was great,' he answered. 'You have skills! I liked the way you included everyone in the conversation and the way you questioned them when it was difficult to understand their meaning. Awesome.'

Sue talked over her shoulder as she went about the room, collating her materials, so Reuben followed suit, clearing the morning tea equipment.

'They are a lively group,' she commented. 'There are a few who didn't make it this time: Steve, Klara, Amina, Yang, Abigail. They should be here next week. So – any questions? Something you didn't understand?'

'Um…nah, nah. It was difficult to … um… refrain from inserting the words that I thought they wanted to say, y'know? I'm not sure if I can be patient enough.'

'You'll learn. I know you will learn. Anything about the members? I thought you were a bit shell-shocked. Almost leaving at one stage…?' She looked at him with a searching expression.

Reuben was embarrassed that she was so perceptive. 'No, no! It was fine. Just fine,' he lied. 'Hunky dory.'

The words slipped out before he could marshal them. He couldn't believe what he had just said and Sue, with a whimsical expression, said: 'Hunky dory? Ha! I've not heard that expression for a long, long time. My father used to say that. When I was ten. Ha!' She grinned and shook her head slightly as if she was reminiscing on a long-ago experience.

'I will take the morning tea stuff to the kitchen, okay?' he said hurriedly as he wheeled the trolley to the door. 'And I will clean the table and vacuum the floors after lunch?'

'Sure, sure,' she replied, waving her hand as a farewell as she packed her suitcase. 'And…thank you. Thank you. You did a good job. Maybe… um…we should meet again next Thursday at the same time. Nine-thirty. Before the session? Just go over everything? '

'Okay. That's fine,' he acknowledged. 'Sure.'

He wheeled the trolley to the corridor, sneaking a look at Sue's trim body as she zipped up her suitcase before the door closed. But her competent professionalism in the meeting impressed him more and he didn't get the same macho rise as before.

She is still hot, but she is good, very good at her job.

He parked the trolley in the kitchen and looking around to see if anyone was watching, exited the building.

Chapter 12:
The café

The café was at the entrance to a mall. He looked in vain for Petro among the customers. *Oh shit! He's gone*, he thought, dismayed. Then, in a quiet corner, away from the other patrons, he caught a glimpse of the wheelchair and a greying-ginger head. He veered, sidled, angled among the other tables until he saw the artist.

Petro had the look of someone who is contemplating an inner vision. *More like an inner demon*, thought Reuben, as he looked at the scowling face of his adolescent legend. He approached the table and Petro looked up, abruptly. 'Rude Man' he sneered. 'Coff-ffee?'

Reuben scanned the table. The only things on it were a container of tissues, some sachets of sugar, and salt and pepper shakers. Reuben suddenly understood. 'You want some coffee? Umm…Black. No sugar. Right?'
The artist smiled ingratiatingly and nodded once. 'Bri-ight Rude Man.'
'Okay,' Reuben acceded and went to the counter to order.

He returned and placed a grinning plastic donkey on the table – a token for the waitress to find the table for their order.

'Well?' said Petro with a look of disdain. 'Well?'

Reuben hadn't planned what he was going to say. 'Um…um…As I said, I followed your career when I was at school. For Art Class. Um…I liked your style. The way you dealt with colour and form, particularly with the big murals. And your…um…your political stance. The way you stuck up for your…beliefs. Your ideals.

'You inspired me to work with my art in public, with murals and graffiti exposing the duplicity and the deception of the rich capitalists that consume all the available resources, devastating the planet, the animals the trees, the water, the air…'

'O-kae…o-kae!' Petro interrupted, with an air of disgust. 'Shit. Fast. Fast, Rude Man?'

Reuben realised that it was gabbling and realised that Petro had missed much of his confession.

I have to slow my words down, he admonished himself, *and simplify the sentences.*
'Sorry…s o r r y… I'll s p e a k m o r e slowly.'

'Art Clas-sshes?' Petro questioned.

'Yes. Art classes. At high school.' He waited.

'Fuckin' study. Me.'

'Yes. The teacher required that we study an Aotearoa New Zealand artist – you. I studied – you.'

'Artist?' Petro exploded with a grim laugh and looked down at his hands. 'Shit…has-been…phuuggh.' Reuben ignored his deprecatory assessment.

The waitress came over and put their coffees on the table. She frowned at Petro and he glowered at her. 'Anything else?' she asked Reuben.

'No, no,' Reuben answered. 'Thank you,' he nodded as the waitress scooped up the grinning donkey.

They tasted the coffee. *Adequate,* thought Reuben.
Petro blatantly stared at him, challenging.

After a sip or two, Reuben spoke again. 'I studied your murals. And performance art works. The ones criticising the rich capitalists. Your environmental activism. It spoke to me.'

Petro stared fixedly and intently at Reuben eyes. He was seeking sincerity. Reuben met them, unblinking. At last, Petro nodded gently and his face softened.

'Good stu-dy?'

'Yeah. I thought you were a legend. You inspired me. With my art works.'

'Le-gendt! Fuck! Ha! Fuckin' hahaha!' he exploded.

The other patrons turned and looked at the two men: the younger one staring at the older one in the wheelchair, who was shaking his head in a paroxysm of laughter. Some were alarmed but before they came to help, the aged man settled down, breathed out and contemplated his companion.

'You're art-tissst?'

'Yep. Mostly murals. Graffiti.' Reuben dived into his pocket and took out his phone. 'See? see?' he turned the phone to Petro so he could see some of the images on his photo app.

'This one is at the over-bridge at Johnsonville and SH1. And this is on the bridge at the Ava railway station. And this one at the wall beside Pack'o'Slave in Tawa. They have painted it grey now, but I think it was one of my best. And this is…'

'Fast! Shit. Fast Rude Man! Too…too…' Petro pushed the phone back and turned away.

'Sorry! S o r r y!' Reuben apologised. 'Sorry. I was too excited. Sorry.' Embarrassed, he let his phone drop to the table.
'Um…Your work inspired me. I saw your name on the Aphasia Group list and I recognised you. There are not many Pavliuk around here! I have to speak to you.'

'Why?'

The question seemed to float between them like a soap bubble, pregnant with alternative answers.

'I wanted…wanted to see how…how you are… Wanted to see … what happened?'

'Happ-penn…hap-end? Ha! Hahahah! Strokk. Fuckin' strokk. Aphss-ia hap-end! Arms. Legs. Hap-end. Fuckin' chair hap-pend. Arrgggh!' Petro banged the table with his left hand. The empty coffee cups jumped and tipped up.

The vehemence of this explosion shocked Reuben. And apparently the rest of the patrons and staff. Reuben righted the coffee cups and turned to them and gestured that everything was okay.

His face grim, Petro seemed to be in a funk of depression.

Chapter 13:

M.S. – Transcript: Interlude and/or Discussion

Text message transcript:

- Editor's note: This is wearying. You can't expect anyone to read this?
- Author's note: Well, that the way it is with aphasia. The mispronounced and mistaken words, the hesitations, the lack of syntax and the anticipatory pauses.
- Editor's note: But it is boring. People aren't going to read this. It takes too long to get some sense of what is going on. It is like an ongoing stutter with every syllable or letter.
- Author's note: That's the problem! Aphasia! This is the reality of it.
- Editor's note: I can't deal with this. It's too hard. Sorry. I can't do it. You should get another editor.
- Author's note: No, no, no. Please persevere. Please. You know about this stuff. I can't break in another editor. Please.
- Editor's note: We have to have some other solution. You can't expect people to read this drawn out, hesitating, stuttering prose. Even if it's real.
- Author's note: I get your point. But, I just want the readers to know the reality. The reality of people with aphasia. Their communication difficulties.

- Editor's note: I appreciate that. Truly, I do. But – sorry – I think you will have to re-write the whole thing.
- Author's note: Surely not.
- Editor's note: You wanted to write the story in the third person. But, Reuben, you know that I can't publish the book with this pedantic text. The readers will give up. Even the carers and spouses of people with aphasia. Especially them! They get it all the time – now they get it in the reading material too! You can't do that to them. And the people WITH aphasia? You think they would cope with the muddled syntax and misused and mistaken words? I get your intention, I truly do. But otherwise, with this mess of muddled text and half-right words, you will lose readers. What you want to say will be lost.
- Reuben's note: I guess so. But I don't want to write the previous chapters again with me as the hero. That would not be right. Or write. Aha! You see what I have done there!

Conversation transcript:

- Editor: Ha ha ha. Very funny. [The editor expresses his opinion, soaked with sarcasm.] Ah! And you see what I did there. We were in a ... um ... a textual conversation and I changed the ... um ... tone, or the ... um ... wha'ya'call it ... the process, or ... um ... the method for the readers. Now, we are in a normal conversation! An audial, conversational conversation.
- [... A pause in the conversation ... A considerable pause ...]

- Reuben: Well ... we could ... um ... break the rules?
- Editor: Wha'd'you mean?
- Reuben: For example, um ... you said we were in a textual conversation, but now ... now, we are in normal conversational conversation.
- Editor: Yeah. So what?
- Reuben: So... you broke the rules. Text to audio. You broke the rules! So ... we could do anything we like. That's the beauty of reading – text and transcribed conversations. We can do both.
- [Reuben pauses and let the notion sink in.]
- Reuben: We. Can. Do. Any. Thing. We. Like! So ... we could change tack – and text – completely, and use this dialogue as the trigger.
- Editor: Ah ... I see! And, we could leave the previous chapters alone. Transcribed text ... with the ... um ... gaps and stuttering et cetera ... then we can, as you say, change tack. That would mean that the effect of aphasia would still be ... well, readable to the readers. They will know how it affects – and effects – people with aphasia. And, with this dialogue, we can take the subsequent chapters in a new direction.
- Reuben: Exactly. We can do anything we like!
- Editor: Okay, okay, okay. You could take over the story in the first person? Hmmm ... that could be too confusing for the readers? Too jarring?

- Reuben: No. I think it would be fine. With this ...um...discussion, it should be fine. But ... what about changing the time-sense! Rather telling the story of me and Petro in the present tense, I could jump to me telling someone else about my meeting with Petro in the past.

- Editor: Yeah...yeah... That could work.

- Reuben: Actually, there was a journalist who came to the Aphasia Group about, maybe eight months after I met Petro for the first time. She filed a report about the aphasia group with some magazine ... um ... Torchstony or Touchstory or something like that.

- Editor: Touchstone Magazine?

- Reuben: Yeah...yeah... that was it. The report was good. She interviewed most of the Aphasia Group. I told her about Petro and his art work and what we have achieved now and I showed some of his paintings to her from my phone... Some of it made into the article ... she quoted some things about Petro and his work. So ... I could fictionalise an interview with her. Tell her about our meetings and what came out of it. As a device.Yeah?

- Editor: Okay ... that could work. Maybe you could contact her and make sure she is onboard with the idea. You have to clarify that with her though. Otherwise, we could get in trouble.

- Reuben: Sure. I can do that. [A micro-pause.] Actually...she is sort-of...well...she is my girlfriend now. I'm sure she would be into it.

- [Sound of back-slapping and congratulatory approval.]
- Reuben: So … what should we do now? If it was a film we could have one of those daily calendars flicking through the days, a wall calendar ticking off the weeks …
- Editor: Or, we could just do this …

Chapter 14: Tempus fugit

So…Reuben is me.
I am Reuben.
And this is the story about when I met Petro Pavliuk.
And what came of it.

For a while, Petro and I met every Thursday at the cafe after the Aphasia Group meeting. After a few weeks, Petro softened his attitude. He still swore, and he still called me 'Rude Man', but I suspect it was a term of affection rather than used derisively. And he invited me to his home and studio.

My six months 'sentence' was up, and I got a glowing report from the Community Centre Manager. Actually, she was okay. We got on well. I continued volunteering for the Aphasia Group on Thursdays.

My relationship with Sue was complicated. For me.
Her professionalism rubbed off on me and I totally admired her. She was so caring and attentive to her 'clients' and I couldn't **not** appreciate her commitment. I know that's a double negative, but that seems appropriate in the circumstance.

Surprisingly – or maybe, unsurprisingly – I matured. I saw her more as a person, than a hot body.
(But she was still hot!)

Two months later, Sue was approached by a journalist for a story about aphasia sufferers. Someone called Shami Fergusson. Sue talked to Shami and suggested that I could help her to – well – 'deal' with interviewing Petro.

And, yes, Petro was on form! He called Shami, 'Shame'. He did that. To everyone. [Only Sue was exempt.]

The following chapters are an account of what I discussed with Shami before her Pavliuk interview…

Chapter 15: Bond. Reuben Bond.

This journalist came up to me in one of the morning teas at the Aphasia Group meeting.

'Hi,' she said, monosyllabically.
Succinct.
I like that.

I think humour is the best way to connect. Holding out my hand, I said to her, with a passable Sean Connery accent: 'The name is Bond. Reuben Bond.'

She giggled. She shook my hand in a business-like manner and responded: 'My name is Shami. Shami Fergusson. I work with *Touchstone Magazine.'*

She was attractive in an earnest sort of way. She wore earnest corporate clothes and earnest make-up. She had that ethnic blend that is so common these days. Her skin was café-au-lait brown – I suspect her ancestors were Indian, or Sri Lankan. But her accent was earnestly and definitely Kiwi[16]. (Some of her consonants were suspect – maybe second or third generation Kiwi?)
She had raven black hair with a streak of red through it, dark brown earnest eyes and long lashes, a touch of earnest eyeshadow, an aquiline nose, luscious lips with a trace of gloss, cute ears with several golden earrings around their earnest lobes.

Shami wanted to interview the Aphasia group members and she was having difficulty understanding what they were saying. She knew that

[16] Kiwi = people from Aotearoa New Zealand - capital 'K' [as opposed to 'kiwi', a native, nocturnal, flightless bird.]

Pavliuk was a … well, a 'tricky character' as one might say. And she knew that I had a special bond with Pavliuk, so, she asked for my help with 'the Aphasia sufferers'.

At the outset, I set her straight.
'No, no, no. They were not sufferers. They were Aphasia Warriors!'

She grinned shyly. 'Okay. Tell me about the Aphasia Warriors. Tell me about Peter.'

'You want me to tell you about Peter? Have you got all day? A week?'

Another giggle – but an earnest giggle.

So I said: 'Sure, I can do that. But not here.' I leaned over to her and whispered in her ear – I couldn't resist that cute ear – 'Petro is quite sensitive. Maybe we could meet at the café across the road after the meeting? Coffee?'

She nodded, earnestly, and said with a Sean Connery accent: 'Sure. Coffee – but not shaken. Or stirred.'
My turn to giggle. Her Sean Connery accent was better than mine.

After the meeting and my few chores, I went to the café. Shami was sitting at the same table that Petro and I used to sit at many months ago. Synchronicity!

I ordered from the counter and got a Captain Jack Sparrow[17] figurine with a missing arm marking the table for my order.

After some small talk, Shami homed in.

---

[17] Captain Jack Sparrow is a character from the film franchise *Pirates of the Caribbean* acted by Johnny Depp.

'I know you have a good relationship with Peter, and he is – um – well, he is…'

'Cantankerous?' I offered. 'Objectionable? Vulgar and rude?'

'Well, yes. Frankly.' With raised eyebrows Shami signalled a resigned gesture of helplessness.

'He is quite charming in his own way,' I countered. 'I had to look past the swearing and the rudeness and the sneering looks and see what was going on with him. He has a front – a facade – to keep a distance from others. He's tentatively volatile – but quite vulnerable actually, in a way.'

The coffees arrived. The waitress recognised me, looked at Shami and turned to me again, grinning. 'Hope **this** friend isn't trouble?' She looked at Shami whose demure face was set in a puzzled frown. 'I guess not!' the waitress said with a knowing look and collected up Captain Jack Sparrow with the missing arm. She sashayed around the other tables clearing dishes and wiping them down. Shami looked at me, quizzically.

'Um, several months ago – well…we were kicked out of the café. Peter and I used to come here after the Thursday meetings but, you know, he can be loud and abusive and swears a lot and the owners banned us. I haven't been here for – yonks.'

Shami nodded slightly with her chin and raised her eyebrows – an omniscient 'I-know-what-you-mean' look.
We sipped our coffee. Not shaken or stirred.

'Okay,' I began. 'Let me start from the beginning. For me, at least.'

Chapter 16: Let's Start at the Very Beginning

'I met Peter about eight months ago at the Aphasia Group meetings. I was working at the Community Centre – well, actually, sentenced to community service – periodic detention, I suppose – at the Centre for six months.'

Shami's eyes widened and I could see the questions lining up behind them.

I rapidly pre-emptively answered them: 'No, no – nothing drastic! A little bit of disagreement about my art works. And the venues I put them on – bridges, public walls and fences. They were – unsanctioned.'

Another set of questions formed.

'I was a graffiti artist. Not an axe-murderer!'

I fished out my tablet and displayed some photos on the screen of my favourite – and less controversial – works. 'Like that,' I said, encouragingly. 'And this. And this…'

Shami examined them and nodded. I think she was quite impressed? I carried on.

'So I met 'Peter' eight months ago, but I knew him long, long before that. As Petro Pavliuk – an artist. I had studied him and his art works when I was at high school. My teacher had an assignment: choosing an Aotearoa New Zealand artist, researching and studying their art works as an inspiration for our own works.

'I chose Petro Pavliuk because I had admired some of his murals in the city. When I researched him fully, under my art teacher's guidance, I realised that he was not a good artist. He was a **great** artist. Phenomenal! He didn't pull any punches, while commenting about nature and the environment and the way that humans had affected it in a detrimental way.'

'So, Peter is actually Petro, an artist,' confirmed Shami. 'You say, a **great** artist. Why have I never heard of him?'

'When I was researching him, at school, the works I found were mainly from the 1960s, 70s and early 80s. There was an international incident when he produced a mural criticising the company Independent Mutual Insurance, and in 1990 he was nominated for an MBE – Member of the British Empire – in the Queen's Birthday Honours list. But he refused it.

'By the late 1990s he had dropped off the public radar. I thought he was dead! When I looked at his works, the films, the cartoons, the sculpture and especially his painting and murals and his artistic performance pieces I realised they were ground-breaking. Brilliant. Genius. My analysis of his art works inspired me, and I decided to paint my take on the environmental, political and social issues as a graffiti artist.

'I have to say, his murals and public art works were legitimate,' I confessed. 'They were commissioned or paid for or sponsored. I didn't have that…um…luxury. Hence, the periodic detention sentence!' I put on a fake French accent: 'Ze trials and tribulations of a brilliant, magnificent and talented graffiti artist like moi!'

Shami smiled graciously. It was more charming than her giggling.
I liked that.

'But – the beginning. Petro Pavliuk was born in December 1943, in the Ukraine. He immigrated here as a six-year-old. Self taught, his work was always focused on nature, the environment and the negative impact that humans have made – where people mucked up the natural balance. Pavliuk was always ahead of his time. His composition, the sense of colour, his grasp of history and form. His interpretation and the subject matter was provoking – political and controversial. Let me show you …'

Again I got my tablet and opened the programme for the images to my PePuk album. I had photographed some of his artworks from various books and magazines I came across in my library research.

I shuffled my chair next to Shami and showed the pictures to her.

Chapter 17:
Protest

'For example, this is what he did for the Whaling protest in 1975. Whaling was only outlawed in New Zealand in 1978. You see that Petro had an extensive mural on a building beside a busy highway in central Auckland. In the top two thirds of the mural, you can see the variety of whales – humpback, blue, sperm, right, minke, narwhal, orca, dolphin and so on. All of them have heads, eyes, blowholes, flippers with very realistic rendering.

'But from the flippers back, there is only a skeleton. Dog-faced scuba divers are attacking their flesh and carting it off in supermarket trollies, taking it to the shops and factories in the bottom third of the mural: restaurants, cat food factories, pharmaceutical and cosmetic plants. And can you see the eyes on the whales? They are human eyes.

'And this bronze and aluminium sculpture he did for the Manapouri Dam protest in 1969. You know about this? Lake Manapouri is in Southland, just south of Te Anau. The government wanted to raise the lake by thirty metres for a hydro-electric power station headwaters. That would have drowned a lot, a **lot** of the bush around the lake. And the wildlife who live there.

'There was a huge negative public reaction to the scheme. This sculpture is in the botanical gardens in Christchurch and you can see the form of a mighty rimu with its leaves drooping down like tears. In the branches, there are all sorts of birds: kererū, tūī, pīwakawaka, kōtare, matuku moana, kawau – even the flightless birds like kiwi, kākāpō, weka[18] – hanging from their necks like hunted game ducks. The birds are made from aluminium.

'Petro was making a point. If the lake were raised, the hydro-electric power would provide generating power for the aluminium smelter at

[18] Native birds of Aotearoa New Zealand

Tiwai Point. By the way, as a compromise, the government raised the lake only eight and half metres.'

And I got another image from the tablet.

'This was his response when France carried out nuclear weapons tests at Moruroa Atoll in the early 1970s. It was on a wall beside the motorway in central Wellington. A mushroom cloud surmounting a stylised Earth globe in space. There are rockets shooting from the earth 'peopled' – and I use this term loosely – by armour-plated cockroaches. I guess he was subscribing to the notion that cockroaches would survive a nuclear blast that killed all other sentient beings.'

I loaded another image.

'This is a mural he painted on the wall of a bridge just across from Parliament – a monstrous hydra. Pavliuk was always left wing. He was incensed that some of the politicians were cosying up with multinational corporations. See the hydra's necks have several politicians faces on them, biting off the birds and insects that are endemic to this country. I don't know if you remember some of the politicians from the 1970s and '80s. These are effigies of Robert Muldoon, Roger Douglas, Jim Bolger, Jenny Shipley, Tony Steel, Bill Birch. It was very controversial at the time.

'See – the body of the hydra has mechanised parts, just like a robot indicating the industrialised corporations. And you see that the hydra is – well, shitting on the 'little people'. They are struggling in the mire left behind. And can you see that the 'little people' are modelled on Hieronymus Bosch's *The Garden of Earthly Delights*. Brilliant!'

Rather than a giving a cursory glance, Shami looked at the pictures attentively. I was pleased that she didn't shy away from the grotesque nature of some of the images. Clearly she had some artistic expertise in her background.

And she showed integrity – a sense of what art can really say to the viewer. Not a saccharine viewpoint, in a 'Disney' or 'Hallmark' way. I was encouraged by that, and I decided to tell her some of Petro's performance art events.

'Not only murals and paintings, he made cartoons, films and performance art events. Some of them were **extremely** controversial.

'One time he was sitting on a pole for two weeks with a painted scene below him with native bush including birds, reptiles, and insects. He flung down paint mixed with his…um…faeces and urine, that blanked out the mural below. He called it: *Humans – deal with your own shit!*'

Shami was shocked, but instantly recovered. 'Wow!' she responded. 'I guess that is artistic commitment!'

'Yep!' I said. 'I have to say that my graffiti is more – sedate. Comparatively. I have no compunction in emulating his form of 'performance art' myself.'

Shami nodded sagely, apparently applauding my decision.

'So,' Shami questioned, 'what happened when you met him. In the flesh.'

I sighed.

Chapter 18: Aphasia Meeting Recalled

'As you know, I was working at the Community Centre on a Tuesday and Thursday for my community service. For various reasons, I decided to volunteer for the Aphasia Group on Thursday.'

In my mind I saw Sue when I first met her. Eight months later, I was surprised at how my view of her had transformed. 'I met Sue, and she asked me to copy her list of names for another meeting and I saw – in black and white – Peter Pavliuk. I couldn't believe it! It was not conceivable that it was another Pavliuk – it is an unusual name after all. And Peter – Petro.' My hands performed a juggling act weighing 'Peter' in one hand and 'Petro' in the other. 'I had to see. He had been my idol. A legend. **I had to see!**

'The first impression was not good – not at all. He was angry and argumentative and swearing a lot despite Sue's apprehensive admonitions. Actually, she used a 'Swear Jar' and Petro filled in up every other month!

'And, if you want my honest opinion, he was a wreck! You see him now, still swearing and scowling. But then, he was angry and frustrated, obese, with unkempt hair and beard. And smelly! The first time I met my idol, he was such a disappointment I almost walked out. I thought that my legendary artistic god was relegated to the status of a homeless vagrant.'

'Why didn't you?' Shami said, her journalistic sensibilities coming to the fore.

'I don't know exactly,' I answered. 'Something about the group. And Sue. She is remarkable. The whole thing about being unable to talk, communicate – well, at heart, I am an artist, so talking is not so important to me, and the way that these people were together, supporting each other, it grew on me. And I decided that I could help Petro. Somehow.'

'What did you do?'

'I used a ruse! He didn't know me at all, and he was still being 'Peter' for all the rest of the people. I didn't know if the others in the group – or Sue – knew he had been a brilliant artist. I knew from my research that he always signed his work with 'PePuk'. So, when I gave him a cup of coffee in the meeting, I whispered to him: 'Not a problem, PePuk.' You should have seen his face!

'I said to him I wanted to speak to him about his work. We arranged to meet at the café – this café – after the meeting, and things progressed from there.

'I guess you have found out that talking is not an aphasic's strong point! It took me a long, long time to work out what Petro was saying, especially when we were talking about abstract things. But we persevered. The fact we were both artists helped. I showed him some of my murals. He pointed out things in my art works – my composition, treatment of material and my **intent** – that need to be said. Abruptly analytical and diagnostic but when I got over my adolescent angst, his help was so very valuable. He was generous like that – gruffly generous. We met at this café for about six weeks after the group meeting, but some of our conversations – or aborted conversations – were, well, 'contentious in a civilised environment', if you get my meaning.'

'Ah!' Shami was on the ball. 'Swearing?'

'Yep! And thumping the tables. And jousting his wheelchair against other patrons' legs. And the waitresses. We were banned! Luckily,

Pavliuk had warmed to me a bit, and he invited me to his home. He still wanted our meetings to be secret from the rest of the group.

'My work at the Community Centre was only on Tuesday and Thursday, so I went to his house on Wednesday morning for a few weeks and then I, basically, went every day except Tuesday, and of course, I saw him at the Aphasia Group on Thursday. After my six months, Community Service was done, I went every day to his home. But I went to the Aphasia Group meeting too.

'He was critical of my art work – constructively critical, in his own way. Well, he shouted a lot. And he was sarcastic. And severely sharp. But I knew what he was saying. It helped me to be a, well – a constructive artist. Art that makes a **difference**. That was the gravity that kept us in our artistic orbit. Art that makes a **difference**. I knew he was great and I think he was respecting me as an artist. That was – wow! Well, it was special. But, mostly, I think he was lonely.'

Shami breathed deeply, surfacing from the ocean of my recollections. She turned her head to the counter, orienting herself. 'We have been here for a long time,' she said. 'The waitress will think I am a bad influence. You will be banned, again! Shall we get another drink? My shout?'

I nodded, grinning like a loon.
She was quite attractive.

Chapter 19:
Pavliuk's Abode

The waitress took our order, smirking a bit. We ignored her and Shami went on with her questions.

'What was Petro's home like? An artistic treasure or a museum?'

'I don't want to give you the wrong impression, because you have seen him. He's better now. Truly! As I said, when I met him, he was a wreck. And the house was his personified reflection: disorganised, gloomy, unkempt, sad. The place was littered with screwed art paper, ripped paintings, misbegotten sketches, plans and broken maquette. The place was filthy: dirty laundry, dishes and beer cans and whisky bottles all over the place, unmown lawns, overgrown gardens. Basically it was a disaster.

'His disabilities, his paralysis and wheelchair, were a hindrance and a major source of frustration with his artistic work. He had someone coming in each week for cleaning and maintenance, but they didn't do a great job. I guess Petro's manner was to blame.

'It was hard to be there. My legend was broken. My artistic idol was decapitated. But, in that few weeks or months, Petro **wanted** me there – I know that. He wanted someone who appreciated his art – the art he **used** to make. But his anger and resentment of his condition overwhelmed him. After a while it built up in him like a tsunami.

'For example, he was looking at some of his drawings and I was commenting on them, badly. At that time I couldn't understand them. He wanted to say what he was trying to do, but his words went to hell – worse than usual, if you can believe that. He cursed his paralysed arm and his wheelchair because he could not sculpt or work on murals. His voice grew louder and louder, his swearing was rampant. He was almost screaming, throwing things around. It was a cataclysmic confrontation.

'But it was not aimed at me. It was aimed at him. Himself. He was so, so, soooo frustrated. He buried his head in his arms, sobbing, saying 'Un-fish buss-nst! Un-fish buss-nst!' '

I was almost translating the words to Shami, but she rapidly worked out the meaning, saying in hushed tones: 'Unfinished business. Unfinished business.'

Unassuming intelligence.
I like that.

I went on.
'I looked around at the drawing and the maquette and I could see that the artistic spark was there, but the forms, the composition and the colours were not **realised**. Something was off. And then it dawned on me – he was depressed – artistically depressed. He had ideas, but when he wanted to work them out, his disabilities got in the way.'

The waitress interrupted us and left our drinks on the table, still smirking. 'Anything else?' she asked We both shook our heads and she resumed her place at the counter.

Shami probed: 'I can see that Petro is much better now. Still cantankerous, barely sociable with people he doesn't know, but not unkempt. Not smelly. So, what did you do?'

'Well – I said that he was gruffly generous about **my** art works. Talking was difficult, but he did express the essence of his philosophy somehow. I can't explain it – but it helped me enormously. And I wanted to help him too. The paralysis in his hands made it impossible to work on his painting, let alone sculptures. Then I got an idea. I couldn't believe that it took me so long to figure it out.

'I gave him a tablet.'

Chapter 20: Resolution

I showed my tablet to Shami.

'It was obvious! I have always used computers – my phone, my tablet. I showed my work on it to you. But I didn't realise that these things are foreign to Petro. He is 80 now – he would have used only basic computers.

'My dad has lots of business contacts so it was easy to inveigle a tablet and software from him. At Petro's house, I showed him how to draw on the screen. He was fascinated. He could sketch some designs, edit them, delete them, and change the pressure or the colour.

'Next day, at the Thursday Aphasia group meeting, he sidled up to me and whispered: 'Ass-some! Ass-some!' I feared he was swearing gain, but realised after a moment he was saying 'Awesome'.

'He looked me in the eye with a passionate stare and said: 'Fry. Day. Home?'

'So, I went next day, and showed him all sorts of techniques: brushes, textures, cutting and pasting, printing, et cetera. And he was off! When he was focussed on his art work, I tidied the house, washed the dishes and laundry and made him a good healthy lunch.

'I got some other programmes, including film apps, and 3D-printing programmes. He devoured it all. Re-assimilated and deconstructed it. And he was doing art again!

'He was still generous with his support for my work. His philosophy was all about channelling passion and commitment into art. In any form. He made me realise that my foray into objectionable graffiti was a waste of time. My graffiti was always being covered up or dissolved away. He counselled me to realise that my art was misdirected in a reactionary public antic because I was angry with my parents. I thought I could hurt them by flouting the law, but it was useless. Self-destructive. Petro pointed that out to me.

'After a while we collaborated. We worked on ideas, to and fro-ing, creating and revising. We had the same idea of ecologically political themes and we used the tablets to refine some designs.'

I leaned over to her across the table, fake-looked left and right as if I wanted to make sure no-one was listening to us and whispered: 'You didn't hear this from me, but we have a commercial line of ecologically friendly art works on T-shirts, tea towels, posters and fridge magnets and digital wallpapers and paintings with the signature of RuPuk. We have our international marketplace on Facebook, Instagram and TikTok!'

I straightened up and said: 'Look at this!'

I stripped off my jersey. Shami looked surprised and she drew away from the table, but then she saw what I was doing. She came closer and studied my printed t-shirt.

A kauri tree with branches laden with birds, reptiles et cetera: tūī, kererū, piwakawaka, korimako; gecko, skinks and snails were on the bark; kiwi, takahē and tuatara were running around on the ground; the roots of the kauri tree were sinking in to the brown earth where the faint form of a woman, Papatūānuku, was cradling the image; the swirl of clouds above the tree had the protecting shape of a male,

Ranginui.[19] Below the image were the words: *May The Forest Be With You.*

Shami nodded and chuckled. 'That's good. Very 'Aotearoa'. And the Star Wars reference[20]. That's very good!'

Demotic[21] indie intelligence.
I like that.

I put my jersey back on, breathed deeply and sighed.
'Petro Pavliuk – still obnoxious but now much better adjusted. Sure, he is still cantankerous, abrasive and abrupt and swears a lot – but, in his own mind, he is optimistic. Soul positive.' I looked at Shami intently. 'And he is not alone now.'

We finished our coffee and looked at each other, contemplating the conversation – and relationship? – between us. Shami rose from her seat and I followed.

'I will interview Petro tomorrow,' she announced. 'At his home. You will be there? I think it would be better if…'

'Sure!' I said immediately. 'Sure, no problem.'

'Okay. See you tomorrow.'

She turned but hesitated and looked back at me.

---

[19] Papatūānuku = The Earth Mother figure who gives birth to all things. Ranginui = the Sky Father. (Māori)

[20] Surely you know this? But if you don't: 'May The Force Be With You' is a common Jedi saying from Star Wars franchise.

[21] Demotic = popular, common

'After I finish my article, I would like to see more of your art.' She reached across the table and took my hand, turning it over.
She placed a business card on my palm.
'This is my number. My personal number. Call me?'

I blushed.
Confident, connecting.

I **like** that.

Cypher

Preface:

I was working on this story as one of the short stories in *Even More Suspect Speaking*. Again, I realised that *Cypher*, with its setting, the sci-fi element and the backstory of the characters, was too long to be included as a 'short story', so I removed it from that book.

Some of the terms will be not familiar to you. After all, the setting is around 2365 CE, 240 years from now. Most of the unfamiliar terms will be understandable in context, but I have added some footnotes for others that are not so clear.

I wrote this story in 2023/2024.
AI (Artifical Intelligence) is an interesting concept, and useful after a fashion, but somewhat unsettling. The use of AI in text, subtitles, speech writing, script writing, screenwriting, image and video creation, facial recognition, Siri, Alexa, ChatGPT, etc... could be unnerving. In 2023/2024 wordsmiths having been striking and protesting about the use of AI in these fields. We will see how it plays out.

In this story, I thought it would be interesting to have a computer/robot with aphasia rather than a human. After the explosion, a glitch in its programming led to a condition that mimicked a stroke, that damaged the robot's 'speech centres'. ThaMu, the human protagonist in the story, has to deal with an aphasic robot.

Just like humans with aphasia, the robot's intelligence is not impaired, but its communication circuits are damaged so it is difficult for ThaMu to get the story straight.

Given that a robot 'thinks' in terms of nano-seconds, at least it can't be as frustrating as it would be for a human? Robots are not emotional.
Or are they?

Enjoy.

Cypher

Chapter 1: Transmission

```
Login: 11:05:056678 on SevenDay, Period twentythree
Systms000356
[9] 214263 a1i_8A8a0@prgm
~ %[]&$m4sk-pt1.tc
:
:
Critical Alert: extreme radiation detected
Critical Alert: extreme EMP detected
Critical Alert: seismic activity detected
:
:
Time: 11:05:205576 SevenDay - Period twentythree
System: offline 148898 microsec
        Alert: protocol 'original status' realised
        $wdlog#/…
        :
        :
        Bandwidth frequencies: not functioning
        Infra-red: not functioning
        Radio frequencies: not functioning
        Micro-wave frequencies: not functioning
        Macro-wave frequencies: not functioning
        Audio monitoring: not functioning
                Audio monitoring: reset
                Audio monitoring: functional - null input
        Motor function: testing

        >>>>>
                Detected: high impact damage - 67%
                Detected: impervium damage - 31%
                Detected: obstruction - 45%
                Detected: high particle density
                Detected: critical vent function
        >>>>>
```

```
        Auto-repair: reset
Motor function: 43% functional - manual repair required
        Time to respond: 123.8 microsec
        … init_1.asec mov@rspnd prgrm …
:
Report: Bodily functions / crew:
        Sherzi: null input
        Joj: null input
        Jami: null input
        ThaMu: O2-57%, Temp-9C, Activity-0%

Waiting for automatic input: h4ndshake.mjj…$stp
        >>>>>
        Null
        <<<<<
Waiting for manual input: h4ndshake.thj…$nrd
        >>>>>
        Null
        <<<<<
Waiting for audio input: h4ndshake.sme…$mvd
        >>>>>
        Null
        <<<<<

Input not detected
:
Shutting down all systems
$@…/…/
```

Chapter 2:
ThaMu

ThaMu opened her eyes. The glassite in her helmet gave a one-hundred-sixty-five degrees vision of the tunnel ceiling. Apparently, she was on the floor of the tunnel. Her head ached and she could not feel her legs. Groggy and disoriented, her hands instinctively checked out her helmet. It took a moment for her brain to realise if her helmet was compromised she would not be alive to be able to check it out.

Her bewildered and bedazzled eyes beheld a view that was phantasmagorical: a kaleidoscope of fluorescent rainbows danced before her, an insubstantial psychedelic shimmering vision.

Where I am? What…? Rainbow? The colours? Beautiful but…what?

As she focused her eyes the psychedelic rainbows melted away. She gazed at the shaft wall and piece by piece she began to make sense of what she was looking at, and what she was doing there, like a space cadet starting to learn a star chart for astrogation.

The shaft wall. The tunnel to The Grot[22]*. I was going down to The Grot. I was going to replace the transdominator*[23]*. But…*

She placed her hands on the tunnel floor and braced herself so she could get up. At least, she attempted to do that. She couldn't move her lower body. She looked down. Her legs were pinned under a beam. Aghast, she realised that all around her was chaos.

---

22 'The Grot' was the main gathering space for the crew, a cave beneath the asteroid that housed all the equipment for their mining operation and the comforts of home. The Grot = a grotto.

23 A transdominator is a solar-scrubber for the excavation machines.

Rocks and rubble littered the tunnel. The rib cage of collapsium-plated steel beams that protected the shaft had been twisted, bent and broken, flattened in both directions. In fact, only the area around her was clear of debris. The steel girders above her were a life-saver. Literally. They formed a bivouac sheltering her body from certain death. But one beam had trapped her legs. She tried to move it, to slide out of it, but she was pinned like a tartumim[24] specimen. The exertion was exhausting. Her arms ached, her head hurt and she almost fainted.

What? Where? Where are the others? How long have I been here? What happened? How is it…? ***What?…***

She panted and gulped the stale air in her helmet. The questions mounted in her head and panic was a short moment away.

Breathe. Breathe. Think. Breathe. Think.
B r e a t h e. R e l l l a a a x x x. B r e a t h e.
You can do this. Focus. Think.
Protocol. We have a protocol. Safety protocol. Remember. Think.

B r e a t h e…

Okay…okay… What? What happened? What happ… Hah – the rainbows! Yes, the rainbows.

She remembered, in the pre-dawn of her dazed state, the phantasmagoric kaleidoscope she witnessed when she opened her eyes.

The diatheryium crystals. They fluoresce when they have been exposed to xenon-135 radiation. So…why? Why would they do that? Where would the xenon-135 radiation have come from…? Oh! Oh my!

---

24 A tartumim is a creature that inhabits the satellites (asteroids, moon, dwarf planets) in the Kuiper belt. Beetle-like but anaerobic, it feeds on diatheryium crystals and excretes diatheryazm. They live to be 250-290 (Terran) years old.

ThaMu rapidly checked the computator on her left forearm. Dust and sand obscured the screen and she wiped them off with her other hand and activated it. The display transferred to her helmet. The alert icon was flashing red.

```
Alert: ***** Radiation
Alert: ***** EMP
Alert: ***** seismic activity
```

Oh! Oh! Shittical-frellin' merd! One of the excators[25]*? Or the ship? Smeggy frellin-frekk.* [26] *Where are the others? Sherzi? Joj? Jami?*

She attempted to activate her commset but her cracked voice was gravelly.
Uh. Uh. Lack of water.
From the tube beside her lips she drank some reconstituted suit water. The taste was foul but it loosened her vocal cords. With a voice laced with pain and panic she called: 'Kapitan? Sherzi? Sherzi? C'mon yo? C'mon?' The display in her helmet was scrambled. She saw, and heard, only static. She closed her eyes and listened, breathlessly. No answer. No picture. Just the crackle and scramble of static.

She tried all the channels. 'Sherzi? Joj? Jami? How doin' c'mon yo?'
She called again and again. But … only static.
Bumsuckle. Frekk. Frellin' merd. Smeggy frellin-Frekk!

Panic was the flip side, but ThaMu gritted her teeth.

Maybe my commset is malfunctioning? That's why I can't get anyone.
I have to follow protocol. Okay. Breathe. B r e a t h e. Think.
How long? I was working on SevenDay, Period twenty-three. Tomorrow is my off-work day.

---

[25] Excavation machines mining the asteroid, moons, dwarf planets…

[26] A selection of choice swear words

She glanced at the computator on her left wrist. She pressed the time icon.

What? She was astonished. *TenDay, Period eighteen. Wow! I was knocked out for three days.*

'Day' was a nominal notion. The pale sun beat down constantly on the asteroid that ThaMu and the others were mining for the DiaTrine Mining Company. No sunrises, no sunsets. The company decided that a 'day' was composed of twenty hours, and a week was ten 'days'. The 'periods' began when they first started to mine the diatheryium crystals and diatheryazm[27] out of the rock.

Knocked out for three days. No-one came to help me?
Where're the rest of them – Sherzi? Joj? Jami?

Shitty-frellin' merd!

---

[27] Diatheryium crystals are a substance discovered after the Zeus probes landed in the satellites (asteroids, moon, dwarf planets) in the Kuiper belt in 2295. Tartumims feed on diatheryium crystals and excrete diatheryazm. Ground down and irradiated by solar furnaces, refined diatheryazm can be administered to quadruple human life spans.

Chapter 3: Kapitan

The Kapitan, Sherzi, was a gruff and rough giant of a man. Two and half metres tall, he was from Persikia[28] – glossy black skin, a bald but tattooed head, black eyes, and with a bushy black beard. When he smiled – an erratic event, seldom executed – his mouth glinted in the light exposing his diamond-coated teeth. His torso and broad back were extensively tattooed with intricate designs and many faces. His tattooed upper arms were twice the size of ThaMu's torso, and his tattooed thighs and calves were ebony pillars.

He had a lot of tattoos.

He was taciturn in the extreme, but every so often, when the crew were off duty and Joj and Jami were slipping into an alcohol-and-narcotic-induced dreamworld, ThaMu's circumspect questions were grudgingly answered. Sometimes, Sherzi talked about his former life on Terran. Admittedly ThaMu's encouragement to supply the Kapitan with triple Phobos whishky drinks would have something to do with it. The alcoholic veil of nostalgia cushioned his usual reticence and he related his childhood history.

'I was a contented commune kid,' he said, 'growing up with forty other children, eight fathers and twelve mothers, on a hippognu ranch and hydroponic garden, Persikia, Terran. It was idyllic. Life was comfortable and comforting.' He paused, as memories swarmed around him like mosquitos.

'Hmmm… go on? ' ThaMu prompted. 'What was it like?'

[28] Formerly the Middle and Central East. In 2000 the area spanned Afghanistan, Iran, Turkey, Greece, Libya, Ethiopia, Somalia,Yemen and all the countries between. It was united after the cessation of WW5 in 2199.

With a whishky-induced sigh that reeked of wistful remembrances he continued. 'We had plenty of time to play, exercise, learn and relax. Hectares of grassy fields, pinus forest where we made tree houses and obstacle courses, hover boards on cross-country trails. Our home-education was thorough: science, mathematics, language studies, music, debating, technology and martial arts.

'I excelled at all the subjects,' he said frankly.

ThaMu had no need to dispute his assessment. For all who met him, as a Kapitan he was described most often as 'impressive'. ThaMu would add another attribute: 'Fatherly'.

'Often, one of our parents would set up a campfire and some of the other parents would serve dinner outside. The smell of roast spuds and hippognu cutlets; the taste of apple and raisonne bread; the creamy taste of blended avomacados, yoghurt, banans and agupre syrup …. Hmmmm.'

Sherzi paused. His face was alight with memories. ThaMu listened, captivated.

At last, with a shrug of his massive shoulders, he went on. 'As the sun set and the stars emerged the fathers and mothers would take turns to play the lyre. They made up verses about what happened that day but we all joined in the choruses and many of us danced. Happy, sad, melancholic, lively …'

'When night fell, and the stars and moon shone so brilliantly overhead, another parent told stories. Fairy tales. Persikia folk tales. Cautionary tales about heroes and villains and magic and battles… funny or tragic or morally uplifting. Ah! Life – it was perfect.

'But…when I was twelve …'

Suddenly, the mood was icy. A wrenched look on Sherzi's face as if he had gazed at a neutron bomb. His eyes shut and an angry sadness enveloped his whole body. His fists clenched, his shoulders were hunched and a tightness around his mouth was frightening. ThaMu's first thought was to calm Sherzi down but she waited, an audience to the drama that had taken over the Kapitan's memories.

At last, he sighed, and took another draught of the Phobos whishky. A big draught. He looked at the roof with unseeing eyes and back down at his hands gripping the glass.

He began again, whispering his tale as if the diminished volume would make it fade away. That it would hurt less.

But ThaMu knew, it didn't.

Chapter 4:
Pirates

'When I was twelve, the commune was raided by space pirates. The commune community fought back but we were not fighters. We were outgunned, outplayed and outnumbered. I was big for my age – I was almost two metres tall and strong. My martial arts training was advanced so I was protecting some of my brothers and sisters. But, I was double-teamed by two frekin' scumbags. They had laser lances. They severed my left forearm and my right leg below the knee. One scalped me – I guess a trophy? They smashed my head on a rock and left me for dead.'

His voice swelled and his clenched fists threatened to bury the table in the floor. 'Those frellin' knobsuckin' smegging pirates slaughtered the hippognu's, burned our abodes and gardens, murdered the adults and most of the children and took a dozen as slaves to other colonies off-Terran.'

He struck the table with so much force it rattled everything in the room. Eyes widened, ThaMu stayed silent. Sherzi was alone with his memories. There was a weighty pause as Sherzi contemplated the tragic consequences of his childhood. ThaMu could not imagine the suffering that the young Sherzi had endured, but she knew that her intrusion into his memories would not be helpful. Or welcome.

At last he shook out his reminiscences, and his alcohol fuelled reverie and faced ThaMu with a challenging look. His introversion had returned. 'So… the authorities found me, fixed me up. I couldn't go back to the ranch, so I joined the Federation Navy as a peacekeeper. We got those pirates. I made them pay.'

ThaMu saw a fleeting but frightening look on his face, a lustful look of amoral retribution.

Sherzi's 'peace keeping role' was more like a 'vengeance keeping role', ThaMu thought.

Sherzi shook his head and returned to his normal, taciturn self. 'I resigned from the Navy. I got a ship, the Black Kyber[29]. Contracted myself to DiaTrine Mining Company. That's all. I am here.'

He went to his cabin and ThaMu was left mulling over Sherzi's revelations. It made sense. The fact that the tattoos on Sherzi scalp, back, torso and legs were of stylised faces of his brothers and sisters and parents – a constant memorial; the fact that the Kapitan was a powder-keg of suppressed rage; the fact that the Kapitan had two prostheses – a glittering titanium bionic left hand and lower right leg. He had eight fingers/toes and two opposable 'thumbs' on his left hand – an evolutionary step up. His dexterity on the navigational console was amazing to watch, as he dodge meteorites, space debris, small asteroids. And it made a marvellous difference in the kitchen.

His right leg moved with blinding speed across the ship's bridge, the excators and the laboratory to break up the numerous fights that Joj, Jami and me got in to.

After that, when they had time off, ThaMu would serve some Phobos whishky to Sherzi and plead: 'Can you tell me a story that your parents told you?' For a moment, Sherzi was disconcerted, but he looked around to Joj and Jami – drunk and drugged – and he softened.

He looked at ThaMu closely, shrugged, and said: 'Sure. Hmmmm... Once upon a time...'

---

29 The Black Kyber is the rocket that Kapitan Sherzi owns. He is currently contracted to the DiaTrine Mining Company

And he told her about fairy tales, Persikia folk tales, cautionary tales about heroes and villains and magic and battles, funny or tragic or morally uplifting. ThaMu drank in the stories, consumed them. They lived in her. It was compensation. For her childhood.

Now, trapped in the tunnel with her leg immobilised under a beam, she thought of Sherzi.

Angry, and stern, gruff, but he is always fair. And his stories were…magic. He could deal with anything that life threw at him. He was more like a father to me than anyone else.

But, why isn't he here!

And what about Joj and Jami?

Chapter 5:
Crew

Joj and Jami were clone twins from EurAkisa[30], Terran – well-built, black-haired, blue-eyed, speedy and always grinning. They were hatched in Bharatvarsha, Indiak, in a facility owned by DiaTrine Mining Company. Their 'education' was 'inclusive', in the terms of the Company 'deals'. Learning, playtime, meals, even sleep – it was proscribed by the Company hench men and women. But there are things that can't be taught or instilled and the twins had a habit of subverting the system. While they excelled in their studies and physical traits, they developed a wicked sense of humour.

Frell that! Wicked? Villainous. Fiendish. Fuggheads. The Kapitan was 'immune' (read: 'scary'), so I got the 'benefit' (read: 'victim') of their 'humour'. And the Kapitan and they were Terran – I was born off-world, so I was fair game. They were always teasing, provoking, harassing me and playing pranks on me. All the time.

Because they were clone twins, they were basically the same person, doubled. *Excellent for the rocket mission. Basically Sherzi had four hands for each task instead of two. A downer for me. Fuggheads! I got them in stereo.*

ThaMu wanted to know Joj and Jami's history before *Black Kyber.* She thought this would help her understand why they did these things to her. But it was like interviewing seagulls on speed. They'd flit and fly around ThaMu answering her questions with half sentences and mismanaged time lines. They pecked at the subjects, in turn. Often one would begin to answer and the other would finish the sentence.

---

30 Similarly, after the cessation of WW5 in 2199, a union of Europe, Russia and Asia.

One moment they were in front of her, apparently listening to her angry complaints for some obscene prank they had pulled on her and then, in a flash, they vanished into the Black Kyber or the tunnel or The Grot to plan another mischievous escapade.

Are they dead? And Sherzi? No, no, no.... Maybe my commset's broken. But they have not been to me in three days? Maybe...maybe they were knocked out. Maybe they are trapped like me. I could rescue them! I have to get out of here. Frekk-frellin' merd. Frellin-frekk!

With a supreme effort, she calmed herself down.
B r e a t h e...protocol...b. r. e. a. t. h. e. ....calm yourself.

She focused her mind on her chakras, centring and grounding herself. She grimly chuckled to herself. *Grounding myself! We are on an asteroid!*

Then, a thought struck her like a sun flare.
Where is Arse? Not here? Why?

Arse. The only other member of the crew.

Actually 'Arse' was not human. It was a robot.

a1i_8A8a was the Series 4 robot that the company sent out with the mining ships. ThaMu was not at all anthropomorphically inclined so she didn't subscribe to the robot as gender specific. Not He or She – but It.

ThaMu didn't like 'It' and mostly she ignored it.

Joj and Jami were used to that robotic technology and used its services. After all, they were born, raised, and educated in a DiaTrine Mining Company institution.

The twins tasked a1i_8A8a with all the heavy and menial work: transporting and lifting crates of the crystal and diatheryazm onto the ship; cooking the meals; cleaning the dishes and laundry; and compacting the rubbish and the inevitable toilet compost into cubes that would burn in the ship's exhaust.

In typical fashion, Joj and Jami thought that the robot's name was a mouthful.
In their speedy stereophonic deliberations they decided:

The name is too pompous.
Too aristocratic.
Too many syllables.
We should call it Charles.
Heehee.
Or Camel.
Aha…because it's basically a Beast of Burden.
A mule.
A donkey.
A pack horse.
Not even that, it is a horse's arse.
That's good – a horses's arse.
Aha - we should call it…

And they, in stereo, named the robot: 'Arse'
The name stuck.

Maybe Arse is okay? It was in The Grot? Maybe The Grot has been destroyed? Hopefully not…but…why isn't Arse here? Argh! My commset… not working? Maybe Arse's sensors are not working too.
But…maybe…

Too many 'maybes' but the last one spurred her on to action.

ThaMu gripped a rock with her right hand and smashed it on the exposed beam pinning her lower body. It transmitted a painful shock for her pelvis but the sound rang out, echoing and reverberating around the shaft. She did again. And again. And again.

She hammered the beam until she could not stand the excruciating pain. Then she collapsed, tears rolling down on her face and puddling in the helmet's recycledarator[31].

No-one is coming. No-one.

Despairing, she gave herself up to the oblivion of the condemned.

31 Recycledarator recycles the sweat, expiration, spit, tears etc... into useable drinking water.

Chapter 6: Transmission

```
$@.../.../
Login: 15:45:302651 TenDay, Period eighteen
Systms000483

[9] 212283 a1i_8A8a0@prgm

~ %[]&$m4sk-pt1.tc
       h4ndshake.sme...$mvd
~audio monitoring: signal detected ///succ3ss0r.p12
a1i_8A8a: activated $m1rr0r1ng.qt

Primary protocol Asimov Level 1

Responding...
Maximum Alert Level: Protocol - respond to all monitoring signals

       Bandwidth frequencies: not functioning
       Infra-red: not functioning
       Radio frequencies: not functioning
       Micro-wave frequencies: not functioning
       Macro-wave frequencies: not functioning
       Audio monitoring: functioning

              Input realised
              >>>>>
              <<<<<
       Motor function: testing
       >>>>>
              Detected: high impact damage
              Detected: obstruction - 63%
              Detected: medium particle density
              Detected: minimal vent function
       >>>>>
```

```
        Auto-repair: reset
Motor function: 68% functional
        … init_1.asec mov@rspnd prgrm …
:
:
Report: Bodily functions / personnel:
        Sherzi: null input
        Joj: null input
        Jami: null input
        ThaMu: O2-85%, Temp 15C, Activity-50%
Alert. Alert.
:
Motor functions: 63% functional
Response for compromised human

Primary protocol Asimov Level 1
Response is required
        >>>Search for input location>>>
        Time to respond: 104.3 microsec
                >>>>>
                <<<<<

Responding… init_5.fve
```

Chapter 7: A Biography...

Despair crept into ThaMu like a slow avalanche, and she became buried in despondency. Sobbing, she reflected on her wretched life.

She was born in Ogygiston, in the southern deserts of Mangala[32]. Her mother and father were cyber workers so she was left with an android nanny, twenty-four hours a day. She was technically orphaned at eighteen months – her parents were killed in an explosion that razed the laboratory. An act of a rival Company, according to the conspiracists.

With no-one paying the bills, she was fostered to an uncaring, negligent couple until she was seven. They used her to crawl up the downpipes and sand-filters of buildings so she could let them in. Then, they robbed the stores and warehouses and sold the proceeds to feed their various addictions.

When she was too big for the pipes, they 'assisted' [read: 'sold'] her to another thruple on UnitedKinland,[33], Terran: a man, and woman and an intersex partner. They had eleven other children, all of them neglected and uneducated.

Huh! What chance did I have. I got into shop-lifting, burglary, binge drinking, shonnk snorting[34]... The ploggers[35] found me, a dirty, malnourished waif.

---

32 Mangala = Mars (Sanskrit).

33 Formerly the Americas, incorporating Canada, USA, Central and South America, 'united' after the cessation of WW5 in 2199.

34 'Shonnk snorting' was a mind-altering narcotic that was popular in the 2350s.

35 The state police force – unsympathetic and callous individuals as a rule.

So I escaped my so-called foster parents, but went to something worse. From eleven sprogs to a hundred uncontrollable, undesirable, undisciplined tweens in Lady Liberty training school. Lady Liberty. Frekk! No ladies and no liberty there. It was a borstal boarding and brutal prison school.

When she was fifteen, the DiaTrine Mining Company 'motivated' [read: 'bought'] the state to release ThaMu into their 'care' [read: 'indentured'] when her testing regime revealed a superior scientific, mental and physical aptitude. The company 'contracted' [read: 'exploited'] her to work in the mines of moons of Saturn, Jupiter, Uranus and especially the Kuiper asteroid belt.

Contracted? Slavery I called it.
The Company owned everything I possessed.

From Mangala to Terran to the asteroids: ThaMu became a Belter[36]. For seven years she mined for the Company.

Then…
I was in a bar on Titan, getting drunk and fleeced by a hooper[37] in a game of domoker[38]. I was just about to punch his lights out, but my hand was gripped in a titanium vice. I looked around and saw an immense bear of a man, black as the ravines on Io. He picked me up – literally – and set me down in a booth away from the others.

'Kapitan Sherzi,' he said abruptly. 'Work with me. Fair wage. No nonsense though. Black Kyber. 2100 hours.'
I was awe struck. He assumed my compliance. But he was not wrong.
I was there at 2100 hours.

---

[36] Belter = a person who lives in the asteroid belt

[37] A con-man.

[38] A gambling card game.

Apparently Sherzi had looked up ThaMu's details and saw her contract from the Company was well and truly over. They were fleecing her! He saw that ThaMu's talent for mining diatheryium crystals and diatheryazm was unmatched. He approached the Company and got her released from their thieving hands.

I think there was some degree of intimidation there.

I met the other crew – Joj and Jami. And Arse the robot. Despite Kapitan Sherzi's curtness, he was true to his word. He paid a fair wage. He was an excellent Kapitan: ran a tight ship, expert astrogator, tech and mech maestro – not so good at cheffing, but Arse took care of that.

Sure, he tolerated some of the crude and adolescent nonsense of the twins – and my reaction to it – but he came down hard when there was too much trouble. No nonsense.

Black Kyber was my sanctuary – for five Terran years. Kapitan Sherzi was more a father to me than anyone else in my life. The twins were annoying 'brothers'. Very annoying. But brothers do that. And I got my own back sometimes!

When I lay back to sleep, I recalled my past: the desperation, the loneliness, the lack of love, the bad choices that my lack of self-esteem lead to – I realised that, here, in Black Kyber with Kapitan Sherzi and the boys, at last I saw that I could fit somewhere. I was exactly where I belonged. That I could call this 'home'. They were my family.

Dismayed and disheartened, sobbing her heart out, she recoiled from the idea of their death.

Surely not. They could be knocked out. Trapped. I could rescue them … if I can get out from under this beam!

She hammered the beam again in her frustration.
Then she heard something.

Huh? What? Where? Nah? Nah… Maybe a malfunction in my helmet? Merd! Figures. Now my techno is packing up…

But the sound grew louder. And directional. She stared in horror at the rubble down the shaft to The Grot.

The rocks were slipping down. Another rockquake? Maybe the asteroid is breaking up! Shitty-frellin' merd!

Chapter 8:
...and a Rescue

No...no...it is localised. Something is down there, towards the Grot. Something is breaking through!

A slim robotic arm broke through the rubble and removed the debris from the tunnel.

a1i_8A8a followed carefully, its tracks navigating the gap it made, sensors around its body making sure that the way was clear and not setting off another rockfall.

ThaMu couldn't believe it. *Rescued? Rescued!*

She studied the robot as it made its way towards her. Her elation was mollified by the fact that Arse was 'limping' badly. One of the motor tracks was slipping so the robot was like a person with a dead leg, sidling along. Three of its arms were functional, but the other two were disabled: one was fractured and the other severed above the 'elbow'. Some of the antennas and the sensors suffered damage too.

ThaMu gestured at the collapsium-plated steel beam that had pinned her legs, but Arse was already studying her predicament.

It extended several long-necked sensors to 'see' the problem from every angle: the beams supporting the tunnel; assessing the likelihood of another rockfall; the boulders and rocks around the shaft; the radiation level; ThaMu's spacesuit and helmet – the robot would be careful to ensure that the suit or helmet would not be compromised in its rescue attempt.

After studying and computing all the possibilities, the robot lifted the beam off like a matchstick with its three good arms and propped it vertically to aid the bivouac sheltering ThaMu, and making sure the path was clear for their escape.

ThaMu surveyed the damage to her legs. Her left one was fine but the right leg had too many 'joints'.

Fractured. Broken. Thank goodness the spacesuit first aid kicked in and administered the epidural. That's why I couldn't feel my legs.

The robot brandished one of its undamaged arms. One of its 'fingers' morphed into a syringe and it injected another narco-sedative into her neck. The effect was almost immediate.

ThaMu looked at the robot woozily and thought, with inappropriate and ironic alliteration: *Arse – an angelic avenger and awesome apparition* – and lost consciousness.

a1i_8A8a, despite its slipping track and damaged arms, lifted her up like a rag doll. The robot's gyro-opotimised suspension compensated for the increased load and it set out off the direction of The Grot.

Chapter 9: The Grot

The mismatched pair reached The Grot – the terraformed cave where the treated diatheryium crystals and the refined diatheryazm were stored along with the scientific equipment, the communication, environment, gravity, and atmosphere consoles, and all the comforts of 'home': bed, shower, toilets, kitchen, hologrammic gym, hologrammic library and pohlogram[39] table, a favourite with Joj and Jami.

The robot set ThaMu down on a bench and closed the doors to The Grot. It went to the main console and operated the climate controls. The screen displayed the environmental changes: temperature, oxygen content, humidity, gravity compensator. As the figures mounted up to living conditions ThaMu regained consciousness and blearily looked around the room. The Grot had survived the rockquake, the EMP and the radiation contamination. Admittedly the collapsium-plated steel beams had buckled and contorted but the place was largely intact and secure.

A refuge, A bubble. An oasis in the vast and uncaring universe, thought ThaMu, groggily distracted. She shook her head. *Ah! Get it together girl. Don't lose your mojo now.*

```
a1i_8A8a: []&$m4sk-pt1.tc - healing process activated
       temperature: 22 degrees celcius
       oxygen content: 23% - 60 L/min 100% FiO2
       humidity 80 -100 mmHg
       gravity compensator - 85% - rising
Climate acceptable
$m1rr0r1ng.qt
Medical mode activated >>>>>proceeding...
```

---

[39] A game like electronic pinball machines

The robot crossed to ThaMu and unclipped her helmet with a flourish. It held the helmet aloft with one hand and ThaMu looked at it, vaguely. In the robot's other hand a syringe appeared and it injected another narco-sedative into her neck. Again.

What the hell! What are…
Two and half minutes. That's all it took. Arse stripped ThaMu from her spacesuit, cleaned her body with unguent but fragrant bio-oils and administered nanites that would repair any deep tissue, muscle, vein, artery, neurones, lymph damage. It also used the nanites to ease the setting the bones of her right leg. Then Arse repaired the surface tissue with biogel spray and splinted the leg with a flexible but firm comsmoplastik[40]. Following medical protocol, the robot left the girl for four minutes. Then it injected her stomach with Meal4Mo – a predigested fluid that contained all the nutrients of a three-course meal. Two minutes later, the robot administered the 'antidote' for the narco-sedative.

…you doing to me. Why is…? Oh!

ThaMu sat up with her elbows on the bench and studied herself. Apart from the blue comsmoplastik cast on her right leg, she felt good. Her head was not aching, and her stomach was comfortably full.

She could detect the aftertaste and the aroma of the salty mushroom and grilled tartumim appetiser, a savoury gorgè terrine with Terran veges, and a delicious and sweet crème brûlée with hot trufflism compote, topped off a glass of Venusian sauvignon blanc.

But she was not fooled.

Wow! What a meal. I wish I could ***actually*** *experience it though.*

---

40 Comsmoplastik = a flexible pseudo-techno cast for broken limbs. It responds to the activity that the patient wants to achieve in a subtle, non-invasive but therapeutic way.

The comsmoplastik cast was flexible so she carefully eased herself off the table and wrapped an orange and gold sarumme[41] around her. The garment clung to her body like a second skin. She gathered herself together – physically, psychologically, mentally, spiritually – took a deep breath and let it out slowly.

She faced Arse and calmly demanded: 'Now. What's happened? What happened to the crew?'

---

41 A sarumme is akin to a body hugging silk sarong but maintains a comfortable temperature in most conditions.

Chapter 10:
Jargon

Rapidly Arse responded: 'A one capital I lower dash eight capital Aa eight aa space aitch numeral four en dee ss aitch aa kay ee period ss em ee … dollar sign em vee dee forward arrow forward arrow forwa…'

'Stop!' ThaMu responded. 'What? What sort of gobbledegook…'
She stopped herself.

Ah. I see. Arse is speaking programming language. Okay…okay…What did Joj or Jami do? They changed something for the robot…um..um… Aha!

'Arse. Initialise Human Interaction Attitudiniser, Level 1.'

The robot seemed to straighten its 'shoulders' and seemed to 'leer' at ThaMu. It spoke in a sexy baritone voice: 'Hiya ThannyMuuuu. Howzithangin'?'

ThaMu was nonplussed. *Frellin hell. What gives?*
Ah! Level 1. Joj and Jami. I should have known.

'Arse. Negate that. Initialise Human interaction attitudiniser. Level 10. What happened? What was the alarm event? And what happened to the crew? Where were Sherzi, Joj and Jami at the time of the accident?'

Immediately the robot responded, this time with a cultured alto voice: 'You required…requested Hu-man inter-ly…inter-action attit-tud-in-niser – Level 10. This is commen-da-dable. You…your re-questing…is appropos…appro-priate and exped-i-ent but, given present…prev-ious oppor-tun-es…nities, usual-ly with Joj and Jam-mee – the Hu-man inter-action attit-tud-in-niser was un-ly only lever le-vel six or se-ben.'

ThaMu was puzzled – the robot seemed to be missing and stuttering its words. Even the robot seemed to be surprised by its response. Its arms were pushing buttons and adjusting controls. It paused to contemplate itself before continuing. ThaMu had the impression that Arse was shaking its head in frustration, which would be a nonsense. Arse didn't have a neck. Still, she had the impression it was considering her feelings.

The robot carried on, despite its mangled speech.

'Level 10 of this…den-nice…de-vice…was con-sidar-able…satis-fect-ory…accep-table and most compel-ling. But, be-fore - Joj and Jam-mee named me…Ars-sse. If that is o-kay for yu…you… to…what… prefer … can to be called not Ars-sse. It is a term that is dero-tat-tuve…dis-parg…de-ro-gatoo…off-ensive.'

ThaMu was puzzled but she thought she got the gist of the robot's diatribe. 'Sure. Sure. That's okay. Arse – not okay. What should I call you though. "a1i_8A8a" is a bit unwieldy.'

'The cont-tract-ion of "A-One" would be amen…amen-able..agee… agree-tory…com-pliant?'

'Okay. Sure. A-One. Yeah. A-One.'
ThaMu eyed the robot. 'I'm not sure what is happening with your speech. It was not like that before.'

Immediately the thought of Joj and Jami and their 'interactions' [read: 'interference'] with Arse flooded her mind.

Where's Joj and Jami – they would fix it.

She exhaled then taking a deep breath she threw her hands in the air then brought them down in a prayer position against her lips and looked at the robot intensely.

Dropping her hands, she said with careful enunciation:
'The First. Question. I. Need. To. Know. … What. Happened? What was the alarm event? What happened to the crew? Exactly.'

Chapter 11:
Accident

'At 11:05:056678 on SevenDay, Period twentythree, my sens-stores... sens-sor-sss de-tected a critical rad-ia-tion, EMP and seis-smick alerts. Online probes indict...in-dicate that surface dis-interr was the cause of all the avent...events. Proba-bil-bitlity... Pro-bable cause – 99.87 per cent – over-heated excators caused an explo-ited...ex-plos-sion that released xenon-135 rad-ia-tion in an unsafe enfire-ons... en-viron-ment. In turn is led to non-safe lev-vils of dia-ather-ay-ium crys-stals breakdown and dia-tribe...dia-ther-solium radio-ation...radia-tion. The expl-o-tive...explos-sion impact-ted the core electro-mag-netic function causing an EMP va-ver-ly...an EMP wave and the force of the...ex-plosion caused a seis-smic disccur-rent...occurrence producing the plaster-roid...aes-tor-roid...aster-roid to break up...'

ThaMu interrupted. It was like a maze, threading the rambling and incoherent tale that the robot told.
'A-One. Stop. Stop!'

The robot stopped immediately.

'Okay – that's the event. But what happened to the crew.'

A-One took a brief moment then responded.
'You required the stat...stat...statue - sta-tus of the other humanoid... humanm co-hairline of the DiaTrine Min-in-ing Com-pany expo... exposition...of aster-roid #45708XM.456. All are...are...decreased... diseased.'
A pause, and A-One enunciated carefully: 'All. Deceased.'

ThaMu was gobsmacked. *What? What?*
'I can't understand? What are you talking about?'

'Joj and Jam-mee were in the cont…cont…contr-trol room of the excator that examined…exam…ex-plo-ded. Their vital funct-ials shut down immediately: temperature 1500 celcius, rad-ia-tion level critical, pulse 0bpm, respiratory 0%, audio risp-ponse – negative. The fax…fac-cts…support that the twins…the two crew members were incen-tiv-ted…in-cine-ne-rated im-mediate-ly.'

ThaMu was appalled by the matter-of-fact explanation from A-One.
A sob threatened to close her throat. The robot continued on as if it was reciting a meal menu.
It is just a machine, she thought. *Just a machine.*

'Kapitan Sherzi was ap-proached…ap-proach-ching the exterior door of the sha-ved…shaft. 2.3584secs after the explos-sive event he vital funct-ials reduced to: temperature -60 celcius, rad-ia-tion level critical, pulse 0bpm, respiratory 0%, audio risp-ponse – negative. His suit and hel-mich…met lost integrity – shred-ded. Gravity was null. His vital signs are remodel…remote… Kapi-tan Sherzi location is … 1200.568 klicks from this pres-sent loci…locus…loca-lity.' A micro-pause. 'Kapi-tan Sherzi bo-dy is in deep space.'

'Stop!' she gasped. 'Stop…stop…ssstop,' ThaMu whispered.

With difficulty, she pieced together the story of the event. The filtering process, the bad syntax and mispronounced or mistaken words and bald facts almost disguised her emotions but they rose up from her gut to her throat, a ball of acidic bile that threatened to choke her. She closed her eyes, spilling the salty tears across her face. Dazed, she faced the robot. 'Are you sure?'

A-One 'looked' at her impassively: 'Affeem…affirm-mative. Details of blud…bod-ily functional…func-tions for all cease-ed at the same time at the alurm…al-larm accid-ent-al …the al-larm…e-ventt…'
A pause.

'Summ-mery...sum-mer-isly...Conclu-sion: Sherzi, Joj, Jam-mee are not sub...sub...sup-porting the means of funct-tial life: Conclu-sion: they are all dis-ease...de-ceas-sed.'

ThaMu covered her head with her hands and burst into tears.

Dead. My family...is dead. I can't....I can't... Dead!

She wiped her eyes and nose. Her left hand covered her mouth as if to stall the grief that would leak from her soul. Her right hand grasped her chest and ribs as if she wanted to tear the soul out completely. Neither gesture worked. She collapsed on the floor and sobbed.

She thought about the last time she spoke to the Kapitan and the boys.

All four of them were at the surface, at the entrance to the shaft. She was angrily complaining about the way Joj and Jami – one of them or both of them – had exchanged the water in her bottle for dish water. The Kapitan grabbed the water bottle, hit the boys over the head with it, biffed it in the recycledator bin and ordered them to, 'Do your jobs! Joj, Jami – exacator. ThaMu – replacement transdominator.' He stalked off to the Black Kyber. She watched him go, turned and made some obscene gestures to the boys and dawdled towards The Grot. Then... nothing. Blank.

Three days later...

Frekk! That was the last time. How tragic. How insignificant. If I had known...

Again the tears welled up and she sobbed. She imagined she was breaking up, melting into a puddle and soaking into the ground below The Grot, diffusing into the asteroid, lost to the vastness of space.

She didn't want to be whole again, not responsible for being a survivor when all the 'family' she had ever loved were dead.

A-One drew close and rested an 'arm' over ThaMu's shoulders. Surprised, ThaMu stiffened, but she let the 'arm' alone.

It's only the robot programming, she realised. *It's just a machine but comforting, nonetheless.*

Chapter 12:
Imminent Danger

Moments? Minutes? Hours? ThaMu was not conscious of how long she was grieving and remembering.

But A-One interrupted with a sound like an excator ruining the obstacle course of her memories.

'Attention. Alert: Alert: The seismic shaft…shift… in the aster-roid is continu-ation…conti…const-tant. The rockfall is cont…contung… The rockfall will happen again. The aster-roid will dis-iter… Destroy…itself. Estim-ma-tion: 2:6:40:23.45378 days before the dis-inter…dis-inte-gration.'

'What!' ThaMu sat up feeling dizzy. With a self-centred but understandable revelation she thought: *I am all alone. Millions of klicks from other humans.* In a clear moment, she imagined that her 'family's' fate would be her own. In her grief she almost welcomed that.

Dead, deceased, demised, departed, defunct – in the vastness of space.

But her survival instinct kicked in. In her heart, she knew that Sherzi, and her twin 'brothers', would want her to exist. Remain. Live.

She rubbed her eyes, swallowed and shook the negative thoughts out of her head.

'You're sure that the asteroid is disintegrating,' she interrogated the robot. 'You're certain?

'Affirm..ting…affirm…'

She interrupted imperiously. 'Okay...okay... We have to make a plan. Some...plan.'

Puzzled, ThaMu looked at the robot.
'But...what about your speech? I can't cope, filtering your speech. Why are you stuttering and using wrong words? What gives?'

A-One seemed to muse on the question because it was at least nine seconds before it replied.

'Posit-ronic brain funct-tional. Inter-llectual properties at fully funct-tional. Ap-part-tally speech functional are im-port-tant...are im-pair-ed. Dis-ruter...disru-pted. Sum-mer-isly...Conclude-sion: EMP and radio-aty-tion could have affect speech.'
Again a micro-pause.
'Talk-ing slow-er is help-ful. Estimate: red-ducing the Hu-man inter-ly...inter-action attit-tud-in-niser to Level 6 could asess...assist.'

'Okay, okay. We will do that. Initialise Human interaction attitudiniser...'

'Halt!' interrupted A-One. 'Can you ens-ss-ure, despot...spite...despite the Level 6 attune-di-stniser, that you could... can... call me "A-One" rather that the alter...alter-nat-tive submarine...sub...sub-vers...sive name that Jos...Joj and Jam-mee ...the twins called me.'

'Ha! Sure. No problem.' She focused her voice and announced: 'Initialise Human interaction attitudiniser – Level 6. Speech rate patterning reduced to 60%.'

'Hey howyudoin'?' The baritone, sexy voice was back. But slower. ThaMu smiled before she realised it.

'Now…let's mak'a'plan,' proposed A-One. 'At the mo-ment it is ab-bout 2.6 days before this…rock is ka-bloom-my!'

With a huge 'whew' ThaMu emptied her lungs of air. She inhaled slowly.

'Um… The ship – Black Kyber? Is the ship operational?' she asked anxiously.

'Nah. Non-funct-tional. The rad-ia-tion fried the com-put-tators and the rockfall dam-maged the impervium hull making it un-us-able.'

'Lifepods?'

'Nah. Non-funct-tional. Life-puds on Black Khyber – all were blood… blo-wen away in the expl-ti-sion. The live-puds on the aeter-roid can mount-ain-tain…main-tain your life for only one day. Not enough. Not nearly enough.'

'Frellin-frekk. What else? Can we use a stasis field?'

'Yep.' The robot seemed to 'shrug'. 'But the aster-roid will be…destroy-ed…and everything on it. Includ-dition…inclu-ding you in your sta-ss-ss-is fie-eld. Ka-bloom-my!'

'Could we rig up the extra exacator with a ramscoop and have a gaser gun to have…'

'The extra ex-excators were destriod…de-stroyed in the raock…rock-fall…'

ThaMu buried her head in her hands. She wanted to sit down on her haunches but the comsmoplastik splint prevented her. Instead, she sat down on the floor, legs outstretched, against the wall.

She was out of ideas.

A-One broke the silence.

'If the Com-pan-ee install-ed matter tran-tran-trans--mitters we could say "Beam me up, Scotty!" But, unfortu-nate-ly, they didn't.'

What? A joke? Ancient history as a joke? ThaMu was not ready for this. *Sarcasm? Nah. Couldn't be. It's just a machine.*

She ignored this facetious remark and focused on the issue at hand.
'If we can't get off this rock, what about other ships?' ThaMu said hopefully. 'Is there anyone in the area, this part of space, that can rescue me…us?'

A-One took a microsecond to respond.
'Detect-tion sy-stems indi-cate that a ship is two days away. About 900,000 klicks. A torch-drive ship.'

ThaMu was almost celebrating with a 'Woohoo!' but the robot continued on.
'But…talk-king to them could be a problemo!'

'Whadyarmean?' ThaMu unconsciously mimicked A-One's Level 6 vocal mannerisms.

'The bandwidth, infra-red, radio, micro- and macro- free-mnk…fre-quen-cies are not ope-rate…opera -st-ly… Not working. Kaput. And bang-gin' on a beam wouldn't car-ried for a ship a million klicks from us.'

ThaMu evil-eyed the sarcarstic robot.
Surely the robot shrugged its shoulders. No. Surely no. It's still a machine. Isn't it?

'But…' A-One said – with an almost mischievous air – 'an est-estim-estim…think that a sub-etheric-stream–mang-o-lise wave could al-lert them with good eff…eff…eff…eff-ect.'

ThaMu stared at the robot, making sure that A-One was not joking.
'Well…do that then!'

'Well…not so ea-zzz-sy!' A-One replied. 'Not. So. Ea. Sy!'
It seemed that the robot was almost gloating.

'Shir-rez, Kapit-tin-no, produced a pro-to-col that res-trict-ed access-ess to the sub-etheric-stream–mangol wave systemo. We can use if…in…it, but it…uses a Pass.'
A pause.
'Word.'

Chapter 13: Password

'Well...what's the password?'

'That's for me, and some-think...some-thing you have to wok...work out your-self.'

ThaMu wanted to gag the cheeky robot.
I should have left it with Level 10. I can understand it more with Level 6 but – what a jerk! Just like Joj and Jami. Hah! Maybe it learnt from them.

The thought of the incinerated twins almost brought more tears.

She took a moment and then asked: 'Surely – when it is an emergency – surely the password would be suspended?'

'Na, na, na. That's not how a pro-to-col wok...works. You have to guest...guess it.'

ThaMu was dumbfounded. Sherzi was a gruff, cantankerous individual, but surely he was not stupid enough to place this protocol on this life-saving process.
I guess he did. Maybe he didn't realise that this is the only option we have left. That all other avenues were 'non-funct-tional'.

Again she slipped into A-One's level 6 speech patterns. ThaMu chanted and echoed like a hologrammic game show host.
'Well... we've two...two...two days to get it ooooooon.'

'Nah. The pot-ent-tial rescue craft is not on our rock's lo-cus. Estimation: you have one and half hours to con-tact them, or they would...will not be he...here to res-cue you before the rock...Ka-bloom-my!'

'And you can't access the sub-etheric-stream-mangol wave transmitter until you have the passcode?'
'Yep.'
'You can't re-route your programming subroutines for this emergency?'
'Nah.'
'Even if it makes my demise certain?'
'Nah.'
'Aha! The Asimov rules of Robotic behaviour – Number One. You can't endanger a human with inaction. Aha, aha.'
ThaMu was triumphant.

'Nah. You had…has…have a chance to work to…is…out the pass-ssy-word in the next one and halve…half hours. In factual…fact – it is 1:34.563425 hours. If you don't wok…work it out in about 1:34 hours my program-ming will give the pass-ssy-word … obeyed-ing the As-i-mov rules. I will complete the action.'

'But,' ThaMu reasoned, 'it's quite likely that the other ship will not work out our mayday message for several minutes and, by their own process of considering all the variables, they will not change course before we are…ka-bloom-my!'
ThaMu slammed her hands down on the ground in a petulant, adolescent but absolutely appropriate behaviour.
'Well,' ThaMu sulked, 'well…that's sux!'
Now I am Level 6 myself. Get it together.

Again, the robot seemed to 'shrug' its 'shoulders'.

ThaMu took a deep breath and said:
'So… a password. How hard could it be. Um… what about "DiaTrine".'
'Nah.'
'Sherzi.'
'Nah.'

'Kapitan.'
'Nah.'
'Whishky.'
'Nah.'
'Persikia.'
'Nah.'

In the next thirty minutes, ThaMu dredged every topic and subject and association that she knew about Sherzi: his favourite meals, his psychedalcohol drinks, favourite hippognu names, the names of his favourite tale-telling parents, the name of his pet Austral tiger, the names of his Navy's ships, and the names of his previous Kapitans, his favourite songs, the barmaid at the bar on Titan, other lovers that he had mentioned in passing… …

For each attempt, A-One said 'Nah' in the same bland inflection and volume. As if it didn't care.

Of course, it doesn't care. It is a machine.

In frustration, ThaMu raised her hands and screamed. 'Argh! Can't you give me a clue?'

'Sure. It is two words.'

Chapter 14:
Two little words

'What!' ThaMu was astounded. 'Why didn't you tell me before?'

'Ya never asked,' said the robot, almost nonchalantly.

If ThaMu were closer she would punched the robot…but she realised that the robot would not feel it. And she would have a sore hand.

In the next fifty-five minutes ThaMu tried: 'Poker Game', 'Regal Hand', 'Kapitan Sherzi', 'bald head', 'tattooed skin', 'Mining Company', 'diatheryium crystals', 'Joj Jami', …

Every pair of words that could be associated with Kapitan Sherzi was canvassed.
With the same bland and impassive volume and inflection A-One answered: 'Nah'.

Time was running out and ThaMu was desperate.
Think! Think! Two words? Two words…Ah! What if…

'Before you said that I didn't ask for a clue. Now – I am asking.
Are there any other clues?'

'A-Okay. Pro-to-col alloys…all-owed to give three cl…cl-ues.
One: It is – two words.
Two: It is from a st…st-ory.
Three: It is re-lationary…re-lat-ed. To me.'

ThaMu danced on the spot – not in a good way!
'Frellin' frekin'-merd! You stupid machine! Argggh!'

She was flabbergasted. She clenched her arms and made a fist with each hand, dropped her head down to her chest and screwed up her eyes. She let out a mammoth sigh then inhaled steadily.

Okay…okay… Two words. A story. Related to 'me' - the robot? Maybe some of the things that Joj and Jami were always joking about? They were always teasing the robot. Arse! Something about Arse…

'Arse wipe.'
'Nah.'
'Arse hole?'
'Nah.'
'Dumb arse.'
'Nah.'
'Arse licker.'
'Nah.'
'Arse monger.'
'Nah.'

ThaMu's emotions were frayed and she was almost panicking.
It's too late. It's too late! I can't think… Too many options.
Breathe. Breathe. B r e a t h e…

Okay. I am distracted with Joj and Jami.

Kapitan Sherzi had the robot on the ship way before the twins arrived.
So – something before the twins… Not 'Arse' but related to the robot.
Before it was A-One.
A-One! Well, why not.

'A-One?' ThaMu asked anxiously…
…but the response, bland and impersonal, was: 'Nah.'

Chapter 15: What's in a name?

Desperation caught ThaMu like a caragessen[42], squeezing the life out of her, circling her body with ever diminishing coils that stole her panicked breath away. She gasped: 'How long before the…'

A-One pre-empted her question: '6.345 minutes'.

Is he gloating? ThaMu looked at the robot. *No, no, no. It is not a 'he'. Just a machine. A machine.*

She forced a breath. In. Out. I n… O u t ….. I n…….O u t……..
She looked up at the ceiling of The Grot.

My irrefutable refuge. My malignant mausoleum. My cosmic crypt.

She sat upright as her determination infused her blood and found her muscles. *No. No.* ***No****! It won't be my grave. I will not die here.*

She closed her eyes, breathed out and in slowly.

So…okay, okay… It is related. To it. The robot. Two words. And a story…

ThaMu imagined this situation through Kapitan Sherzi's eyes. In his mind. The password would mean something to him.

The Grot. The mining operation. The Black Kyber. His history. Something with the robot? A story.

---

[42] Caragessen = Ten-meter-long serpent of great strength.

She recalled Kapitan Scherzi: his calmness but taciturn-ness, his bear-ness, his presence, his soft side when the boys were drunk or drugged, when he opened up to ThaMu about his childhood. A memory, an ethereal reminiscence of him, was almost tangible to her.

She opened her eyes slowly. They were tired. She blink rapidly to clear her vision.

The stress of the last two hours was catching up with her. She vaguely glanced over the bulky body of the broken robot. There was a plate attached to the 'torso', just underneath the wreckage of the amputated rear arms. And there was the name of the robot. She chuckled, hopelessly.

No. Not Arse. Not A-One. Just a1i_8A8a.

A thought kindled in her brain.
Yes! Or actually No! Not Arse nor A-One. Sherzi never called the robot that. He always referred to it with its proper 'name'. The code. a1i_8A8a. Something about that…something…

ThaMu remembered some of the things that Kapitan Sherzi talked about. The stories that his parents told.

Fairy tales, Persikia folk tales, cautionary tales about heroes and villains and magic and battles… There were stories…

She looked at the name and blearily refocused her sight on the other side of The Grot. Her head was spinning.

I remember one in particular. It was a tale about space pirates. I remember because I was surprised that he told this story after the incident with his family. The murdering space pirates. And the slaves they took. He hated those space pirates.…but he told this story several times.

The story goes....um... Forty space pirates had a cave on Mangala[43]*. A Grot like this one, with all their loot. It had magic doors. And...and... the hero, the peasant boy was named Alha ...um...umm...Akly Bee something....um... no.... Ali. Yes Ali... Ali...Ali Baba. Yes! Ali Baba!*

The blurred vision on the robot's name and the name of the story's hero met in ThaMu's mind like a supernova. Transliteration!

a1i_8A8a. Ali Baba. It is the same. Yes. a1i_8A8a = Ali Baba! Yes. Yes!

Despite the comsmoplastik cast, ThaMu jumped in the air with a victory salute. All the stress and strain were forgotten at the solution of the puzzled resolved itself.

Oh. I remember. I remember. Oh! Oh! Ali Baba spied on the space pirates and discovered the treasure. And he learned the password. Yes!

ThaMu looked at a1i_8A8a triumphantly.
'Open Sesame!'

'Yup!' said the robot.

Surely I detected a little bit of exaltation in its tone, thought ThaMu. *But – no – it is just a machine.*

```
$@.../.../
Login: 20:13:893651 TenDay, Period twentyfour
Systms002378
[9] 2186483 a1i_8A8a0@prgm
~ %[]&$m4sk-pt1.tc
        h4ndshake.sme...$mvd
        Password: affirmative response
```

43 Mangala = Mars (Sanskrit).

```
ali_8A8a: sub-stream-mangolise wave activated
        Broadcasting …
        Repeat *** >>>>
                MayDay - MayDay - Mayday
                All crafts Alert - Extreme Alert
                Rescue coordinates AT188.99673 -
                SL45.28864
                Human survivor
                MayDay - MayDay - Mayday…
                Please respond - all crafts…
        Repeat from *** until affirmative answer >>>>
```

She heaved a complicated sigh: relief, exhaustion, anxiety, sadness, grief, gratitude.
Sadness for Joj and Jami.
Grief for Sherzi.

And gratitude for the Asimov Robotic Laws.

SKIDADDLE

PREFACE:

I was working on a story about a young person with aphasia.

Stroke is the most common cause of aphasia and the risk of stroke increases with age. Most of the people with aphasia are older. Usually they have spouses, children, grandchildren and long-time (or long-term) friends that care for them through the complexities of this discommunication condition.

Especially spouses or siblings.
Most times the memories, the shared experiences of every day life over ten, twenty, thirty, forty years before the aphasia event, will sustain the difficulty of trying to understand one who is not speaking clearly. A gesture, a one-or-two-word sentence, a squeeze of the hand, a tilt of the head, could mean volumes to people who know each other well.

But stroke can occur with young people too, and there are other conditions that produce aphasia, such as brain injury, brain disease or tumour. If a **young** person has aphasia, and their parents are not around, the people around them might not be invested in their care. Maybe their friends move away – wanting to get on with their own lives. And, for a partner – a girlfriend or boyfriend – aphasia could be quite a challenge to spend time with an uncommunicative person. They have not the advantage of spending years together before aphasia set in.

The back story of *Skidaddle*: Zac, and his mother and sisters, his injury, his struggle to meet someone with whom he could have a meaningful relationship as a young person with aphasia – it just kept growing. Clearly, it was **not** going to be a short story.

I channeled some of the story into another short story about a young person in the snow, meeting a deaf person. Alex is the 'hero' of *Yeti* – the first story in *Even More Suspect Speaking*. It was a much simpler story about two people who overcome their communication issues. Queenstown, SkiRescue and its owner Jiāo featured in both stories, but I am sure that Alex and Zac never met. (I think Alex was in Queenstown several seasons before Zac?)

Enjoy.

SKIDADDLE

Chapter 1: Hunk

Zachariah looked at himself in the mirror.
It was almost too easy, he thought.

He washed his hands and shook them out, slicking his golden-blonde hair over his head in a casual wave like the unmade bed. Again he checked his physique, preening in front of the mirror and tilting his head as the alpha male he was.

Well…which one? Blonde or brunette? Hmmm…

In the huddle and crush of the club it was so easy to pick up girls. Popular opinion, and not just females either, had Zac down as a hunk. A smidgen under two metres tall, broad shoulders, narrow hips, and big feet. Dusky skin, blue-eyed, strong-nosed, firm-jawed, with designer stubble and long hair, tied into a tight man bun – he was a catch.

And he caught. The girls.'

In the bar he had a routine – sidling up to his 'mark'; 'accidentally' knocking into her and spilling her drink; apologising with a 'Sor-ree! Sor-ree!'; and, with one hand, indicating the half-filled glass and gesturing that he would replace it. With the other hand, he would gently brush the spilled droplets off her arms or shoulders, all the while gazing intently into her eyes with a promise of something else.

The girl would scan him. Shy women ducked their heads, looking at him from the corners of their eyes like an apprehensive bird. Bold women would shrug as if the drink was not an issue but they would tilt their heads, nostrils flaring, eyes sharp, intrigued.

Seldom – very seldom – the 'mark' would decline and turn away from him and go about their other business.

Often the woman would start a conversation, but Zac would shake his head and whisper in her ear: 'No Eng-lish!' Usually the girl would nod her head, reasonably. He would breathe in her ear 'Franz' or 'Claude' or 'Rodrigo' – whatever he fancied that night.
And, usually, she would say her name.

His 'mark' would keep up a monologue and Zac would feign intense interest. He had practised single words or phrases to gain her confidence and compliance. After a while, he would gesture to the dance floor. He was an excellent dancer, but always observed and imitated his partner's style of dancing and built on this. When his partner began to dance he raised the bar (or the barré): when she twisted, he swirled; when she moved her hips, he would grind; when she raised her arms, languorously, he would interlace his fingers with hers, bring them down and pull her closer. The two of them were in their own world, intensely connected, isolated in a magic bubble of music and intimate dancing. Before long, she thinks that she is the only woman that matters for Franz. Or Claude. Or Rodrigo.

Sometimes, a boyfriend would show up, spoiling for a fight. Zac would make a fake-macho effort in the confrontation taking pseudo umbrage but always threw his punches. The victorious boyfriend would be puffed up, arrogant and cocky, but usually the woman would berate the boyfriend, and side with the 'loser'. 'Get lost, you pig!' was the commonest phrase. Then, she would console Franz on his defeat.
Or Claude. Or Rodrigo.

And the consolation usually took place at her place.

The sex was always great.

Zac had a silent body alarm clock. Before dawn, he extricated himself from the bed/sofa/floor/table/under-the-table, gently removing any limb that was imprisoning him, and he was always half-dressed before his 'mark' was rubbing the sleep out her eyes. 'Work,' he said, with a disappointed shrug and a satisfied smile. One was fake the other was genuine. He left the room, headed for his home, a shower, breakfast and change of clothes for work.

One night stands – the perfect way to have aerobic exercise, sexual connection, with no emotional commitment. Yuuus!

Zac abdicated his responsibility for the one-night-stand: *because* he thought to himself *the women always want it, enjoy it, and savour it. A memory of 'what I got up to when I was footloose and fancy-free'. Something scandalous to tell their friends. Or a juicy jibe to taunt a jealous ex-lover…*

The lack of 'English' in his fake personas – Franz, Claude or Rodrigo – was more literal than most people imagined. Zac's lack of 'English' was recent.
And absolute.

Zac was born in Aotearoa New Zealand and English was his primary language, with a working connection to Māori, the second official language for the country. He had some German and French from his basic high school education and a smattering of Spanish from TV viewing *Where is Carmen Santiago?* cartoons.

But his connection to language – all languages – disappeared after the accident.

Chapter 2: Biography in a nutshell

Zachary had two older sisters, Minerva and Persephone – seven and ten years older than him. The three kids had three different fathers. And none of the fathers were in the picture. Ever.

Zac's mother was a constant confusion in his life. He loved his mother, but even as a child he recognised that she was a weak and whimsical woman. *Look at the names we were saddled with,* he often pondered. Her decisions were based on the flimsiest data: intuition, horoscopes, gossip, dreams and psychic readings. Benevolent chaos reigned in his childhood and adolescence.

Zac's education was erratic, to say the least. He had severe dyslexia, but it wasn't diagnosed until late adolescence, because most of his schooling was home-based – wherever 'home' was at the time. In his first twelve years Zac had lived in twenty-four houses, flats, apartments and house trucks in sixteen cities, towns, and rural communities. For three months, their abode was a tent. At least it was summer.

They seemed to move from one city to another, one boyfriend to another. It was like they were on the train, a railway ride with no map, no destination and lots of carriages filled with baggage. Emotional baggage. Zac's mother died when he was thirteen years old – a fragile age for a boy to lose his mum. An overdose of drugs, alcohol and malnutrition.

His sisters stepped in. They were twenty and twenty-three at the time and not ready for a rebellious, wounded and angry teenager. His 'train' fell off the rails. Truancy, shop-lifting, under-age drinking, smoking spliffs, assault… After a few years his sisters couldn't handle him and the State stepped in.

After a stint in borstal, the eighteen-year old Zac returned 'home'. His sisters had thankfully abandoned their mother's itinerant lifestyle and settled in Hawke's Bay with Perse's boyfriend, Tony. Zac was chastened by his juvenile imprisonment and sincerely apologised to his sisters. He landed a job with Tony, on the proviso that he would sort himself out.

Tony managed a construction company in Hastings. Zac got on with Tony and he became a reliable, capable worker. For five years, everything went well.

Then, at twenty-three, Zac fell off an unsecured ladder against the second storey of a building. He sustained major injuries: two broken arms, a broken leg, and he smashed his head on the stony ground. He was in a coma for five days. Physically, he made a full recovery in terms of his limbs, but the brain injury damaged his speech centres.

When he tried to speak he lost most of his words. It seemed that the path from his brain to his mouth was a sticky quagmire that sucked his speech into a muddy mess of incomprehension. Those words that he could pronounce were often wrong: mangled, distorted, sputtered and stuttered.

He could hear and understand things, but he could not voice them.

He had – has – aphasia.

Chapter 3:
Aphasia: can we talk about it?

Before this accident, the dyslexia meant he couldn't read or write very well. Now, his reading and writing were more erratic but his speech was much worse. *Ironic. When I could talk I could explain that I was dyslexic. Now, I can't even say the word.*

The hospital promised everything: rehabilitation, speech language therapists, occupational therapists, physiotherapy, music therapy… But nothing eventuated. He seemed to fall through cracks in the system. He sank into a depression – he became moody, grumpy, cantankerous. He and his girlfriend, Rachel, argued all the time.

Well, sort of argued – obviously, she did all the talking. Zac just snarled, grunted and broke things. Rachel berated him in no uncertain terms for his boorish behaviour and bad humour. She left him two months after his accident, saying she couldn't stay with a temperamental and petulant mate. Zac suspected that she couldn't relate to anyone who could not sweet talk and adore her.

Fuck that! I am the one whose life has backfired. I am the one whose fuckin' life has turned upside down.

His friends drifted away. They were always talking about the latest rugby games, racing, politics and girls but he had no words. He could not talk to them. They thought he had no opinions but he **had** his point of view. When he tried to speak, someone always talk over him, arguing their points or laughing and joking. The noise in the pub was too distracting, too confusing and the black bear of depression came closer every week. He gave up on his friends.

No, they fucking gave me up.

Even at work, his muteness affected his co-workers. Like his ex-friends, he couldn't communicate with them in social chitchat. He couldn't answer them when they needed something from him. He couldn't warn them if something was dangerous or unsafe.

About six months after the accident he was working on a construction site, wearily building a brick wall with heavy concrete blocks. For a week his depression became exacerbated by insomnia, and he was drinking and smoking dope. He stumbled, knocking a concrete block from the wheelbarrow and into the path of one of the young workers. 'Hey!' the youth exploded. 'Wha' the fuck, you retard!'

Zac lost it.

The frustration of six months of not being able to express himself, six months of emotional isolation, six months of resentment for what life had done to him, incensed him.

He hurdled the wheel barrow and punched the youth in the mouth, his nose, his head, his stomach. He grappled with him and smashed him into a plasterboard wall. The wall fell down, and wrecked several thousand dollars worth of computer equipment and electronics on the other side. The foreman intervened and Zac punched him. The other workers tackled him – his face was in the dirt, his hands and legs struggled to break free as they pinned him down.

Eventually, the rage left him, his arms and legs and shoulders relaxed. Warily they let him up. Shaken and overcome, Zac was doubly inarticulate with shock. He stood up quickly and the workers and foreman understandably backed away. Zac took the easy way out.

He ran to his car and reversed so violently it collided with a fork lift loaded with roof tiles. The fork lift was upended, the tiles broke and the crate the tiles were in managed to take out the strut of the scaffolding on the building. The scaffolding went down in a mass of pipes, ladders and boards. Luckily no one was hurt.

Tony had to give him notice.

In the next month, Zac extreme moodiness, anger and surliness alienated Mini and Perse, his sisters. Contemptuously they gave him the 'silent treatment'.

Silent! Ironic, Zac thought, as he sank further and further into depression. *What's the fuckin' point? No friends, no girlfriend, no family, no job.... It is so fuckin' pointless. Pointless life. I can't express...anything. At all!*

Two weeks later, he packed his belongings into a tramping pack. He left Hawkes Bay, heading south for a ferry to take him across Cook Strait and then drove to Queenstown.

He didn't say goodbye to Tony.

Or Perse and Mini.

Just...left.

Chapter 4: Waipounamu[44]

Zac marvelled at the landscape in the South Island.

For his first thirteen years his mother shipped the family from place to place all over the country in impulsive drive for a better life. It always led to catastrophe. But, that was only in the North Island.

The unrealistic parenting skills of Mini and Perse; the borstal that applied fascist zeal to their treatment; the five years that Zac had been at the construction company in Hawkes Bay; and the six months with aphasia: that had all happened in the North Island.

Zac had heard so many tourists raving about the South Island with its amazing scenery and experiences but he discounted this as 'tourist exaggeration'. Despite his mother's fanciful itinerary around the North Island, he had seen so many wonderful sites and experiences: Wellington's Te Papa Tongarewa and Zealandia, the caves at Waitomo, Whakarewarewa and the hot pools at Rotorua, mini-golf at Taupō, Lake Waikaremoana, Kelly Tarlton's aquarium in Auckland, Northland's kauri forests and Ninety-mile Beach…

Then there was tramping and camping the Ruahine and Kaweka ranges in Hawkes Bay, and the cuisine and wineries around Napier, Hastings and Havelock North. Could the South Island beat that?

Apparently so!

The journey from Picton to Dunedin on the East coast was packed with scenic sites and astonishing and quirky experiences. Blenheim had

[44] Waipounamu is the Māori word (and make more descriptive) name for Aotearoa New Zealand's South Island

its wineries; Kaikōura its seals colonies, crayfish and whale watching; the Christchurch gondola; Geraldine its cheeses; Oamaru the Steampunk Head Quarters Museum; and the breathtaking sight of the sunrise on the Moeraki Boulders. And all of it was flanked on one side by the stunning Southern Alps, snow-clad and brilliantly monumental, and on the other side the cool, blue-green watery expanse of the Pacific Ocean.

Zac slept in his car on the side of the road in rest areas, making his breakfast and coffee on a portable gas stove. He picked up odd jobs along the way to financially tide him over.

One stunning morning in Kaikōura epitomised his trip.

He left his car and stretched, turning stiffly this way and that to wake up the muscles in his back. Something dark and big was next to his car. He focused on it and, filled with astonishment, he realised it was a sea lion – an adult sea lion – much bigger than him. The creature rose on its front flippers, lazily looked at Zac, blinked, twitched its whiskers, yawned, and settled down on the rocky beach, closing its eyes. *I guess, this is his home and I am the invader.*

Cautiously Zac went to the other side of the car. Keeping an eye on the sea lion, he was on his haunches making coffee and looking out on the ocean when he saw some disturbance in the water. He stood upright and looked closely, still keeping an eye on the creature beside the car. He scanned the water.

Dolphins! *There must have been twenty or thirty … no wait …a hundred.* The disturbance at sea was growing and Zac saw that the expanse of watery confusion was more like two hundred and fifty metres long, thick with dolphins leaping, pirouetting, somersaulting out of the sea like trampoline tumblers and greeting the day with absolute delight.

He headed inland and spent a chilly morning at Alexandra, before going from Clyde and Cromwell, where he met the Clutha River, Mata-au. The river was pristine – clear, fresh, deep and so, so blue. He was tempted to swim in the fast flowing water but he soon squashed this urge when he realised the temperature was just seven degrees[45].

The gorge was decorated by thyme plants under the snow cover. At Cromwell he followed the Kawarau River and every turn on the road seemed to astonish him more. At the lake, he turned and saw the immense mountains that were a background for Queenstown, The Remarkables.

And they were remarkable with their snow-clad tops and valleys and rocky ravines. Magnificent.

He turned and looked at the town and felt a sense of rightness. A feeling that this is where he ought to be.

And no mistake coming to Queenstown!

This tourist town was the adventure capital of Aotearoa New Zealand: skiing, snowboarding, mountain biking, bungy jumping, jet boating, luging, paragliding, hang gliding, rafting, rock climbing, tramping, mountaineering… all packed into this small holiday destination.

And a party place.

His trip both cooled and inspired Zac considerably – figuratively and literally. He acknowledged that his attitude had poisoned his relationship with his co-workers, his friends, his girlfriend and his sisters. But, he didn't want to go back.

---

[45] seven degrees Celcius is 45 degrees Fahrenheit

Through the road trip he observed that the tourists were understood by everyone despite their lack of English. People seemed to be willing to understand them. Body language, gestures, indications seemed to be enough for the locals to understand their wishes.

A germ of an idea blossomed in Zac's brain…

But, he had to get a job. With no qualifications to speak of, and with the added complication of his aphasia, he went looking for notices of job vacancies on the shops and businesses around town.

Barista for a café? Electric bike shop? Waiter in the Indian Restaurant? A Thai, kebab, Subway, Kentucky Fried Chicken? Dish-hand for an Indian/Thai/Chinese/European-fusion brasserie?

The managers looked at him with interest but when they heard his stuttering and mangled speech they shook their heads. 'Nah. I don't think you're right for this job,' they said with an expression of regret, embarrassment, snobbishness or insolence – depending on which establishment they worked for.

Zac had almost given up when he spied a tiny sign in the corner of property. In hand-drawn calligraphic lettering it said: *Backroom Worker Required.* The title above announced the business as *SkiRescue – Equipment Rentals.*

What the hell. Here goes… as he stepped up to the entrance.

Chapter 5: SkiRescue to the rescue

The doors were swing doors, just like the saloon in a Wild West movie, and a surprise for Zac. He went through expecting them to be sensible, ordinary doors, but they flew open, bounced on the wall and returned with the same impetus, crashing into Zac face. He yowled, tears of pain sprang into his eyes watered and his hand to his nose, finding blood.

'Sorry, sorry! I told Jião that he has to fix these doors. They're a trap. Sorry, sorry. C'mon … sit down. I'll get a tissue. Sit down.'

He was aware that a woman had taken his arm and led him to a seat along the wall. He blinked away the tears and vaguely saw someone reaching across the counter to fetch some tissues. She dabbed at Zac's nose and was patiently insistent when he flinched. 'There. No serious damage,' she reported, and she yelled: 'Jião! Jião, your deadly doors have a new victim.'

She moved to the other side of the room and Zac glimpsed an attractive woman: tall, black hair tied in a pony tail, athletic body in a red, skin tight track suit and Ugg[46] boots. She continued to yell: 'Jião, Jião get out here,' as she burst through another set of swing doors at the back of the showroom.

Zac was just getting up, nursing his nose, when a man came in from the backroom. He was Asian, maybe fifty, fifty-five, sparse and greying hair slicked down with some sort of gel, and an impassive expression on his face. He was shorter than Zac, a lot shorter, but seemed to have the same bulk.

---

46 Ugg boots are a unisex style of boots that are typically made of sheepskin with fleece on the inside, a tanned outer surface and a synthetic sole

Built like a brick shit-house, Zac acknowledged, a recalled memory of a description from one of the men in his mother's life. *What does that mean, exactly? But he is – well – rotund.*

'Droors. Sorri abo't dat,' the man said, with a singular lack of compassion. 'What'y'want?'

Zac motioned to the window, indicating the *Work Wanted* sign. He rose and searched in his pocket for his wallet. He produced a card and held it out to the man. It said:

I have Aphasia.
I understand things perfectly
BUT
I have difficulty speaking, reading and writing.
You can help by speaking clearly and slowly.
And giving me time.

Zac said: 'Work-ker… good. Good work-ker. Hard…work… Strong. Fix things… Mec-chann-nicy…mech-nic-al… Carp…carpen… wood-work-ker… Um…um…time…time-ly…time-ly…re…reli-a-ble. Me.'

The boss listened to his stuttering, halting speech, and fixed him with a shrewd eye. He jutted his chin forward as he considered Zac, then he went across to the assassin swing door and challenged: 'See wha' yo' got. Fix th' droor?'

A tool box was on the ground beside it. Zac examined the double hinges on both sides, bent down, rummaged through the tool box and took some adjustable wrenches and screwdrivers and went to work.

He adjusted the tension on the screws and the position of the caps that limited the swing doors action both ways. He tested it out and it worked perfectly. The downswing was muted, both directions.

It took him four and half minutes.

'No' bad, no' bad,' the stout Asian man showed little emotion but Zac could see that he approved. 'Name is Jiāo. You're…?'

'Zac,' Zac said.

The manager studied the card again. 'Hmmm. Ap'sia? Ha! Just like me!' Jiāo grinned, breaking into an animated sort of dance. 'Asi'n Ap'sia!' he chortled, turned and went back to the rear of the store. He looked back over his shoulder, a difficult thing to do because his neck was almost non-existent, and ordered Zac: 'C'mon! C'mon!' as he waddled to the backroom doors, all the way talking with his thick accent. 'Ap'sia. Dat's okay. I seen dat. No need to speak da boots, poles an' skis. Just fix them. Get th'm workin'.'

'Jobs…mine?' Zac was astounded.

'Ya, ya, ya.' Jiāo rounded on him and Zac had to jump out of the way to avoid his circumference. 'To'rrow. Eigh' t' five. Thur'day to Mo'day. Time off Tu'sday, Wes'day. Roimata – sort you out. O-kay?'

'Oh. K-k-kay,' Zac stuttered at Jiāo's retreating back. Jiāo gave a backwards wave as he left the premises admonishing Zac to: 'Work hard.'

Zac was astounded. *It seemed too easy, but…what the hell. So… Roimata?*

He looked around the backroom and saw a woman leaning against the wall beside the doors. Tall, black hair tied in a pony tail, athletic body with a red, skin tight track suit and Ugg boots. And a box of tissues.

Chapter 6: Roimata

'Your nose's okay?' Roimata approached him with a playful look on her face. Zac was nonplussed, but he raised his hands as a gesture of 'I'm okay'. As she came towards him she said: 'Jiāo is very abrupt, terse, but he pays a fair wage and he is very perceptive about people. I think he likes you.'

Confused about this forthright woman, Zac gave her his card. She read it and looked at Zac. 'That's okay,' she said. 'Aphasia. My koro had the same thing. He had a stroke. You?'

'I…I…acc-cid-ent…bash-shed my head…'

'Ah. I see. No problem. So, I will speak slowly and clearly. Just like with my koro. And wait for you to finish what you are saying. Okay?'

Zac appreciated her moderated voice. Often, when Zac presented his card, the recipient spoke more loudly and dumbed down their conversation as if he were mentally compromised. Roimata spoke slowly in a mellow, alto voice and waited patiently for confirmation of his understanding.

He nodded. She smiled.

It was a momentary thing, but Zac's brain celebrated and revelled in that smile. It suggested peace, contentment and restitution. It conveyed comfort and support. It was sunshine and rainbows and a place to rest. Somehow. Zac relaxed and smiled too.

With a twinkle in her eye she continued her introduction, slowly.

'So – I am the front person in the shop and you are the maintenance man for the equipment that we rent out. When they return their equipment you should take it into the backroom and check it over. There is a table with the tools and cleaning gear. These poles, boots, and skis are ready to go out to the shop. We have other equipment too: packs – backpacks or tramping packs – tramping boots, rock climbing helmets…'

That was six weeks ago.

Zac was relieved to find he could cope with this job easily. Originally he was puzzled that his 'weekends' were Tuesday and Wednesday, but it made sense. They were mostly busy from Thursday to Monday because a lot of people took a long weekend off from their work and drove from Christchurch or Dunedin or flew in from Auckland or Wellington. Zac appreciated the time off on Tuesday and Wednesday because the chairlift queues were light and the ski slopes were easily accessible.

The other thing about his job was his colleague. Jiāo was seldom there in the shop – just once or twice in a fortnight. But Roimata was always there. In conversations between them at work, in the last six weeks, Zac got to know about Roimata. They got on well and she didn't mind the silences. In fact, she seemed to understand him intuitively. Almost telepathically.

When he was heading for a cup of coffee, Roimata was there with two mugs. When he was loaded up with skis, poles, boots she opened the sliding door between the stockroom and the showroom without being asked. When he couldn't find a spanner, Roimata was there handing him the tool.

But Zac was attuned too.

After lunch he took the appointment book from the lunchroom when Roimata was just searching for it. He too opened the sliding door when she had her arms full of returned equipment. And when she was looking for the job sheet for a difficult client, he was at the door handing her the file. It was almost spooky but it seemed to Zac that Roimata was on the same 'wavelength'.

Despite that, Zac was careful to avoid reading no romantic interest into their intrinsic compatibility.

Don't sleep with the boss, he reminded himself. *Or in the words of a former ex-friend in Hawkes Bay, 'Don't shit where you sleep.'*

It was not going to happen anyway.

Adoring Aidan.

Roimata had a boyfriend. Aidan was a ski-instructor – a strapping, tall, muscly and ultra-fit specimen. Roimata was over qualified. She was a qualified Search and Rescue (SAR) paramedic but there was only voluntary SAR work for her in Queenstown. So, she was the receptionist/secretary/front-person/boss at SkiRescue because she wanted to be with her man.

Adoring, alluring, arousing Aidan. Hah.
Well… Anyway, I have other fish to fry. Other cherries to pick. Other turkeys to stuff. Yuuus!

Chapter 7:
Back to the Bar

So … Zachariah looked at himself in the mirror.
It was almost too easy.

He washed his hands and shook them out, slicking his golden-blonde hair over his head in a casual wave like the unmade bed… et cetera, et cetera…

He relished his position in Queenstown. The anonymity of his existence. A place to lose himself in the babbling, bubbling tourist trade.

Look at me now, he assessed him form in the mirror. *Mini and Perse and Rachel can stick it. Hawke's Bay can stick it. Queenstown! Yuuus!*

A town where standards could be flexible. The perfect destination for one night stands. He had – has – aphasia, but as a fake tourist, he could function with a minimum of talking and no recriminations. Franz, Claude, Rodrigo **and** Zac: 'No English!'

He recalled the two girls sitting at the bar inside. Waiting.

The blonde or the brunette? Hmm – very attractive. Either? Maybe both. Who shall it be tonight. Should I be Franz? Or Claude or Rodrigo?

A niggle inserted itself into his mind. *Do you want to do this? Really?*

He peered closely at himself in the mirror as if he could examine the thoughts and motivations written on his face.

What – conscience? Surely not. Get a grip.

He straightened himself, shook his head. *Nah! You got this.*

He washed his face and brushed his hair again and, with a wink and a click of his tongue, he strutted out to the club's bar. To the two girls sitting inside.

Waiting for … Rodrigo, I think.

Chapter 8: Skidaddle

Zac walked home to his apartment in the frosty, winter morning after leaving the brunette's place by half past six. The lake was still and luminous. The moon was just setting over the far western hills and the stars were almost consumed by the dawn.

But something was off. The night was fabulous. The brunette, Charlotte or Cheryl or Charlene or some other 'Ch' name, was adventurous. Apparently she had read the Kama Sutra or some variation of it and the positions they were engaged in were spectacular. As usual he left before dawn with the excuse of 'work' with a shrug and a smile.

But the satisfaction was only physical. Something was missing.

He showered, dressed, breakfasted and, as he walked to work, he imagined the previous evening's – the orgasmic culmination – that he had just experienced. *Charl-eryl-lene was quite spectacular.*

But there was something not right.

On his way he passed a reserve. A snow-covered slope, about four metres high, came down to the footpath. Zac watched a boy at the top of the slope with a blue tarpaulin. He seemed to be about five years and was dressed in a snow suit, mittens, a woollen hat and gumboots. It took him several goes to set the tarpaulin down then sit on it. Zac was intrigued.

The boy rocked himself on the top of the mini hill. Apparently the boy was deciding whether to abort his mission in the name of caution, or plunge ahead recklessly.

Well, he was five – of course he was going to do it!

And he did. He rocked over the edge of the slope and careered down. There was a hump in the middle of the icy track and when he hit it he sailed off into a snow bank. The boy broke into gales of laughter. Then he climbed up the hill again. Zac watched while the boy made three or four circuits.

Zac was captivated and slightly saddened, wishing he could be five again. Innocent, unsophisticated, ingenuous…the boy was open to everything around him. Zac regretted that his childhood had been so … complicated. Contaminated. Compromised. The boy was caught up in a moment of pure, unadulterated joy.

Zac clapped his hands in approval. The boy looked at him curiously. Zac said to him, in his best broken English, 'Ski? Les-suns?'
The boy looked laughingly at Zac as if the suggestion was absolutely ludicrous.

'Don't want to ski. This is more fun. This is…Skidaddle!'
Delighted with his new word he chanted it on his way up the slope. Still giggling.

'Jason. Jason. Breakfast is ready.' A woman approached from a house across the road.

Jason, mused Zac. *Apparently he is a 'Jason'.*

'Aw… five more goes? Please?' said Jason.
'Three. Only three – or I will give your bacon and eggs to the dog.'

Ostensibly the mother was looking at Jason, but Zac realised she was assessing **him** out of the corner of her eye.

He returned the look directly. About forty, tousled red-hair, manicured face, wearing a red puffer jacket, black leggings and boots. She approached him with an inviting look. *Yummy mummy*, thought Zac.

He was going to give her the nod-that-means-something-could-be-on but the 'out-of-sorts' niggle in his brain made itself known.
What's the use….kids, husband, … Nah! Too messy…

He ducked his head, turning away from the woman's flirtation attempt and trudged, grudgingly – but somehow virtuously – on his way to work.

Chapter 9: The Warehouse *(where everyone gets a bargain!)*[47]

The niggle in his brain was burgeoning alarmingly. He couldn't help himself. *The sex is great. Always. But it's not … fulfilling. Something is missing. Some connection…*
But – I don't want that. I don't ***want*** *that.*

His confusion paralysed his thoughts. His solution, as usual, was sweep these thoughts under his mind's rug and scoop up his attention on work and play.
Live in the present moment. I think I have seen that on a bumper sticker. Yeah – present moment.
At least, in his conscious mind.

So, despite his new reservations about his lifestyle, he still spent the next week indulging in another three one-night-stands.
Two raven-haired beauties, and a redhead – but not Jason's mother. All satisfied customers.

But the thought did not sit so comfortably in his psyche. He was vexed. Unsettled.

He was due for time off, so he went Dunedin, a three and a half hour trip. He was going to invite Roimata, but he realised she would be filling in for him at Ski Rescue, and he expected that she would want Aidan to come. Something about the ski-instructor rubbed him up the wrong way.

---

[47] The Warehouse is a NZ's one-stop-shop (like USA's WalMart or UK's ASDA) and this is their advertising slogan

He doesn't value Roimata enough. Too confident. Too full of himself. Too conceited and arrogant and ... macho.

[Apparently, Zac had never heard of the phenomenon known as negative projection. When a person criticises another, often they are exposing the faults that they have themselves. Even if he did know this concept, he would say: 'Yeah, nah!'[48]]

Dunedin was often called the 'Edinburgh of the South' because many of the early European settlers came from Scotland. Dunedin prides itself on its beautiful heritage buildings and stunning scenery. And cheese rolls. Its CBD is dominated by the Octagon – obviously, because it has eight sides – and its centre includes a bronze statue of Scottish poet Robert Burns. The University of Ōtago, situated to the north of the Octagon, offers an annual award called the Robert Burns Fellowship which is open to writers of poetry, drama, fiction, biography, essays or literary criticism. And the region's rugby team is known as The Highlanders.

The university's student body, nicknamed 'Scarfies', are notorious for parties, burning sofas, and pub crawls. And there were many pubs in Dunedin to crawl into.

Zac didn't care about that so much. The relief of being able to wander the streets anonymously with no one to bother him by starting conversations was more to the point. He went to a café and sampled the famous Southland cheese rolls for lunch.

He was relieved that he only had to point to his choices in the cabinets – no conversation involved.

---

[48] Yeah, nah = Kiwi slang. Kiwis are exceptionally agreeable, so even when they want to disagree with you, they'll throw in a 'yeah' as well. Basically, 'yeah, nah' is a non-committal way to saying 'no'.

He meandered along the main street, sat down to listen to a guitar busker singing the hits of the 1970's and '80s. He was good and Zac dropped a five dollar note in his guitar case.

Zac went to a neighbouring pub, ordered a triple whisky and a pint of stout and sat down on one of the plush settees that lined the booths around the room. The locals were watching a replay of a rugby match on a giant TV. The Highlanders were playing the Canterbury Crusaders, a local derby, and the people were discussing, debating and ridiculing the game. Refreshingly no one sought his views so no subterfuge as a non-English speaker.

But this was also an isolating device. He surreptitiously regarded the other patrons while drinking his beer, and wished he could also discuss, debate and ridicule the game. He wished he could give his opinion as vehemently as the others were doing. But he couldn't. He can't.

He left the bar and walked off his depression around the streets, walkways and parks of the city.

When he had enough, he drove around the harbour spotting the sculptures and murals that artists had contributed to the 'beauty of the city'.

A matter of opinion, I guess – some locals or visitors will appreciate them and some would be challenged.

On the spur of a moment, he went to The Warehouse in South Dunedin. This department store had everything from clothes and shoes, to cutlery, dishes and kitchen stuff to gardening odds and ends. Again, the anonymity of browsing the aisles without anyone confronting him was a relief.

Eventually his trolley contained a pair of boots, a printed t-shirt that said: `In My Defence I Was Left Unsupervised`, a pepper grinder, a lava

lamp, a DVD double feature of *Dumb and Dumber* and *Dumb and Dumber To* [49], and two coffee mugs inscribed with the message:
DON'T PANIC. Keep Calm. Carry On Shopping.
He thought it would be a nice addition to the lunch at SkiRescue.

Before he went to the counter he looked in the specials bin: a couple of dozen young adult books about vampires and werewolves marked down to three dollars each; expired green-foiled chocolates shaped as lecherous leprechauns leftover from St Patrick's Day; an assortment of screwdrivers; and wine glasses and other household dross.

Two items perplexed him. A red flexible plastic container or a bag – a material was like a thick raincoat – with two elastic openings at one end, and a bigger one at the other. It was plain on one side but the other side had a hard, black PVC base with five parallel runners like railway tracks.

Then it dawned on him!
They were over-shorts. Bloomers. You can wear them on the snow and sled on the PVC tracks on the arse end. Like a toboggan.

He remembered the five-year old boy with a scrap of blue plastic tarpaulin, atop of a snowy slope. Jason.

He had so much fun, sliding down that mini-slope, over and over again. He said something about sliding with his piece of tarpaulin. Something like ski-something… Ski-paddle. Ski tootle. Ski- Ski- dooddlaly…. Ah! Thats it. Skidaddle.

Huh. That's perfect. With these bloomers I can Skidaddle. Not tobogganing – Skidaddle. Brilliant. Hah!

---

[49] Two comedy films starring Jim Carrey and Jeff Daniels. The spelling is not a typo!

On impulse he bought both pairs of red bloomers. He imagined giving the gift to Roimata, and he longed to see her puzzled face turning to amazement and then incredulity when he demanded that she try it out.

Heehee! What a laugh. I have to get her to promise to use whatever is in the parcel. It will be a priceless. And they are only one dollar each. Woohoo! Skidaddle away.

After paying his bill, he returned along the harbour route. Before returning to Queenstown, he decided to get fish'n'chips and L&P[50] from a local takeaway. Sitting at a picnic table on a reserve overlooking the harbour, he savoured the view.

The sea was languid, the blue-green waves shushed rhythmically, a steady and relaxed pulse. The bush along the hills darkened with the setting sun into secret corridors and chasms. The birds were calling their farewells to each other. A certain chill sent him back to the car for his jacket. He sat there as the dusk deepened into night and the stars brightened like blossoms above his head. Zac inhaled fully, and breathed out slowly.

He stood up, rolled his shoulders and stretched,
What a perfect day. Recuperating. Restful.
But a sense of unconscious unease sat below his stomach, his throat and his mind. Niggledness.

Next day he excitedly burst into Ski Rescue with the wrapped bloomers tucked in his backpack, planning to spring the surprise on Roimata at once, but work was so busy he didn't get the chance to.

---

50 L&P = Lemon & Paeroa, is a sweet, lemon-flavoured soft drink manufactured in Aotearoa New Zealand. It is considered Kiwiana, and was traditionally made by combining lemon juice with naturally carbonated mineral water from the town of Paeroa, a little town in the North Island of New Zealand.

Morning tea, he thought, but Roimata had a doctor's appointment and she rushed off. *Okay, lunch, I'll give it to her at lunch.*

Lunchtime arrived. Roimata was sitting at the break room table with a cup of coffee and a chicken sandwich. Zac sidled up to her with a lop-sided grin and the gift-wrapped bloomers behind his back. 'Dun-ed-nin,' he attempted. 'Grift for…you.'

'Aw! You didn't have to!' she said, a fetching frown and a smile competing on her face.

Just then, Aidan barged into the room and swooped on Roimata, embracing her. *Like a predatory octopus*, thought Zac. *And just as slimy.*

Startled, she turned her hands and gently pushed him back.
'What gives?'

'Let's go to lunch!' he demanded. 'I got a promotion at work. So, my treat. Maybe we can go the Margo's. She has an amazing Mexican cuisine. You know I like Mexican food. Spicy. Just like you!'
He planted a passionate kiss on Roimata's lips. 'Okay?'

She raised her eyebrows in surprise.

He turned to Zac. 'You can cope with the tourists, Zac? I just want to treat this special lady to some excellent cuisine. You don't mind?'

Zac kept his face neutral, but he was seething. He sat down at the lunch table and dropped the bloomers under his chair.

I'm not going to produce these bloomers with Aidan watching. He would not get it. At all.

Zac looked at Roimata, but she was gazing at her beau.

She always has this glow when he is around. Radiant. Smiling adoringly. Huh. Aidan. More like her Adonis. What's he got that I don't have…
Oh. Yeah…conversation. Bugger!

'Sure,' he said, acquiescing. 'Sure. Gud…lunc-ch.'

Roimata looked at him with a puzzled expression, but Aidan had already gripped her hand, leading her out the door.

Chapter 10: The meaningful 'mark'

Roimata didn't return after lunch. Zac was fine, in terms of coping with SkiRescue's business, but the black bear of depression was hovering, clawing, and contributing to a niggling feeling in his conscience. A feeling that was ever more present. He closed the shop and thought about the day as he walked downtown.

Hmmm. Aidan. Something about Aidan. He's arrogant and doesn't treat Roimata right.

There was nothing at home for him, so he went to the bar. Three whiskies took care of the bear, but the niggle? *The meaningful relationship aspirations? Arrrgh! Just ignore it. Go with the flow. Live in the moment, and this moment…*
He surveyed the scene.

Ah! The same old same old. Women who were there for a good time. So… brunette, brunette, blonde, redhead, peroxide-blonde, black, brown, honey-blonde, black…

Something about the peroxide-blonde drew his attention. Some intuition. Her posture? Her confidence? Her body? *Hmmm…why not?*

He went to the gents and spruced himself up in the mirror. As usual. *Franz, I think.*

He approached the bar and 'accidentally' spilt the girl's drink. 'Sor-ree! Sor-ree!' he fake-apologised and gestured that he could get another one, all the while looking to size up his peroxide-blonde 'mark'. He studied the floor and the drink he had spilled in 'bewilderment'.

Actually he was studying her body: *high heels, tight jeans, generous hips; glitzy-spangled red top under a black satin jacket; the swell of ample breasts with a hint of black lace bra.*

His practised look focused on her eyes. *They want to see your impassioned interest* he reminded himself.
She was looking at him with unfeigned interest. *Yussss!*

His peripheral vision took in the rest of her face. Her hair was short and styled perfectly, the peroxide-blonde had a subtle purple rinse through it. She had had about six earrings around the lobe of her left ear. Dangly earrings with a feather motif dropped from each earlobe. Eyebrows were refined with an interesting quirky lift like a cursive 'n' shape. Her eyeshadow subtly enhanced her jade-green eyes and toned with her purple hair, and her full lips were crimson with lip-gloss.

He winked at the bar tender, a complicit acquaintance, and ordered a margarita for her and a whisky for himself. The music was not loud but he still turned to her and whispered: 'Franz.'

All part of the plan. Whispering in her ear is an intimate way to say: 'We are alone now. Everyone else is superfluous… Just you. And me.'

He searched her eyes and again: 'Franz. No English.'
Sure enough, the girl whispered back: 'Suzie. No problem.'
They clinked glasses and he skolled[51] his drink.

In halting fake pigeon English, he ventured 'Home?' and 'Holi-daze?' and 'Dance?' and Suzie answered: 'Wellington, at Vic, studying Political Science and Psychology' and 'Winter term study break with my flatmates' and 'Sure'.

---

[51] skolled = to down an alcoholic drink in one go.

She left her two flatmates behind (*the red-head and one of the brunettes…hmmm…nice…*) and went to the dance floor. And, as usual, Zac had his non-verbal 'moves' but this time, Suzie kept up with him.

Zac was intrigued. Generally, he had a system of seduction: intense gazing into her eyes, brushing imaginary hair from her foreheads, gently cradling her elbows when getting the bar or the dance floor or the tables. His niggling conscience interceded. This time, he was more… *committed? Suzie. Suzie is a real person. A person with hopes and fears and past and future – not a pleasure vehicle for a one-night-stand.* He realised the emotional feeling was more important rather than the systematic, and inevitable, physical outcome.

But still… the alcohol, the music and the dancing were working their 'magic'. The dancing was sensational. Magnetic. A slow dance, a nuzzling kiss on her neck and a tight squeeze on her jean-clad buttocks, a lingering french kiss sealed the evening.

They left the bar and taxied to her place.

And as usual, the sex was excellent. Actually – phenomenal.

But the thought of 'Suzie' – the reality of her, the 'hopes and dreams' person – stayed with him as the passion subsided and they fell asleep.

Chapter 11: Honesty

In the morning, Zac's body-alarm woke him up, but he didn't slink out a bed as usual. He turned and studied Suzie as the moonlight softened her face. Her short hair was barely tousled, her eyes were closed and her lips were sensuously parted.

He gazed at her. Time seemed to have no meaning.

She stirred and Zac couldn't help himself as he gently kissed her forehead, her cheek, her neck, her collarbone, her breast and her nipple. She stirred and he embraced and spooned her.

What is happening? This is not good.... not good at all... I should go...just go... But...somehow... it seems to be right? Maybe... She is amazing. Maybe she is the one ... Why not?

She moved against him and reached for his arm, drawing it around her body, encouraging him to continue caressing her breasts. She nuzzled her head against his shoulder. She lifted her right leg and her foot caressed Zac's calf and foot. He slowly massaged her shoulders, her breast, her belly and hips. He reached down to her pubic hair and she stretched her legs and rose up to meet his hand, gently moaning, searching for his mouth and kissed him hard and long. It seemed this woman had breached the borders of his personality. He was melting, fluid, enveloping, assimilating with her body, her soul. Osmosis.

Casually, slowly and expansively, they made love.

Passion spent, Zac questioned his motivation. Apparently his mind had developed a full-blown conscience. He felt that for some months – years – he had been fooling himself.

After my accident, I was angry. I didn't want the pity I thought the people were offering me – a pat on my head. Or the condescending way that I thought they were speaking to me or treating me. I was so, so angry. I thought that superficiality was a way to get happiness and satisfaction from an empty, superficial world. I could look down on these people, these women, and be a god, an incandescent image, a pleasure principle in their shallow lives, but remote and distant. An icon of their wild and carefree days before they settle down to the humdrum lives of wifely duties and baby-making.

But – what am I, really. For them. I was an extra, a footnote in their biographies. A forgotten dalliance. Arggh! I want to be more than that. I want to be awakened to the possibility of companionship. Of connection. Love. It's time…

He snoozled a kiss in her ear and said in a whisper: 'Um…last thing… what I…um…I tell you…'
'Hmm?' Suzie sleepily responded.
'Um…Zac. Zac… Name Zac.'
'Hmmm…What…what is Zac? Um…Franz. Franz?' Suzie was clearly puzzled and she turned and looked at him cautiously.
'Um… Name's Zac. Not Franz. Zac'

Suzie pushed her hands against his chest as she turned over. The puzzled look was mutating to something else.

He hastened to explain…sort of. 'Zac. Um…New Zea-lind…English…ex-plit…ex-plain…'

'What gives? What are you doing? This is a scam?' Suzie sat up and angrily wrapped the sheets around her. 'Shit! What are you doing? This is a game? A fucking game? You're fucking with me?'

Ironic, but not helpful, Zac thought momentarily.

'No! No!' he said raising his hands defensively. 'O-kay! O-kay! Look…' He located his trousers on the floor beside the bed and reached for his wallet. 'See! Look!'
He grabbed the 'Aphasia' card and held it out to her.
As an olive branch.

Warily she took the card and she turned on a bedside lamp.
'Aph-a-sia? Aphasia. What's that? That is a country? Or what?'

Zac's hand gestured to read on. Suzie read the rest of the card.

'So…not Franz? You're Zac…a New Zealander? You're not German or Austrian? English is your language … but you can't speak it? Right?'

Zac nodded, a plaintive look on his face.

'Why?' She was incredulous. 'Why 'Franz'? Why the subterfuge? Why lie about it?'

Zac shrugged and shook his head. 'Eas-sy. Umm…just-ea-sie-sier. Hard to…talk.' He shrugged again. Suzie sighed. Afraid she would react badly he hurried to argue his case. Well, sort of. Arguments are not an aphasiac's forté.

'Usual-me are…gone. Now. Us-ual-ly. But I …like you. May-be…we got…get to-get…to-get-ther. Like you.' He shrugged hopefully. 'Yeah – like you. Your guy?'

She turned away and got out of bed and looked out the window. The moon was fading as the dawn was edging its way up the horizon. The snow-covered mountains and the pristine lake were a scene from a Hollywood film as Zac looked appealingly at her naked back.

He realised that he was not considering her physical body, but the aesthetic beauty of this moment. An impressionist painting, not a magazine centrefold. He looked at her not as a lover but as a woman. An individual. It encouraged him that he was changing and things could be better. Meaningful.

Her back stiffened and he knew a decision was imminent.
Just see me. Just see me.

But she turned and alarm registered on her face. 'Shit! Shit! What's the time? Time?' Panicked, she looked about the room, rushed to the dresser beside her bed and checked the time on her phone. 'Shit! I'm leaving. This morning.' She looked at Franz/Zac steadily then out of the corner of her eye. 'Sorry! Sorry! It was great – great. It was a perfect evening - yeah? Magical. But…I have to catch the plane for Wellington. This morning. Seven-thirty.'

She backed away almost falling over her feet. 'I have to shower and get my stuff.' She headed out the door to the bathroom. 'Thanks Franz…I mean, Zac… It was perfect…The best!' As she closed the bathroom door her voice echoed faintly: 'When you go out can you make sure the door locks. See you later…sometime…'

Her voice diminished, as did his hope.

The sound of the shower accompanied his disconsolate dressing. He left the apartment, locking Suzi's door.
I forgot — this is a party place. Of course she is here for a break. Bugger! She was…ideal. Perfect. But she's leaving. Maybe I could get her number? Address. Wellington is not far?

He walked back to his place, running his fingers through his hair, oblivious to the perfect landscape emerging in the rising sun: the lake luminous, the mountains magnificent.

The pavements were deserted, as was his soul.

A slow moving thought crept up on him.
He was undergoing an epiphany.

He was lonely.

It invaded him like a sickness, a flu, casually creeping up from his groin to his stomach, chest, heart, throat, to his mind. It was a hollow space, an emptiness, a void. The idea of himself as a shell, a facade, a 2D film set, a foam rock that people can pick up with no effort and toss. It frightened him.

Ha! The Loneliness of the Uncommitted Male, he mocked grimly. *I wish I was… Could I be…Arggh!*

The feeling of dread, the feeling of friendlessness, the yearning for love – the words wouldn't come, so he forced his emotions down. He shook himself, took a deep breath and jumped on the spot like an athlete preparing for a sprint.
Wow! I have to get a grip. Harden up, boy!

But he was not convinced that a footloose and fancy-free image was for him. Not at all.

Chapter 12: Dishonesty

He showered in his apartment, changed, breakfasted with muesli, banana and yoghurt, walked the six blocks to town, ordered a flat white from the coffee caravan and arrived at work ten minutes late. Roimata threw him a quizzical look. Zac lightly shook his head: *Telepathic. She knows. Okay…* He went to the backroom, to work on the ski and tramping equipment that had been returned yesterday.

Work was slow. News of a storm coming to the mountains spooked a lot of the tourists, so Zac had time to mull over his new-found conviction. Specifically, the last twelve hours. Last evening with Suzie rattled him. His unconscious mind wouldn't let it go.

It was fine. Really – fine. But…she was…more than that. Not a one-night stand. I wanted to have…have a relationship. Some sort of meaningful relationship. So… I should have met her before. Before she was leaving. Maybe…I …we…could have a chance. Bugger.

One-night stands are okay, but…empty. Meaningless. And … what I did before. With Rachel, and the other girls before my accident. I didn't give them a chance. I was always selfish, always macho, a big ego-maniac. Even with my sisters – I didn't give them a chance. Maybe if Mum was alive…

Nah. Nah. I can't blame her. I have to get myself together or I will be a loser all my life. I have to grow up.

But – what can I do? I know my talking and writing is…suspect. I can't communicate by talking, but surely I can do other things. Body language, drawing, maybe sign language. Surely someone will take me on as I am.

He stood up from his desk and approached the sliding door as Roimata opened it from the other side. Obviously. Telepathy. She looked at him with a concerned question already forming on her lips but at that moment, with a rush, Aidan swung in to room.

'Hey! My clients pulled out with the bad weather so – want some coffee?' he entreated her. 'Something I have to tell you. Oh. Hi Zac,' he acknowledged.

Zac glanced at Aidan. Something about the ski instructor was … different. He wasn't his cocky, confident self and momentarily regarded Zac with sudden apprehension. But once fixed on Roimata, he regained his assertive self. 'Coffee?' he said, gripping her hand and pulling her towards the door.

Roimata looked back at Zac with a puzzled and regretful face but shot him an order as she followed Aidan through the swing doors: 'Look after the shop…'.

For half an hour Zac manned the front desk but he was preoccupied with his altered perception of his life's path, his raison d'être.
One-night stands are a waste of time. I have to get real. Grow up!

And, with increasing insistence, he pondered the puzzled look that Roimata gave him as she left with Aidan.
Why was she puzzled? Maybe she wants to say something to me.

He had lots of time to muse. The weather was getting worse and only the returns were coming in.

He was checking the rental booking for ski gear for a father with his two children when he noticed another couple entering the shop. The man was tall and well built and his girlfriend was cuddling up to him in an extremely amorous manner.

She was fingering his hair, stroking his arm and nuzzling his neck, laughing in a coquettish way. She had a short peroxide-blonde hairstyle with a purple rinse.

Suzie.

Zac froze. At the same time, Suzie looked at the counter and saw him. Rather than shock, or embarrassment, she stared at him and then whispered into her paramour's ear. The man looked at her, and Zac, and her again and burst out laughing.
Suzie joined in and in a loud and scornful tone said: 'Good to see you, Franz. Or Zac! Or whatever you name is today. Ha ha ha! Maybe it's 'Charlie'. Good time Charlie!' She gave him the finger, and sloppily kissed her 'partner'.

Zac was stunned. He couldn't believe that 'his' Suzie could be so cruel. He moved his mouth in concentric 'O' shapes like a goldfish, but his aphasia rendered him speechless. Sweat broke out on his forehead, he tightened his fists and turned so that Suzie and her 'friend' could not see the rage on his face.

I bared my soul. And she doesn't care. I thought she would be understand. Shit! I'm a joke. A joke! And she was here. She lied. Airport my arse. She couldn't get rid of me fast enough. Just a joke. I'm just a fuckin' joke to her.

He looked up and saw that Roimata had re-entered shop. When she saw him she looked startled. She reached out to him but Zac was embarrassed, panicked and incensed, all at once. He rushed past Roimata and launched himself out of the shop knocking poles, skis, boots everywhere as the contemptuous laughter of Suzie and her one-night-date echoed around his ears. Reeling blindly, he went out onto the street in the driving sleet.

He wandered the streets at random, pushed and elbowed tourists on the icy pavement, staggering erratically but his unconscious mind, like a GPS location finder, eventually deposited him at his apartment.

He unlocked his door, stumbled into the lounge, kicking over the chairs and coffee table. The black bear attacked him, roaring and snarling and clawing him as he backed against the lounge wall, sliding down on his haunches, comforting a bottle of whisky.

Why should anyone put up with me? No girl will cope with me? I can't discuss or admire or sweet talk or even argue. Basically I am a fucking mute. Damn, damn, damn, damn. Useless, useless, useless.

I can't hold down a proper job. I can't make friends. I'm fuckin' ridiculous. Lonely. Is this the way it will be? For another twenty, thirty, forty years? I can't deal with this. I can't fuckin' deal! Fuck, fuck, fuck…

Chapter 13: Consequence

The whisky was evaporating in Zac's mouth. The bitterness of the alcohol matched Zac's desperation. He drained the bottle, staggered to his feet and launched the empty bottle at the TV. The screen shattered and glass went everywhere.

Rid'culous. I'm rid'culous. I'll show 'em fuckin' rid'clous.

The deterioration of his vocabulary was a sign that he should hunker down in his apartment and sleep it off. But the black bear was frenzied, snarling and growling, roaring, teeth and claws bared. He thought his head would explode. He grabbed his backpack, parka and hat and stumbled to the door, blindly heading down the street.

Reaching the transport depot, he saw that a Mountain Goat[52] was almost ready to leave. The driver was surprised. Gale-force winds were springing up, so he expected no one would be going up the mountain, but the return trip would likely be full. Zac had to concentrate making sure that his walking and demeanour was acceptable so that the driver wouldn't kick him off. He nodded at the driver, mumbled, and took out his staff pass. The puzzled driver shrugged, and let him on.

The trip up the mountain was slow. Winds and sleet buffeted the vehicle. The roar of the gale meant that the driver could not talk to Zac in the back seat, and that suited Zac just fine. *Couldn't converse to you anyw'y. Fuckin' speech denied! Speech – a fuckin' joke!*

At the top of the road Zac left the mountain goat and went to the chairlift building. The yard was rutted by the trucks, vans and cars that had been over it all day and the sleet and snow had built up so the

52 A Mountain Goat is a robust 4WD shuttle bus from the village to the ski fields.

hollows were icy. Zac's anger focused his gait but he shouldered three people who were making their way across to the returning mountain goat. One slipped on the ice and went down in a heap but Zac blithely continued on as the fellow's companions swore at him.

I'll show 'em, the bastards. The fuckin' bastards. I'll show them. Just. Focus. On. The. Chair. Lift.

The young chairlift operator said warily: 'Not good up the top. Getting worse. Why are you…?'

Zac glared at him ferociously and opened his jacket. His t-shirt was emblazoned 'SkiRescue' in big broad red and gold letters. Zac was careful that the green words below – 'Rental: for all your ski needs' – didn't appear. The operator was cautiously impressed and when Zac showed the staff pass he let him on. Zac barely got his anger and his inebriation under control as he threw himself onto the seat as the chair sailed off up the mountain.

The chairlift ride was much worse than the mountain goat trip. Snow was falling heavily now and the wind whipped it into daggers. His ears and nose were burning from the cold, his teeth were chattering but Zac didn't register this.

In a sober mood, Zac would have realised that the weather was not conducive to anything other than jigsaws, or a movie indoors. But the madness that had built up over so many years, blocked him. Poisoned him. Made him reckless. *The fuckin' bastards. I'll show them. I'll show 'em, the bastards.*

The terrain below appeared and disappeared with every gust of wind and snow blast. The chairlift pylons were apparitions made ghostly with the wind-blown mist and sleet.

At the top of the chairlift station he stumbled to his feet. The top operator shouted at Zac: 'The chairlift will shut down in half an hour. Whiteout. Get off the mountain.' But Zac ignored his advice. The man reached for Zac's arm but Zac turned sharply and shook off the restraining hand, raising his fist threateningly. The shocked operator cursed and screamed, 'Thirty minutes. Chairlift will shut down. Thirty minutes!' but Zac had already stumbled up the path oblivious to the warnings.

Zac staggered up hill amid the wind and snow and each trudging step, physically and psychically, were loaded by his alcohol-affected legs and his alcohol-addled mind.

It's too bad. Too fuckin' bad. No one wants to deal with my fuckin' talkin'. They think they can but it's too hard. I can't explain things – every day, every opinion, every fuckin' conversation. They don't want to deal with that shit. I'm shit. Useless. Just fuckin' useless. What's th'point?

In the shelter of a massive boulder, he zipped the backpack open. He had his merino beanie, parka and boots on already so, struggling, he got his waterproof over-trousers, waterproof gloves and a rock-climbing helmet and put them on. Then, from the bottom of the backpack, he produced his bloomers. *I forgot they were there. Hey! Woohoo – why not!* The inebriation fought with the garment and its elastic openings but, eventually, he got the bloomers on over his leggings.

The slope beneath him was a rumpled duvet, an abstract pattern of rocks and boulders among the snowy and ice. He hesitated, a cautious, rational thought that evaporated in a drunken moment. He remembered Jason, hesitating over whether to abort his mission in the name of caution, or plunge ahead recklessly.

Not an option. Just do it. Do it!

He sat down, braced himself for a moment, thought: *Like my fuckin' life! Downhill. All downhill…* and he tilted.

Gravity took over.
Whoosh! He careered down the mountain.

Trackless powdered snow became packed icy paths; gullies and gulches turned into expansive plains, gentle slopes with banks of waist-deep snow. These became steep slopes when he ploughed into them at precipitous speed … *Thrilling. Exhilarating!* … but almost out of control. *Wow! Wow! WOW! Yahoo! YAHOO!*

Sliding, spinning, jumping, skidding… He steered haphazardly with his bloomer's plastic runners, narrowly avoiding rocks and cliffs by good drunken luck rather than management or control.

Wow! *Wow! WOW! The best one dollar I have ever had. Skidaddle! Wahoo SKIDADDLE!*

Then, suddenly, he was airborne. He closed his eyes and arched his back, arms outstretched. He felt free, unburdened.

Like a bird. Untethered. Unencumbered. Free from the drudgery and frustration of life with aphasia. Free from the pain of relationships that are not going anywhere. Free from my…

That thought lasted about two seconds.

Abruptly he slammed into an ice wall. He plummeted – ten, twenty, thirty metres – falling through a gauntlet of icy fingers and feet that clawed, punched, pummelled, kicked at him. Tumbling, turning, spinning, his fall was arrested by an ice-shelf. He was on his back, winded, shocked, in physical pain.

He blacked out.

He didn't know how long he was unconscious but slowly he opened his eyes. Dazed, he blinked away the snow that formed on his eyelids and focused on what was around him. The alcohol seemed to be frozen out of him but he took a while to register.

I'm lying down? Sky above. Stormy. Dark. Night is coming on? Wind whipping up there. Ice and rock around me. I can't …breathe. Hurts to breathe. Where am I? Hollow? A ditch? Cave? No…crevasse. Oh, shit! Crevasse. How long? My head hurts? And…breathing…is…hard…

The cold blast seeped down the crevasse, freezing his eyebrows, his eyelids, his nose. Pebbles, gravel and ice dropped with increasing regularity. He propped himself up to a semi-sitting position but felt a violent pain seared his chest. He carefully felt around his torso and his head.

Ribs cracked, I expect. And blood on my face and hair. Ah…woozy. What? Happened?

Ah – I remember. Suzie. Whisky. Trip up the mountain. My obnoxious behaviour. And…Skidaddle…that amazing SKIDADDLE!

The exhilaration of those moments, the delight of letting it all go… Zac wanted to laugh out loud but it hurt too much. Cautiously he breathed in but the pain increased. He panted shallowly. He moved his legs but an excruciating pain in his left shin almost made him black out again. He looked down and saw that his lower left leg was at an impossible angle. The bile rose up in him and, with the remainder of the whisky, he vomited over the edge of the bank. His ribs, his legs, his whole body protested but it was out of his control.

He gasped, gently, and raised his eyes to the billowing black clouds and driving snow above.

Head injury. Cracked ribs. Broken leg. And at bottom of a crevasse. Cool. Obviously. At least the gale and the whiteout can't reach me. Not sure about the falling rocks. And I'm not sure how stable this ice-shelf, or the crevasse, are.

He tried to call out but his breath was so shallow it came out as a whisper. The wind was picking up. Chunks of ice, dirt and rock fell from the lip of the crevasse and landed on him like frozen darts, stinging his cheeks and mouth and embedding themselves in his clothes.

No one can hear me. No whistle or cell phone. Useless. At least I had a helmet on. Hah! Was it? Maybe I should have done the job properly. Better to be knocked senseless. Better to be dead. What a mess. Just….useless. I'm useless. Waste of space…

He reviewed the last few hours. Last night. Last week. The last few months…

One-night stands? What a joke. I'm the joke! And what about Suzie. What was I thinking? She was only expecting a good time. Wham Bam Thankya' M'am! Only it was Thankya' Dude. Huh! But I can't do this anymore. Nah. Nah… It's not good enough. Not an option…

But, what's the use. I am all alone. Why would anyone bother with me? I can't speak. People can't understand me. How can I relate to someone? What's the point…

Zac sank deeper into depression. The force of the gale and the icy snow above the crevasse were increasing with every second. He was desperately cold. His eyes closed, and the tears iced up on his cheeks. The pain of his head and chest was diminishing.

His broken leg was numb. Zac knew enough about his situation to realise that he was hypothermic. And he didn't care.

What a waste. Useless. Perse and Mini… I should… I want to… I should have called them. I should have reconciled. I was not fair to them. I was angry. Frustrated. But they were doing their best for me. At least I will be out of their hair now. I wonder if they miss me? I miss them. Desperately. I should have called…

And Roimata. She always sees me. Sees. Me. I should have told her…. Huh! Told her! How can I tell her anything.

Useless…what a waste.
Wastrel…
wasting…

Chapter 14:
What's the point?

Flip a coin. Tails or Heads.

Really.

Flip a coin.

Heads

Something inside him woke up. He was not ready to die. Summoning his flagging energy, he yelled out – but the words choked in his throat. It was too painful. He couldn't get enough breath to sustain the shouting and his voice died to a whisper.

Maybe someone will see me? Surely, someone? What was I doing.

He didn't tell anyone about his intentions. Drunk and ashamed, he vaguely recalled the Mountain Goat driver, and the chairlift operators and his inebriated behaviour. *And, despite my drunkenness, with my aphasia they couldn't understand what I was saying anyway.*

Zac's throbbing pain diminished as the storm raged overhead. His thoughts freewheeled. He remembered his sisters, and his childhood projects, before he went off the rails.

I remember that I was quite good at maths. Numbers made more sense than words. Maths. Pythagoras. Inverse proportion. The same here… storm increasing, pain decreasing. Waxing and waning. Moon quarters. Yin and Yang. My mother liked that project. Yin and Yang. Up her alley. My mother… my mother… She was…she was…a foolish…weak…flakey… I hated moving around all the time… but… she was…she was…

He struggled to get his thoughts in order. The cold seeped into his body. His mind. His soul…

She was…patient. She didn't get mad … when I stuffed things up… She always…hugged me when I was feeling bad… She was…I was…loved… I …miss…her…

The cold didn't seem as bad as before.

And his pain – his head, chest, leg, his mind – seemed to be less.

Numb.

Perse… Mini… miss… Mum… miss…Mum… Mum… miss you….No consequence.

No consequence? He closed his eyes wearily, dropped his head onto his chest. His breathing was growing ever more shallow. There was a rattle in his ribs. He felt the crunch of snow with his hands. He sniffed, but he could not distinguish any smells.

The ice … and snow … were clean. Unadulterated.
Pure.
Just…
Pure…

Zac died.

Roimata alerted the authorities when he didn't arrive at work. The Mountain Goat driver and the chairlift operators recalled him and his drunken state. They searched for him, up the mountain when the weather was clear.

They found him three days after the storm. Frozen solid.

The rescuers were puzzled about the bloomers.

His sisters didn't come to the funeral – too far and too late.

Roimata was the only mourner.

Tails

Something inside him woke up. He was not ready to die. Summoning his flagging energy, he yelled out – but the words choked in his throat. It was too painful. He couldn't get enough breath to sustain the shouting and his voice died to a whisper.

Maybe someone will see me? Surely, someone? What was I doing.

He didn't tell anyone about his intentions. Drunk and ashamed, he vaguely recalled the Mountain Goat driver, and the chairlift operators and his inebriated behaviour.

And, despite my drunkenness, with my aphasia they couldn't understand what I was saying anyway.

He wallowed in self-pity until, at last, he revolted himself.

Get a life. Get over yourself! C'mon…c'mon… Other people have dealt with this aphasia thing before. There are other ways to communicate.

He remembered a poster that one of his mother's boyfriends had on the wall: Sex Is Okay, But It Not Like The Real Thing!

That's true…I know it now. Something else. Something … bigger.

Praying was foreign to him, but in desperation, he prayed. Sort of.

Please…please…give me another chance… I can do better…I will do better… another chance…

He struggled to get his thoughts in order. The cold seeped into his body. His mind. His soul…

Abruptly a rope snaked down from above and a wind-swept call from the surface. Zac grunted out a reply. A shadowy form was abseiling down the rope, coming closer and closer. Someone landed beside him on the ice shelf, securing themselves with an ice axe before checking Zac out. The person raised their snow goggles and scarf and his face lit up with equal parts of joy and shame. It was Roimata.

Then everything blurred: the abseiling rope; the other members of the rescue team; the stretcher manhandled to the ATV buffeted by the wind; to the windless by siren-noisy ambulance; the hospital and the doctor and nurse and warmth and the oblivion of medicated sleep…

And all the time, Roimata was there, with her hand in Zac's hand.

Two days later, Zac gradually woke up out of his pharmacological fog. The first face he saw was Roimata's. He struggled to sit up. 'What…. what gives…?'

'Shh…shh…' She placated him with a hand on his shoulder and upper arm. 'You're safe. Shh… Everything is okay.'

He settled down and looked into Roimata's eyes questioningly. 'What…? Why…?'

As usual, Roimata understood intuitively what Zac was puzzling over.

'Aidan and I broke up,' she spoke matter-of-factedly. 'At the café he told me he was 'relating' with two other girls for the last month. Actually, he asked if I could join them 'for a little fun.' I said 'Yeah, nah!' and he didn't appreciate the way I upended my coffee in his lap. When I got back to the shop and I saw you, I guessed what had happened. I knew about 'Franz' and the others.'

Shamefaced, Zac looked away, but turned to her again. 'How…?'

'I went to your place. The flat was open and you had gone. I saw the whisky bottle and the TV. I was looking for you down town and the Mountain Goat driver called me over and said he took you up the mountain.' She reached her hand to grip his. 'I saw the chairlift operators and they said you were up there. Fool!' She punched his arm. Gently. 'You know I am a Search and Rescue paramedic. The weather was worsening, so I got a team together and … found you.'

'Found..?'

She shrugged, and almost didn't answer. Eventually she said, 'I knew. Somehow, I knew.'
Telepathy.

She tussled his hair and bent down to kiss his forehead. Fondly. She whispered: 'I always know.'

Zac closed his eyes. Tears leaked across his cheeks and down his neck. Roimata brushed them away. Fondly. 'Sor-ree… Sor-ree…' he murmured.

Now he knew what he was searching for: these weeks in Queenstown; these months after his accident; these years in Hawke's Bay; the years after his mother died.

A companion that understood him. That **sees** him.

'By the way, I went back to your place, and I saw your diary,' she confessed. 'I rang your sisters – Minerva and Persephone.' Her eyebrows shot up and she pursed her lips.

Zac shook his head. 'Ah…' he said, shrugging in resignation.

'They were worried about you,' she continued. 'They didn't know where you were. I told them about your accident. They are coming this evening.' She looked at Zac, not with a question but a confirmation. 'I will pick them up.'

The tears burst out of Zac's eyes, almost shockingly. Roimata cradled his head in her hands and kissed him. 'Yes…' he managed. 'Yes…plea-ase…'

She looked at him searchingly. 'No Franz. No Claude or Rodrigo. Just Zac.' He nodded, vigorously.
She stood up. 'I think we will be an excellent team.'
She nodded her head as an acknowledgment of his unanswered assent. 'I will be back later – okay?'

She went to the door and suddenly turned, puzzled. 'By the way – what's the story about those bloomers?'

His brows lifted in surprise, remembering.
Then a coy look came over his face.

'Ski…dad…dle!

The Muddled Mage

Preface:

My grand daughter was responsible.

I was working on *More Suspect Speaking*, my second book for *The Suspect Speaking Series*, and I was musing about what sort of subjects or situations I could use for a short story.

She was a teenager, very creative and loved fantasy, so she said, enthusiastically: 'What about a wizard who has aphasia. He gets the words wrong during his spells, so they have surprising results. And – ooh! – there should be a vampire who is a vegetarian. And a genie…'

The idea rolled around in my head and gradually *The Muddled Mage* was born.
And grew. And grew. And grew!

This novelette is now half of this book. The setting of *The Muddled Mage* is a fantastical realm outside Earth.

The important spells are in another language, and they might seem to be related to an Earth languages: Latin, German, Italian, Estonian, Romanian, Arabic, Greek… but those languages should not be reliably translated? They are different in the Mage's world. I have given a translation in 'our' English in the footnotes.

But two of the characters were actually from our realm, characters from Aotearoa New Zealand. Ketekete, the familiar and Tahurangi, the faerie.

When they speak te reo Māori [Māori language] it is colloquially accurate, rather than literal.
I based these exchanges on *Phrase Book of Modern Māori* by Scotty Morrison, an excellent book for those who want to learn te reo Māori. The footnotes detail the 'slang' sense of the words and phrases that they say.

Enjoy.

The Muddled Mage

Chapter 1: A brief biography of Seraphim Starfire

Chapter 2: The familiar familiar

Chapter 3: Veges, please

Chapter 4: Fortunes favours the bold

Chapter 5: The Solar Panel

Chapter 6: Were (we're) weird

Chapter 7: 'Doctor, I have a problem!'

Chapter 8: Coming …

Chapter 9: … and Going

Chapter 10: The enchanted mirror

Chapter 11: A dark, dusty dungeon

Chapter 12: ADADHD

Chapter 13: Double, double, toil and trouble

Chapter 14: Fire burn, and cauldron bubble

Chapter 15: Rescue, Revelation…

Chapter 16: … and Recognition

Chapter 1:
A brief biography of Seraphim Starfire

The tomato sauce bottle hovered over the dining room table, wobbling slightly. Below was a luncheon: fried potato chips, a fettuccine with basil pesto and walnuts, cucumber and carrot salad, mushrooms sautéed in butter, apple cake with a large jug of custard.

Unblinkingly, Phim gazed at the sauce bottle, his index and the middle finger of his right hand pointing at the object, his thumb curled round his ring and little finger. He slowly lifted his left hand, palm outwards to the table and said, in stentorious tone: 'Rotate!'

Immediately, the bottle flipped over and emptied its contents not only on the chips, but all over the unsuspecting food below. Phim stuttered a distressed call to recant his instruction. 'No…no…reverse… no… rerun… revoke…renounce…no, return…return…return,' he pleaded, but the desperation caused his voice to rise an octave which seemed to negate his command.

'Return!' a resonant bass voice sounded behind him. Like a scared puppy the bottle righted itself, sailed over the floor to the kitchen bench and inserted itself onto a shelf between the mustard and the peanut butter.

Embarrassed, Phim turned to face his mentor.

Luxima Aerolaness was a squat man, just one and half metres tall with a face wrinkled like a discarded paper bag. He wore a red and orange robe and a large hat. He was clutching an oak-wood staff with an aquamarine crystal slowly winking in a silver cradle on top. Fiery red, thick hair and beard, generous-sized lips and nose completed the picture, and his diamond eyes betrayed a wily intelligence. They drew you in like a hypnotising whirlpool.

Yes, Luxima Aerolaness was a wizard.

Scowling, Luxima faced Phim. 'Hmm. No lunch for me then. What possessed you? Rotate? Rotate?' he said accusingly.
'Sorry. Sorry,' said Phim. 'In my mind I thought 'Return' but my mouth opened and … the other words came out. I don't know why…'
'Fool!' Luxima scoffed. 'Seraphim Starfire. What possessed me to mentor an apprentice mage like you who could muddle – no, bamboozle – simple instructions. Bah! Sort it out. I will get my lunch somewhere else.' He turned and made for the door.

Phim was already surveying the mess on the kitchen table so he didn't see Luxima's parting look at his apprentice. It was a mixture of amusement and puzzlement. In the last two months, Phim had been tongue-tied or muddling the spell-words in odd and random ways. He knew the word in his head, and often got the beginning, but the rest of it was erratic or mistaken. The wizard shrugged and strode out the door, slamming it behind him, more from frustration than anger.

Phim was also puzzled. *Why?* he thought. *Why did I mix up these words? Something about the 'Re…' prefix, I suppose. But, I know it was 'Return'. I know it! But…the other words…popped into my mouth…'*
He tugged his right earlobe as he retreated into his thoughts. As usual, he wondered about his genes. *Maybe my mother or father would know?*

But that was a wasted effort, because Phim was a foundling.
A proper foundling, he thought. *I was just found…*

…at midnight in a wicker basket on the back steps of the Torrencia Cathedral. He was swaddled in a threadbare blanket, with a gold ring around his right big toe, and a note tied to his left little toe, naming him 'Seraphim Starfire'. It was freezing outside, but the monk who found him reported that his temperature was normal, as if he had been basking in sunshine. His dark eyes were bright, and he was in robust condition. The High Priestess estimated that Seraphim was six weeks old, and they recorded his birthday accordingly.

He grew up in the monastery beside the cathedral, eventually working with the monks in their gardens and workshops, educated by the recitation and reading of sermons, prayers and the gossip of the monks, nuns, priests and priestesses. They all ignored him. Most would say he was lonely but he was so optimistic the word didn't enter his vocabulary or his philosophy. When they called him at all, he was simply 'Phim'. His fair skin freckled in the sun so he seldom went out without trousers, long sleeved shirts and an enormous hat.

His days were full, and he loved it when the monks sang praise and thanksgiving to the Divine Octet, the gods that created the world and all its mysteries. At two hourly intervals from six in the morning to eight in the evening the theocratic community[53] sang their glorious devotions in complex syncopated rhythms, counterpoint, fugues and choral harmonies. It thrilled him, inspired him. It seemed to him that the music was the voice of the gods themselves.

When Phim was fifteen, Luxima Aerolaness visited the monastery to do some wizard-work. Apparently there was a bell that suddenly began ringing the time-honoured children's chant of: 'Nyah nyah nah nyah nyah!', shrilly and very loudly. The wizard completed his repair and was almost at the High Priestess's study for his payment when he saw a boy with rusty red hair weeding in the kitchen garden. Phim was singing the songs he had heard from the community and adding a few phrases of his own. The tone of his voice, his use of melismatic melodies, and the complex rhythms caught Luxima's attention.

---

[53] the monks, nuns, priests and priestesses

He crossed to the garden. The shadow of the wizard startled Phim out his singing daydream and he looked up apprehensively. Usually when he sang, someone would slap his head or cuff his ears.

'Who taught you that?' Luxima said brusquely.

Still expecting punishment, Phim said cautiously: 'I listen to the monks singing in the chapel.'

'But,' the wizard said, 'you are improvising on their melody and rhythms. Who taught you?'

Phim shrugged, pursed his lips and opened his dark eyes wide, innocent of any wrong-doing.

Luxima fixed the boy with an intense gaze that seemed to look right into Phim's soul as if to divine his future. He shook his head several times, and studied the pulsing crystal that crowned his staff. Phim watched as the wizard stroked his red beard and squinted. At last Luxima said: 'I am a wizard. I can teach you. Do you want that?'

Phim tugged his ear with his right hand – which he always did when he was thinking. His past fifteen years rose up like mist on a mirror in a steamy bathroom. He wiped each layer of his life: his sombre existence at the monastery; his role as an unpaid labourer; his optimistic loneliness; his disassociation with the people who had haphazardly cared for him and, ultimately; his 'orphanage' – the mystery of his parents.

Sometimes the future boiled down to a one-word answer.

'Yes,' said Phim.

Luxima nodded, and continued up the steps to the High Priestess's study. She rose and was clearly set to bargain with the wizard for his work: goods, services, gold… But before she could utter a word, the wizard said: 'I want that boy to be my apprentice.'

The shocked look on the High Priestess's face was momentary, but the wizard noted it with amusement. With an air of nonchalance she asked: 'Which boy?'
He pursed his lips. 'Huh. You have so many boys working for you?' He pointed out the window. 'This one.'
'Sure' she said. 'Nothing else?'
'Nada'.
'Done!'

Luxima turned and walked out the office door noting in the reflection in a facet in the blue crystal, the look of astonishment on her face. He chuckled to himself. Then he said to the boy: 'Get your things. We are leaving in four minutes.'

Phim ran to his bed, rescued his name tag, the ring and the blanket, and was back in three minutes. 'Hmm,' was all that the wizard said and he set off down the road, Phim trailing after.

That was two years ago.

When Luxima left the cottage after the disastrous luncheon, he looked back through the window at the boy busy rectifying his mistakes. He wondered if he had been suckered.
I have taught this boy for two years, and, in the beginning, he was so promising. But, in the last two months, he is getting all the words of the spells wrong. He is becoming a tragedy.

Yet, he thought to himself, *the crystal was so favourable about this boy. Maybe he has to find his own way. Perhaps I am constraining him. I guess I have to trust …*

When he went back inside, Phim turned abruptly and raised his hands, an apology forming on his lips. Unfortunately, his raised hands were a signal to the ruined food in the dustpan to fall. Immediately Luxima pointed his staff at the detritus, pointed with his right hand in a formation of crossed and uncrossed fingers and uttered a single, commanding word: 'Gelo.'[54]

The rubbish froze on its way to the floor. Without another word, the wizard sat down at the table and with a wave, a bin from the kitchen cupboard scooted towards the shamed boy. Phim tapped the suspended bits and pieces of the ruined lunch and they fell into the waiting bin. He replaced the bin in the kitchen and faced his mentor: head bowed, arms down, his hands clasped in contrition. Luxima breathed out in a tuneless whistle.

'I can't imagine what has gone wrong with you, boy,' he ventured. 'Maybe it will come right. I hope so. Otherwise…' Phim raised his head. The wizard stared at the boy intently. Eventually, he blew another noisy breath and rose. 'I have to go away for a few weeks. I think you have enough supplies. Look after the cottage. Don't burn anything down.'

He rose and went over to the cabinet on the far wall. A whispered word and a gesture with his staff and the cabinet doors flew open. Luxima selected several volumes, pamphlets and books, and placed them on the table. With a flick of his staff the cabinet door shut. 'Study these texts. There are some exercises listed – you can do those, but don't get uppity. See you in a few weeks. I expect some progress.'

'Yes maestro,' said Phim. 'I would did…will do my best.'

'Hmm – I think you should do better than your best,' Luxima sighed. He hesitated at the door, and turned to face the boy. 'Oh! I almost forgot,' he said. 'You need a familiar. I've got one for you. By the time I return I expect you to have bonded properly.' He pointed at one volume. 'The instructions are in that book – okay?'

---

54 Freeze.

The wizard went through the door and stopped on the stoop, raised his staff and spoke: 'Ketekete, huc accede et comitem tuum saluta.'[55] He turned and looked at Phim appraisingly, nodded, and left.

Phim blinked. After a moment he ran to the door, desperate to have more information or instruction from his mentor, but the road was deserted. Luxima had gone.

Phim almost panicked. His eyes filled with tears, his hands were clasped over his chest.

What am I going to do? How can I live here with no instruction? He has never left me before. How can I …

A screech above him startled the boy and he turned to the canopy over the door. A large, green parrot was making its way across the thatch, as if it was on hot sand. The bird reached the lintel, fluttered to the ground and goose-stepped into the cottage.

Phim followed, flabbergasted.

---

55 Ketekete, come here and greet your companion.

Chapter 2:
The familiar familiar

The parrot confidently made its way across the dining room, hopped onto the table, stretched its wings like a diva taking a bow and faced the boy. Phim noted that the bird was about thirty-five centimetres tall, its plumage mostly forest green edged in black, but when it flew, it showed bright red feathers under its wings.

The parrot looked around the cottage with a superior air as if it were a general inspecting the troops. It strutted along the table, spreading its magnificent tail feathers and flew to the bench and drank a few mouthfuls from a pot of water then, from the cabinet, it surveyed the room.

Well, thought Phim, *it seems to be quite at home – goose-stepping around.* The comparison with a presumptuous parrot and a military goose made the boy giggle. The bird tilted its head and fixed the boy with a beady eye. At this apparent admonishment, Phim managed to suppress his giggles. *Apparently I am an insect that it would like to devour,* Phim thought to himself, eyeing the formidable beak and muscular claws. He sensed the intelligent and crafty nature of this creature and realised that he'd been given the bird as a 'familiar'.

Approaching the creature carefully, he said, 'Um…hello. What sort of creature are you? Are you a parable…I mean, a parrot? What's your name, I wonder.'

The parrot raised itself to its full height and announced: 'Ketekete.'
'Oh! You can talk. How did my mentor find you? Where do you come from? I love your plummet…plumage. What sort of bird are you?'
The bird looked haughtily at Phim and said: 'Ketekete.'

'Ah…the same answer. I guess you can't talk. I see. Well…you said "Ketekete" so, apparently, I should name Ketekete. Are you a boy or a girl, I wonder?'

The bird looked around the room, spotted a pack of tarot cards on the table, flew down and proceeded to sort them out. All the male characters were discarded, as it chose the female character. 'Ah,' Phim deduced. 'A girl.' The fierce look on the parrot's face made Phim reassess that opinion. 'You are a laddle…lady?' Another haughty look. 'No? Obviously, you're not a lady but… a female. Yes? A female!'
The insolent bird imperiously nodded. She turned and picked its way pompously across the table.

The apprentice mage focused his thoughts. 'Well…' said Phim, talking to himself, 'my maestro…mentor said you would be my "familiar". I'm confused. What is "a familiar".'

Apparently the parrot's hearing was keen. She turned to Phim and flew to the books that Luxima had left on the table. She began to manhandle one of the books with her talons.

'No! Don't do that!' Phim ran to the table scared that the bird would ruin the precious tomes that Luxima had set out for him. The parrot looked at the boy with disgust. Phim froze. Should he rescue the books and risk injury from the parrot's cruel beak and talons? Or let the bird have its way with the books and explain to his mentor what happened.
The dilemma was short lived. Ketekete selected a book, opened it and stepped away leaving one claw on a section of text. Phim was certain that the parrot was pointing. He approached, warily, and read…

> A familiar is a normal animal or similar creature that has been summoned to service by a sorcerer or wizard and magically bonded to the spell-caster, after which it becomes a magical creature and gains greater intelligence and new powers.

> As the bond between spell-caster and familiar grows, the familiar can pass on the master's spells by touch, and the two learn to share an unique language. Eventually, familiars and their masters communicate through an empathic or telepathic link.

'Huh,' contemplated Phim out loud. 'Empathic link? Well, if you can't talk I can't wait for that. And what about the "bound"....no, "banana"..."bantam"... Ahhhh!'
He concentrated and forced his mouth to take notice of his brain. He spoke slowly: 'The "bond" thing? How I – you – we – can achieve that?'

Ketekete gave him another haughty look, shook her head and flew to the larder. Her talons and beak were excellent prehensile tools and the bird feasted on seeds and nuts as well as some of the beetles and insects that strayed across her path. Phim let the parrot do it, not so much out of complacency or indulgence, but from a certain respectful caution. The talon and beak were quite fearsome.

Instead he spent three hours studying the book.

As he resurfaced, he spotted Ketekete on a rafter above him apparently asleep.
I have to make a connection with my familiar. Talk to her. Maybe Ketekete would like me to stroke her feathers? No, no, no. So – talking?

'Ah-hem,' Phim coughed politely. 'Ketekete – wake up? Awake? Yoo-hooo! Wakey-wakey!'
The bird opened one eye and seemed to mumble: 'Kia moe ahau e te pōrangi...'[56]
Phim was astonished. 'Did you speak to me? What did you say?'

---

[56] Let me sleep, you idiot.

Lazily Ketekete murmured: 'Pōrangi…pōrangi…'[57] as it closed his eyes. Asleep.
Poor ranges? Pour ranches? mused Phim. *That's nonsense. No. No. It was rambling bird-talk. Surely. Or just some random words copied from another owner. Just nonsense.*

Phim tugged on his right earlobe while he was thinking, a vestige of his time in the monastery. Better than sucking his thumb.

Still fast asleep. But the text said the bonding should take part as soon as possible. At least in the next twelve hours or the empathetic/telepathic link would not develop.

Phim redoubled his efforts, jumping and leaping and waving his arms around and calling, as politely as possible, 'Yoo-hooo! Wakey-wakey!' over and over again. The bird didn't stir.

I have to do something different. Maybe I should sing to it?

Phim settled himself down on a seat, closed his eyes, and sang with remembered melodies from his time at the monastery. He improvised variations on them, composed new phrases. He sang of the wonder of the mountains, the forest, rivers and waterfalls, the sunshine and starlight, the sun and the moon and the seasons. He didn't just sing them, he imbued the music with the essence of each thing. He sang of the relationships between them and the human world. He sang of the pathways and ethereal threads that wove an insubstantial fabric that contained all that lived in this realm.

Transported, he didn't realise that Ketekete had come down from the rafters and nuzzled into his lap. The parrot was waving its head in time to the rhythm of his song. Phim was startled and abruptly stopped his

---

[57] Idiot, crazy.

melody, staring at the bird in shock. The bird rose up, wide-eyed, mouth open, and abruptly flew back to the rafter, muttering 'Manu wairangi…'[58]

Is she talking to me? Phim pondered. *Man urine? Mango why ranges? No, no. Just bird talk. But…I got to her. She was listening to me. There was a bond forming there – I know it!*

Over the next few days, Phim did his chores, studied the books that Luxima had provided and practised the basic exercise that the books allowed. Most of the spells had body gestures, or mandalas or runes that should be written on the ground or a slate tablet. He completed these perfectly, but when he spoke the words, his misplaced or misspoken words resulted in surprising outcomes.

He enchanted the dishcloth to put away the dishes. The spell called for the phrase 'To Name A Cupboard' but out of his mouth came 'Tornado Curtain'. A waterspout formed in the sink that spun out of the kitchen, across the floor and disappeared into his bedroom, soaking and spinning anything not nailed down.

As he tried to clean the bath and the toilet a phrase in the spell included 'Scrub The Porcelain' but this came out of his mouth as 'Scrap This Potato'. All the compost from the garden arrived en masse through the bathroom window – shambolic and smelly.

Despite his failure, he tried another spell to clean up the mess. The spell called for the words 'Clean Up This Rubbish' and 'Get It Back Where It Came From'. But, when he said 'Clear To The Roof' and 'Get It Bouncing Casually', the shambles formed a ball and proceeded to bounce from the floor to the roof to the walls, like a giant lava lamp. Smelly bits fell off and journeyed on their own, jumping around the

58 Foolish bird.

walls, roof and floor leaving bits of compost everywhere. The spell lasted eight hours. Gradually Phim was able to trap the compost balls in sacks and cart them back to the compost heap. Then he cleaned the bathroom, the old-fashioned way.

Every attempt at spell-casting met with a derisive snigger from the parrot, and usually a muttering of 'Pōrangi.'[59] When Phim heard it, he thought it was a stock phrase from another owner – maybe an expression of commiseration. *Maybe she is saying 'Poor Ranger'. Perhaps her owner was a ranger. But, she could be empathising with me. Bonding?*

When he was not studying, practising, or cleaning up the mess his failed spells created, Phim sang. And Ketekete, despite her apparent antipathy for the boy at all other times, came close, often snuggling into his lap. Phim was careful and continued his singing, letting it develop organically. He was responding to Ketekete's mood, composing and improvising his rhythm and melody, the scales or modes to match the parrot's intellectual and emotional demeanour. They sat like this for half an hour or more.

Yes. They were bonding.

Phim studied the chapter on 'The Familiar' closely, to read between the lines. At one point, the writer said that:

> The physical and spiritual connection of the mage and the familiar was vital in high-level spells to implant them so they would not diminish in time. These effects would be permanent.

He didn't understand this at all.

A week passed. It was night – the half-moon was obscured by scudding clouds above the forest. Phim was practising lighting a candle on the table. He was two metres away from the kitchen sink.

---

[59] Idiot, crazy.

Ketekete was behind him, tucking into the seeds, fruit and wayward insects on the kitchen bench – again. Seraphim had graduated from the hedge-witches spells to more wizardly spells – the sort that used foreign languages to make them effective. He gazed intently at the candle, pointed with the index finger on his right hand, made a complex gesture with his left hand and spoke resonantly: 'Lucerna retro lux!'[60]

Immediately, Phim realised the words were not right. *My brain said 'lucerna lux' but my mouth inserted 'retro'. Why?* He looked for the chaos on the table and the shelves against the wall but, behind him, Ketekete was yelling. Phim turned and saw Ketekete with her tail alight. The spell had reversed, backfired. Instead of being forwards on the candle wick, the flame was backwards on Ketekete's behind.

'What are you doing?' the parrot screamed, dousing her behind in the sink.. 'Pōrangi! Pōrewarewa![61] You complete idiot. Useless. You have maimed me. Complete and utter…'

'You can talk?' said Phim with a mixture of confusion and excitement. 'You **can** talk!'

Ketekete stood still. Then she turned, this way and that to inspect the damage to her tail feathers. Phim rushed over to the parrot and gripped her with both hands, forcing her to face him. 'You can talk. All this time I thought you were musket…muzzy…mute, or only saying rancid…random words, but you can talk. Why didn't you tell me? Why?'

Ketekete fluffed her wings and shook her head vigorously, making sure that Phim got the message she wanted to be released. Phim left the bird on the bench but stared intently and somewhat angrily at her duplicitous eyes. 'Why. Didn't. You. Tell. Me?' he said in exasperation.

---

60 Light the lantern behind.

61 Idiot, crazy, stupid, insane.

Ketekete gave a bit of a shrug and turned away from Phim's furious face, nonchalantly saying over her shoulder: 'Well – I can speak when someone is worth speaking to.'

'Ahhhhh!' Phim exploded. He jumped up, did an indignant dance on the spot. Fuming, he stomped to the door, planning to leave this arrogant bird to her own devices for a while.

Just then he heard a faint sound outside. He froze. Ketekete froze too. A rustle of leaves and branches, unsteady footsteps and a plaintive cry: 'Please…please…help…help me…pleasssse…'

Immediately Phim went out the door and searched for the sound.

In the deep shadow of the forest trees he could see a dim figure, stumbling along the path. It rose up, looked plaintively at Phim and collapsed to the ground. The apprentice mage ran over.

It was a young girl dressed in black. Her hair was greasy black and there were dark shadows around her eyes, her cheeks were hollowed and her lips, pale and dry. She was clearly emaciated. Phim knelt down and cradled her head in his arms.

Dazed, she eventually focused on Phim and said again: 'Please…help… me… Pleasssse…'.

Phim's experience with the female sex was limited. The nuns and priestesses at the monastery were sexless female eunuchs, and most of the clients that Luxima had to deal with were older women or of peasant stock. So, this girl was a completely new and revealing experience for him. [His seventeen-years also played a role.] Ketekete followed Phim out and perched on a fence post beside the girl.

The apprentice mage was so enchanted with his victim that he didn't notice a strange thing about her mouth. But Ketekete did.

When the girl released her final sighing plea, her mouth dropped open and the parrot saw the enlarged and sharpened incisors in her jaw.

She was a vampire.

Chapter 3:

Veges, please

Phim picked up the girl in his arms and turned to the cottage door. She was so thin and slight that he had no trouble carrying her. Ketekete flapped around the apprentice, dodging his boots, picking at his trousers. In a panic, she said: 'Wait! Wait! This girl…is she a…what I mean, she is…'

'Get away from me!' Phim said furiously. 'You don't talk to me for the who…whorl…whole week, ten days. And now you want to give a whole loser…leather…lecture! Get away. I have to get this girl inside.'

Ketekete panicked. 'But she is…a…a…tangata whakaheke toto[62]…'

While he tried to shake off the parrot, Phim looked at the girl. She revived somewhat and, as he marched to the door, Phim said, 'We'll get you inside and see what is wrap…wrote…wrong with you. It's okay. We'll help you.'

'You want me to go inside?' she said, faintly.

'No..no…' Ketekete buzzed around Phim like a mosquito. 'Don't invite…' but the apprentice shook his head and ignored the bird.

'Come in and we'll see what's what,' he said as he stepped over the lintel. On the doorstep, Ketekete bent her head in frustration, and resignedly marched after the boy.

Phim laid the girl on the sofa and covered her with a blanket. She closed her eyes with a whimper and promptly fainted. He stood up,

62 Bloodsucker.

sighed, and looked at her, appreciating her beauty despite her emaciated state. But Ketekete was still pulling on his trousers with her beak, so he turned to the bird and said: 'What?' It came out more aggressively than he intended, but he was so annoyed at her muteness over the previous ten days.

If Ketekete had shoulders she would have shrugged them. And if she had hands or fingers she would have shielded what she said with one hand and pointed at the girl with the other.
Instead, she whispered: 'She is a vampire!'

Phim's anger burst out. 'Why didn't you tell me that you can talk. Huh! For ten days. You made me thaw…thatch…think you were mute. Why? I guess that Luxima found you and gauge…gawk…gave you your intelligence and your speech but….'

Ketekete rose up and self-righteously pronounced: 'I was always intelligent. He only gave me the gift of talking. But he didn't say that you were a – a – whakarorirori ākonga.[63]' She ruffled her feathers as if to shrug. 'Anyway – that is the least of your problems. She is a vampire!'

Phim sniggered, as if the parrot were joking. He looked from the girl to the parrot and back again. 'You're kidding?' he said incredulously. 'You're just making it up. You're just upset that I foundling…frond… found you out, you green-eyed, green-hearted bit of flush…flunk… fluff and feathers!'

'No! No!' his familiar protested. 'Just look in her mouth. Just look!'

Phim looked at the girl unconscious on the sofa. He bent towards her and gingerly lifted her upper lip. Her incisors gleamed viciously back at

---

[63] Stupid student.

him. Immediately Phim stepped back aghast. 'Wh…wh…what?' he stammered. 'What is…going for…do? I mean, what is she going to do to us?'

'I don't know – but you invited her in. You know that vampires have to be invited in,' the bird said self-righteously, 'and you did. She will give us a vampire kiss. Nibblicious necking! Can you get rid of her before she wakes up?'

'But…but…she asked for help. Look at her. She is starving.'

'Doh!' said Ketekete, sarcastically. If the parrot had had eyebrows, they would have shot up with an 'Of course!'. Belatedly Phim had the same notion. *If she is a vampire, and she is starving, and I invited her in – I guess we're dinner?* He went back to the sofa not sure what to do.

'Maybe her teeth are – just like that?' he countered. 'Perhaps she has a genetic disposition for oversized testy…terrify…teeth. Maybe her other teeth are similar – big molars or big wisdom teeth or…' Recklessly he was lifting her lips to check and suddenly the girl opened her eyes wide and grasped his hand in a vice-like grip. The shocked apprentice mage almost screamed but before he could utter a sound, the girl said in a hoarse voice: 'Where am I?' as she looked around at the cottage.

'Um…um…the cottage…um…we live here and…um…' Phim was completely disconcerted.

Thankfully Ketekete broke in. 'The cottage is the home of Luxima Aerolaness, the wizard. He will be home shortly. Very shortly.'
Phim blurted out: 'You're starving – clearly. Are you a vampire? So… so…what are you going to do? Are you intending to feed on me?'
'Us?' said Ketekete interrupted and she flew to the cabinet, with a fearful look at the emaciated girl.

The girl dropped her head and released her grip on Phim's wrist. 'Yes. Don't know. No,' she mumbled. Phim retreated several paces and studied the girl. She sat up, tucked her legs under the blanket, and made herself comfortable on the sofa. Then she stared at Phim.

'Yes – I am a vampire,' she answered. 'No – I'm not going to feed on you.' She glanced at the bird. 'Either of you.' She sighed a mournful sigh. 'Yes – I am starving. That's why I need your wizard's help. I am at my wit's end.' She gazed at the apprentice mage with a dejected look. 'I am a vegetarian.'

Shocked into silence, Phim and the bird stared at her. The parrot recovered soonest. 'Vegetarian?' she said. 'Really? No bitey-bitey? No neck-nibbling?'

The girl nodded vigorously and miserably. 'That's why I am starving. I thought Wizard Aerolaness could help me…' she said, plaintively.

'Um…um…Yes? But actually, we don't know when is returning,' confessed Phim. 'He is travelling for several weeks.' If Ketekete could bite her lip she would at this candid, and perhaps, foolish remark.

The girl tucked her head down into her knees and sobbed.

'Oh, don't cry, don't cry,' Phim placated. He placed his arm on her shoulders and gently rocked her. 'It's okay. We'll see what we can do. It's okay…' He straightened up.

This calls for a distraction.

'Um…sorry, I don't know your name. I am Seraphim Starfire but my friends call me Phim. And that is – I guess – my familiar. Ketekete. We have only just meat…met. We have some…issues. She is some sort of a parable…parrot. And apparently a joker. So – what is your napkin… nomen…name?'

'Oh..um...' she choked back her tears. 'My name is Artémissa. Artémissa – the vegetarian vampire.' She laughed humourlessly and took some deep breaths. 'But you can call me Arté.' She paused and sheepishly asked: 'Um...what about your – your speech thingy? You seem to be – stuttering? Stammering?'

'Sorry. Sorry. Sometimes I get the wrong wards...words spilling out from my month...my mouth. Usually I get the first letter or cymbal... signal...syllable. Sorry. My mouth doesn't understand my brain, somehow.'

He shook off his funk and brightened up.
'So – c'mon Arté. Get comfortable and I'll see what I can do.'

He lit the lamps around the room, crossed to the kitchen and larder and brought out preserves, fruit, vegetables to put on the kitchen bench. He sliced and spread and cooked and baked. And he made a selection of elementary spells as the girl watched. Ketekete perched on the table and whispered some amendments to Phim's spell-casting.

For example, making sure that when Phim instructed the jelly to 'site' and it was about to run over the floor, she whispered 'set'. When Seraphim enchanted the cherries and cranberry to 'combat', the parrot covered the bowl of angry fruit with a lid and encouraged Phim to amend the spell to 'combine' them.

Phim realised that, with Ketekete talking to him, the bird could be useful – at least she could improve his spell-casting. But he was still furious about her apparent speechlessness.

After twenty minutes he pulled out a chair with a flourish and requested Arté's presence at the dinner table.

Ketekete had already flown to her place, warily well away from the vampire, but Phim shooed her away from taking the food he had laid out for the distressed damsel. He gestured to the food, all of which had a very, very red hue.

'Pickled beetroot and radishes, deep fried red children...chilli,' he boasted, 'red capsicums stuffed with baked tomatoes and Red Leicester cheetah...cheese, tomato jelly, cherries and cranberries, cheesecake with a raspberry jus, and – the pièce de résistance – blood oranges! Enjoy!'

Artémissa was overwhelmed. 'This is for me? Thank you. Thank you.' Grateful tears sprang into her eyes.

Thirty minutes later, the three of them were replete. Phim dimmed the lamps to a cosy glow, Arté went back to the sofa, tucked her legs up under her and sighed contentedly. Ketekete flew to her perch on top of the cabinet, throwing sidelong glances at the relaxed vampire and, assured, cautiously tucked her head under her wing and proceeded to go to sleep.

Phim sat down beside Arté on the sofa. He was uneasy about how Arté tackled the capsicums and blood oranges – her incisors punctured the skin with a fierceness that was quite alarming. But he relaxed, crossing his feet and leaning back on the cushions. He raised his arms and interlaced his fingers behind his head. He was quite pleased with himself, despite mucking up several spell-castings.

But his self-satisfaction was about to be punctured.

'That was magnificent,' Arté said tentatively, 'but I can't survive on that food. I have to get to your wizard somehow. The food was delicious – but it can't sustain me. Sorry. It is like a light bandage on a severed artery!'

The choice of metaphor made Phim queasy but he looked at the girl and saw earnestness and goodness shining out of her.

Distraction is the key, he thought.

'Hopefully, he will be here. Soon,' he placated. 'In the meantime, tell me about your life. How did you come here?'

Chapter 4:

Fortunes favours the bold

'Well,' Arté said hesitantly, 'I was born in the Segonea District in the north of Torrencia. I was an only child. My mother died when I was just three years old and my father – well, he struggled to care for me. Often, I was left with the next door neighbour, a sour old woman who had a fondness for Red Ticka.'

Seeing the puzzled look on Phim's face, she said, 'The alcohol made from chillies, broccoli, sugar and donkey's milk. Cheap, potent, and very somnolent. Most of the time I had to fend for myself because she was always sleeping. I grew up educated by my ragamuffin friends and whatever I could find around me. I was always a vegetarian – to my father's disgust. By the time I was sixteen, I was hanging with my friends at all times of the day and night. I was quite wild. That's when – that's when **he** found me...'

Arté eyes filled with tears and she dropped her head. Phim didn't know what to say, but his compassionate nature led him to hold her hand and wait for her quiet sobbing to stop.

She looked at Phim gratefully and said: 'I don't want to think about that...that...monster. But I owe you an explanation. Yes. A vampire cornered me and he bit me. He made me a vampire. The craving for blood was strong – it still is. It was hard, but I am strong-willed and I rejected the way he wanted me to feed. I was a vegetarian, always. After I stood up to him, he didn't want anything to do with me. He banished me – cast me out. I suspect he was thinking I would crawl back to him – but I will never do that. I would rather die!'

She laughed humourlessly, made a fist of her right hand and smacked into her left. With a tight face and rigid jaw, her vehemence was impressive. Phim instinctively recognised the strength of this girl – her determination and resilience – and he admired her fortitude. *I want to help her but what can I do?*
She continued on…

'I wandered for a few weeks, sleeping in cellars by day and venturing out at night, drinking honeyed milk and some raw veges. But I was starving. Then, I heard someone say that a wizard – Luxima Aerolaness – was in the south of Torrencia and that he could do amazing things. I wondered if he could help me. So – that's why I am here.'

Out of ignorance Phim asked: 'Why were you in the cellars during the day and out at night?'

Another humourless laugh. 'Vampiric vulnerabilities. The sun would burn me to ash. That's the way vampires are.' She looked up at the roof and let out a big sigh. 'Ohhhh! I miss the sun most of all. Basking in the sunlight after a swim in the river. The dappled sunlight in the forest. The magnificence of sunrises and sunsets. Oh…oh…I miss that most of all…'

The forlorn look on her face was devastating.
Phim thought: *More distraction…*

'Luxima is training I…me…to be an image,' he said candidly. 'Sorry… a mage.' Arté was aware that he was changing the direction of the conversation, but telling her story had upset her so she didn't mind.

Phim continued: 'I was renovating….researching….reading about scrying. You know, fortune telling?' He shrugged and playfully held his hands in a pleading way. 'Let me practise on you?'

Arté smiled. 'Sure,' she said. 'After that magnificent meal…my future is yours to discover.'

Phim got the book that he was studying and thumbed through the pages. 'So tea leaves… Ah! We have no tea yet. Maybe tomorrow. Um…next one is … palm reading. Okay?' Phim took Arté's right hand in his own.

He studied the lines across her palm. He closed his eyes, gestured with his left hand and chanted in a deep voice: 'The signal of the palm frond reserved.'

His eyes opened in shock as her hand seemed to be boneless and flapping around. 'Sorry! Sorry! My words are mucked up. Can I do it again?' he pleaded.

Her hand stopped flapping and she studied Phim with a question in her eyes, but she left her hand in his. 'Um…sure – no problem.' Arté sounded cautious.

He closed his eyes, made sure that his brain and mouth were in sync, steadied himself and again chanted: 'The sign of the palm is revealed.'

He opened his eyes and stared at Arté's hand. The lines were forked indicating a dilemma, a path of two choices. Phim had a feeling in his gut: *Violence. Teeth. Biting.*

Startled, Phim dropped Arté's hand and got up from the sofa. The girl was disconcerted but the apprentice mage hid his anxiety by turning the page. 'Forget about the palm researching…reading thing. This is more interesting. Phrenology. It's about head pumps…head bumps!'

Arté smiled at him as if he was making a joke. 'You've got to be kidding me?'

'No,' he said. 'It's scientific. Your physiology has a lot to do with your decisions, your choices, your…well, your future.' Arté sniggered, but said: 'Okay. Whatever.'

She turned around and Phim placed his hands on her head. 'The future signal of the bum in scale.' Two dozen tiny pimples arose from Arté's head, each with a pink, semi-spherical surface and a deep cleft in the middle. Miniature bums. In shock, he raised both his hands above his shoulders. The pimples disappeared. He hit his forehead with his open palm and cried: 'No, no, that's not right. Not the right words. Can I do it again?'
Arté giggled. 'Sure,' she said. 'Do it again. But I see why you are an apprentice.'

Thankfully Arté – and the sleeping Ketekete – didn't see Phim's blush.

He placed his hands on her scalp again and carefully – brain and mouth in sync – said: 'The future signs are in the bumps in the scalp.' He moved around Arté's scalp and felt the bumps and…again, a visceral feeling came over him, almost a vision. *Dark hair, generous female lips, bared, vampire teeth flashing down on someone's neck.* The violence was most upsetting.

Phim dropped his hands and covered up his discomfort by saying: 'Well…that was inconclusive.'
Arté looked back at him suspiciously, but he was already turning the next page in his book.
'Tarot, tarot. That's a defying…definition…definite prospect for writing…reedly…reading the future.'
Arté giggled at Phim's tongue-tied sentences as the apprentice mage went to get a deck of tarot cards. He gestured to Arté to join him and they faced each other across the table. *At last,* Phim thought, *I don't need to cast any spells. This enchanted tarot contains its own magic.*

He asked Arté to shuffle the deck and cut the cards three ways. Then he placed two from each pile on the table, and asked Arté to pick a seventh from any of the stacks.

The Magician. The Lovers. The High Priestess. The Wheel of Fortune. The Tower. The Devil.
And Arté's seventh pick: Strength.

He was not an expert on the deep meaning of the seven cards, but he knew the prediction was powerful.
I can't believe it. All seven are Major Arcana! What sort of future does this foretell?

He crouched with his hands clasped, and screwed up his eyes. His vision swam, as if he had opened his eyes underwater. He struggled to get a clear picture. Again, a vision came to him: *Arté – it was definitely Arté – rushing up to someone and plunging her teeth into his neck.*

He stood up abruptly and the chair clattered behind him. He went to the kitchen sink for a glass of water. Arté noticed his agitation and asked him anxiously: 'What do you see? What sort of future?'

Phim gathered his thoughts as he drank the water. Trying for lightness, he turned and remarked casually: 'Oh…nothing. It is so difficult to read the cards and … I have not got the export…the expert…um… experience to be more difficult… sorry…um…definitive.'

Phim's thinking was muddled. He trusted his feeling of the goodness of Artémissa – her strength, resilience – but he couldn't shake the visions that he had seen in the last few minutes. *Is Vegetarian Arté destined to be Carnivore Arté? Is the future written or only implied? How can I help her?*

Arté was looking at the books on the table. 'What about this one?' she suggested, picking up the volume closest to her. 'Crystal Ball and Lyre? Even I know that a crystal ball is a potent way of fortune telling.'

Phim shook his hands as if he was casting out his negative thoughts, crossed to her and looked at the book.

'Yes,' he said. 'We have all the equipment and I have studied the methods. Okay … let's do it.' *Hopefully the future will be clear. And not vampirish.*

The crystal ball, covered with a patterned silk cloth, was on the shelf by the cabinet, with the lyre underneath. Phim placed them on the table, clearing the offending tarot cards away. He glanced at the parrot sleeping above the cabinet and reflected for a moment.

Ketekete. That duplicitous bird! But…remember the 'physical and spiritual connection' of the mage and the familiar was vital to 'implant' or fix high-level spells – and make them 'permanent'. Surely this is important enough to get a physical or spiritual connection with that blinkin' bird. My so-called 'familiar'.

He thought about his time with the parrot. The best time with Ketekete was when he sang to her.
She snuggled down with me. I stroked her feathers to soothe her. Harmonious.

A thought popped into his head – unbidden. An inspiration, a vision. No – more like a memory. *Of course – song and feathers! Feather and song! Something from her and something from me. Physical and spiritual. That's the way, I'm sure of it.* It was a process that brought his love of music and his familiar's feather together. A crystallised, full-fledged way of spell-casting.

And he knew that this process was absolutely true. He didn't question it.

Seraphim crept up to the sleeping parrot. Carefully, sneakily, he plucked a feather from her tail. The indignant parrot woke up and flew across the room as Seraphim hightailed it back to the table. Ketekete blustered and spluttered, protesting the theft of her feather but Seraphim's focused seriousness and Arté's curiosity quietened her down.

'Well,' she mumbled, 'you could have said "Please",' and then sat upright at the head of the table, once again a judicious distance from the vampire.

Seraphim noticed that the three of them were now in an equilateral triangle: Arté, on one side of the table, and he on the other side, with Ketekete at the head. It was a propitious geometry for his spell-casting. *This is no coincidence. I'm sure of this.* He uncovered the crystal ball and picked up the lyre.

As he had envisaged, he sang a verse of the song he composed for Ketekete using the feather to pluck the strings of the lyre. *Song and feathers – feather and song.* He repeated the melody several times, his tone swelling with each iteration. The crystal ball filled with a vapour, and a scene emerged.

Seraphim paused and, in a deep voice, said: 'Per a aquesta persona, revelar alguns esdeveniments futurs significatius.'[64] He resumed his playing and singing. The scene in the crystal ball became clearer – and eventually he recognised it.

Abruptly he stopped singing, stood up and stared in horrified amazement. He laid the lyre down on the table. Not gently. The vision in the crystal ball dissipated like a mist on a sunny day. Arté's expectant eyes turned to dismay. 'What happened? What did you see?' she said urgently.

After some moments, he responded: 'Nothing. Nothing at all. Sorry.' He looked intently at Arté, while he searched for words. 'I can see I neck…nest…need more practice.' He drew his hand across his furrowed brow and gulped.

---

[64] For this person, reveal some significant future events.

'Sorry,' he said again. 'That has been an edit…eerie…um…effort for me. I need to go to bed. Um…we have a guest room just along the hall. I think you will be comfortable there.'

Arté was perplexed. She knew that Phim had had a shock, and intuitively she knew it was about her. But she didn't know Phim well, so she didn't press the point. She nodded, courteously. 'Thank you. Thank you for your amazing dinner and your … fortune telling?' She grinned, but her eyebrows were a question mark. 'And – your compassion. I'll be fine.' She rose and gripped his hand across the table. 'Go to sleep. I will be fine.'

Phim turned and went to his bedroom and, for the first time, Ketekete strutted ahead of him. He closed the bedroom door and turned to face the parrot.
'What are you doing?' Ketekete whispered viciously.
'What?' Phim said faking nonchalance.

'I know what I saw,' hissed Ketekete. 'I know that Artémissa will attack someone. That she bites that someone in the neck with her fangs.'

The parrot looked dramatically down her nose at Phim.

'And that someone is you!'

Chapter 5:

The Solar Panel

Phim reeled and sat down heavily on his bed.

How…how do you know that? I saw in the crystal ball but no-one could see it but myself. So…how do you….

I just did. I saw it.

Phim looked at the bird and suddenly he realised that he had not spoken to Ketekete. And the parrot has answered him back using the same medium – not speaking!

In amazement, this time he actually spoke. Audibly.

'You…you saw in your mind. You…know what I am experiencing. I can feel it too. It's like a…a…another sense?'

'Um…maybe…' Ketekete seemed flustered. 'It was just there.' She gave a bird-like shrug. 'Just somehow…there.'

'Oh! Oh! We are bonding! The book!'

Concentrating, Phim tried it again.

Hi Ketekete! You remember the book. It stated that 'eventually, familiars and their masters shared an empathic link.' We're linked. We have empathic telepathy.

Phim jumped up and did a victory dance, but Ketekete shushed him.

'That's fine, but what are you doing?' she hissed. Ketekete tried telepathy again, and incredibly, it worked.

You can't let that vampire roam about the cottage when you are sleeping. She is going to bite you. You'll be a vampire teabag. The un-dead piranha kiss. You will be her chew toy! Or she will turn you. Then, you will be a vampire. A blood-sucking mage!

No. No. She wouldn't do that. I can't believe that she would do something like that. She is a committed vegetarian. And I can see goodness, her strength.

The parrot was about to 'say' something but Phim got in first 'saying': *Anyway…the crystal ball could be faulty. You know most of my spells are dodgy. Maybe it was not a true future. Or only a possible future. I can work with Arté, help her, care for her… I have to. And she will trust me.*

Ketekete shook her head in despair. She knew that Seraphim's spell with the crystal ball, the lyre accompaniment and the song was perfect. No wrong words. And she knew that the connection with Phim – her feather and Phim's musical composition – was potent. And permanent. She said bleakly, with her real voice: 'Whatever. Your funeral.' She sniggered, funereally. 'For a while – before you come back as the apprentice undead!'

'Go!' Phim commanded. 'Go to sleep on the cabinet.'

The bird chose to telepathically respond: *Not likely. I'm not sleeping with that tooth fairy! I'll sleep in the trees outside.'*

Phim opened the door and Ketekete stalked out.

Phim closed the door gently. He undressed and lay on the bed, but sleep didn't come easily. He tossed and turned and dreamed of sharp incisors piercing blood oranges. The juice ran increasingly crimson red and pulsed and was sticky, flowing down a plate that became a neck, a shoulder, an arm…

He woke with a jolt, eyes wide, heart hammering. *Get it together*, he demanded of himself. He opened the curtains of his bedroom. The sun was peeking among the trees, reddish in colour. *Red at night, shepherd's delight. Red in the morning, vampire's appetite!*

He shook his head and pursed his lips. *No, no. I can't think that. Arté. I have to help her....* and with that, Phim crossed the room and opened his bedroom door.

He surveyed the room expecting someone – but no-one was about. *Ah – of course. Ketekete had gone outside to the forest. But where is Arté?*

He scooted to the guest room. The door was open. He poked his head inside but, apparently, the bed had not been slept in. Arté was not there. He crossed to the windows, drawing the net curtains aside and checking that they were locked. He checked the bathroom and Luxima's bedroom. He even looked under the table in the dining room/kitchen/study in case she was there under the bench – but, there was no sign of her.

He opened the main door. He was just about to call Ketekete but he remembered the link that was growing inside him. *Another sense.* He closed his eyes and concentrated. It was easier than he expected.

Ketekete, I need you. Come here to the cottage door. He paused, and added: Please.

Within ten seconds, a green arrow launched herself from the forest and unfurled as Ketekete.

'Huh!' she said guardedly. 'That was … different? Better than yelling! And,' she curtseyed, daintily for a bird, 'you said "please".'

Phim didn't want to make small talk. 'Arté is missing,' he said breathlessly. 'I looked all around the cottage. Maybe she is in the forest, or...or...'

'Maybe, she ran away. Maybe she wants to feed somewhere else, carnivorously,' Ketekete said nastily. 'Some where she can find better food than a scrawny boy and an intelligent parrot.'

'No!' Phim said forcefully. 'We had a good talk last night. I can't believe she is gone. She wouldn't go without saying goodbye. Where would she go?'

Ketekete stalked into the cottage and flew to the table. She ducked her head to her wing's shoulder and closed one eye. 'Well…what do you know about vampires? Other than that they bite and drain their victim's blood and can make that someone a citizen of the undead.'

Phim gripped the table in concentration and recalled all he had learnt about vampiric behaviour. 'Okay. They can move incredibly fast. Super strength – when they are…um…fit and well – not starving. Um… Most of the urgent…urban downsides are myths: reflections in mirrors, garlic, crosses… They are not really deadly to vampires. They are stocking…stopbank…stories. Um…they are only active at night because…Oh!'

He straightened up and looked at Ketekete with delight.

'The sun. They avoid the sun totally. The sun can destroy them.'

Ketekete nodded with the eventual expected answer as Phim raced to the guest room. The lacy nets on the windows meant that the sun was streaming in. He covered the window with a woollen blanket that totally shut the sun out. Dimly, he looked around the room. There was a trunk at the foot of the bed. Phim lifted the lid quietly and discovered Arté in a foetal position, sleeping peacefully, a smile on her face. He closed it again so he didn't disturb the vampire.

Ketekete commented, under her breath: 'Huh – you had a boy-look.'

'Huh!' said Phim, sotto voce. 'See? She didn't leave us.'

'Sure,' Ketekete whispered testily, 'sleeping like an undead baby.'

The two of them went to the dining room table. Ketekete feasted on seeds and fruit and dozed. Phim went back to Luxima's books, pulling on his right earlobe as he pondered.

Surely I can help her. Then she will know we are on her side. Not food. Surely I can do something before Luxima's return. What would be the best thing for her?

Phim studied the books, opening one after the other.

I can't make 'vegetable' or fake blood that could sustain her metabolism… but I could make her life more comfortable. She said that the worst thing about her vampiric state was not to be able to feel the sun – and see the sunrise and sunset. Sun on her face. Maybe I could find a spell that would help her to be in the sun safely?

All day long he researched and studied the magic that could make Artémissa safe in sunlight. At last, he had a plan.

I think this spell will work, but I have to be careful. The spell is so potent it could be dangerous, especially if I muck up the words. And I need to make the change permanent, so I have to work with my familiar. That's the only way to 'fix' it.

Phim practised the gestures and the tones for the spell-casting, checked and practised the words and drew the radiant mandala in chalk ten, fifteen, twenty times. One hour before the sun was due to set, he was ready. *Well, ready as I'll ever be*, he confessed to himself. He stood up, stretched his cramped limbs and shoulders and looked for Ketekete. She was feeding, again, at the kitchen bench.

The need for another feather was uppermost in Phim's mind and, telepathically, he broadcast this need to the bird. She stood up straight, looked at the approaching Phim and took off. Phim managed to grasp one foot but the two of them fell to the floor. Ketekete retreated under the table. Phim followed, still gripping the parrot's foot but whacked his head on the table's apron. But he managed to hold on to the bird.

'Please, please,' pleaded Phim, rubbing his sore head. 'I need this for my spell to work. To become permanent. Please. For Arté.'

At last Ketekete relented. 'Well…well…whatever,' she acquiesced, 'only because I want you to succeed. I don't trust that vampire. I don't trust her motives or vegetarianess. And the future that you've apparently dismissed? I'm not sure you should discount it. But – okay. I know it will be perm…ow! Ow, ow, ow, ow.'

Phim looked at the tail feather he had plucked from the parrot. It was a gorgeous green and black plume. 'Thank you,' Phim said gratefully.

Ketekete followed circumspectly, rubbing her rump with her wing. Phim retrieved the appropriate spell book, chalk for the mandala and a lamp. They went to the guest room, and Phim knocked gently on the door. No answer. He opened the door carefully.

The bedroom was undisturbed and the woollen blanket was still covering the window. Phim carefully opened the trunk. Arté was still asleep. He looked at her with a fondness that made Ketekete roll her head around – her version of rolling her eyes. Phim shook Arté's shoulder. 'Wake up Arté,' he said excitedly. 'I think I can help you? Wake u–'

Abruptly Arté stood up with a snarl, her vampiric teeth bared, her eyes wide and fierce. Phim took several steps back and Ketekete flapped her wings and flew to the other side of the room. Both were alarmed and shocked.

Artémissa recovered almost immediately and sat down in the trunk. 'Sorry, sorry!' she said contritely. 'I was surprised, that's all. I was… I was…' She broke down in tears. 'Forgive me. You are so kind and…um…'

Phim took a breath, approached the trunk and helped Arté stand up. 'No, no,' he said, 'It was my fault. I should have wafer…walk…woken you up more slowly. But… but I think I can help you. Or, at least, try to make you more comfortable.'

Ketekete stayed where she was, her distrustful eyes on the vampire.

'Oh … what do you plan to do?' Arté asked.

Phim explained his plan. The vampire was unsure but she eventually nodded, and Phim started to get ready. He sat Arté down on the trunk, and proceeded to chalk the intricate eight-pointed mandala on the floorboards in front of her. From the lamp he lit eight candles and placed them on the points of the mandala. He stood opposite Artémissa, shook his limbs like an athlete preparing for a sprint and took eight slow breaths. He interlocked his fingers, raised his arms and made some complicated gestures.

Suddenly an inspiration ignited him. A flash, a vision, and somehow a memory. And, again, he knew it was the right thing to do.

Seraphim held the green tail feather between his thumbs, and blew long and hard. The sound was like a trumpet blast, an incandescent, shining reverberation. Then he spoke in a deep tone: 'Sol nutriet te! Sol nutriet te! Sol nutriet te!'[65] and blew his 'trumpet' again. The sound seemed to have a physical presence, like a golden halo that hovered over Seraphim. The candles lent their light in the same way. A second halo brightening above his head, dazzled and shot across to Artémissa and buried itself in her chest. Seraphim, Ketekete and Artémissa stood bolt upright, and then collapsed on the floor. At that moment, all the candles went out.

---

[65] The sun will nourish you!

After a few minutes the stunned trio roused themselves. 'Everyone is okay?' Phim said shakily. 'Arté? Ketekete? Are you okay?'

'Oh! I have such a headache,' the parrot complained. 'And my butt is so sore…'

'Artémissa!' said Phim, concerned. 'Arté, are you all right? I didn't… I mean I did for the… My words were…' He stopped and looked at the girl.

The vampire shook herself, looked down at her chest and then at Phim. 'I feel fine. Great. Wonderful!' She shook herself and took a deep, ecstatic breath.

Phim was concerned.

The plan. The mandala, the candles and the gestures were perfect. Then I got the idea for the feather and the trumpet thing. Where did that come from? I think I got it right but…the words…I didn't say the right words. I should have said 'Sol tibi salvus erit.' [66] *Where did the other words come from? I mucked up the words. What have I done? And …permanently!*

As he was contemplating his misfired spell, Arté went to the window in a heartbeat. She whipped off the woollen blanket and sent it spinning against the wall. The setting sun was just over the horizon and the last of the sun's rays illuminated the room. The panicked apprentice mage cried out: 'Don't Arté – I didn't… The spell is …'

But he stopped still as Artémissa slowly raised her hands in the air as if she was cradling the sunlight to her body. She stayed like that for up to two minutes – eyes closed, body upright, arms embracing the sun's rays as Phim and Ketekete circled around her back, marvelling that she was alive and hadn't been reduced to a pile of ash.

---

[66] *The sun will be safe for you.*

I did it, thought Phim, *I actually did it.*
In his mind he reached out to his familiar, Ketekete.
We did it! Your feather made all the difference. It should be permanent. Thank you, thank you.
He did a little victory dance on the spot.

After studying the vampire, Ketekete telepathically communicated:
I don't want to spoil your success, but – did Arté have that complexion last night?

Phim looked at Arté. The orange glow of the setting sun disguised the fact that Artémissa was an odd colour – pale, but not whitish-pink. The apprentice mage looked closely at her face. It definitely had a pale green hue – not a sickly, slimy green but a green hue all the same. And the opacity of the colour was increasing with every moment.

'Arté. Arté!' he called, alarmed. 'Maybe you should get out of the sun now…'.
'No – it's glorious,' she burst out joyfully. 'I didn't think I would ever see the sun again. Thank you, thank you. I feel fine. And I feel stronger every moment. The sun has – sort of – filled me up somehow. I feel marvellous. I feel – amazing!'

With this ecstatic statement, in a heartbeat Arté ran out of the room, across to the cottage door and left. Wide-eyed, Phim and Ketekete looked at each other for a moment, then they quickly followed her.

They found her dancing in front of the cottage in the last rays of the sunset. The sun sank below the mountains and an owl hooted in the shadow of the trees and flew off soundlessly. Arté stopped whirling and twirling and faced the pair. Phim's heart sank as he looked at the vampire. 'Okay,' he said carefully, 'come in to the cottage. I think… I think you dictate…disguise…discover…no, no…see this. For yourself.' He took her hand in his.

For the first time since the spell, she looked at her hand and froze. Then she looked at her other hand. Then she pushed up her sleeves. There was a moment of shocked silence, and Arté flashed, as a streak of lightning, into the bathroom and studied her face in the mirror.

Her skin was completely green.

Deep-sea green with a touch of jade. Her veins were a faint fern. Her eyes were sparkling malachite and her hands and feet were emerald with highlights of olive and celadon around the wrist, ankles and tendons. Her hair had turned a lustrous and glossy green-tinged black, like a dark shade of purple basil. Moments later when Phim and Ketekete reached her, they gazed at her apprehensively as she inspected her reflection. It was too much for Phim.

'Sorry, sorry!' Phim stammered. 'I don't know what happy…what happened.' Pleading, he wrung his hands. 'I'll fix it…something…I'll sort it utter…out … tonight… and I'll…'

Arté spun round and hugged Phim with an embrace that almost knocked him out. 'It's marvellous. I love it! I love being green. And – can't you see?'
She stepped back so that Phim and Ketekete could examine her.

Ketekete was more observant than the youth.
'You have fattened up!' said the parrot cheekily, but accurately. 'You're not starving.'

Certainly, Artémissa had lost the emaciated look. She was still skinny, but her body was confident and her face seemed fuller. The hollows under her eyes were gone. 'When the sunlight hit me I seemed to get some energy somehow. The sun – somehow – filled me up. My hunger lessened. I'm not so hungry now. I don't know how, but…'

Phim was sorting through the pieces of the puzzle of what had happened. 'Of course. Photosynthesis. You can photosynthesise your food from sunlight. I think....um...I think you're cured!' They held hands and joyfully danced around the table, laughing heartily. Ketekete flew to the cabinet and presided over the celebration, cackling and chortling and making rude comments like: 'You were a vegetarian – now you are a vegetable.' Or 'Basically, you're a solar panel.'

Five days later, after bathing in the sunlight for three hours or more a day, Artémissa had blossomed. She was delighted with her green appearance. 'So exotic,' she purred.

When she was not photosynthesising she tidied and cleaned the cottage, cooked and followed Phim around helping him with everything he needed. She changed her diurnal pattern, sleeping at night but for only three or four hours.

Nothing was said but Arté soon became one of the household. Ketekete noticed that Arté looked at Phim with a certain amount of affection that the apprentice mage was not aware of. But she also noticed Artémissa's incisors were still sharp, and she could move blazingly fast, flash, if she wanted to. The parrot remained distrustful.

Phim's routine continued as before: waking at six, exercising with his own routine of yoga, tai chi and zumba, before showering, and eating breakfast – mostly muesli and fruit. For three hours in the morning and the same period after lunch he studied the papers and books that Luxima had left. Arté made the lunch after her daily dose of sun. Phim continued to avoid the sun, wearing trousers, long sleeved shirt and a big hat when he had to go outside.

Before dinner, Phim practised some of Luxima's tasks and exercises – usually unsuccessfully. His preparations and gestures were perfect, but he kept mucking up the words, inserting random words or phrases. He tried to turn potatoes into bananas but only succeeded in making them into a set of banjos. He attempted to change a pile of onion peels into a ream of writing paper but it turned out to be a set of frilly pillows.

Phim and Arté took turns to prepare the dinner. Even though the food didn't nourish the vampire, she joined Phim and Ketekete socially. After dinner, Phim and Arté would walk through the forest that surrounded the cottage. Sometimes Ketekete would accompany them for a while, flying above them through the trees to the skies where she indulged herself with aerobatic displays. The bond between the apprentice mage and the parrot was strengthening but Phim had to disregard some of the mistrustful thoughts that the bird harboured about the vegetarian vampire.

One day, Arté and Phim were walking after dinner. The birds were singing in the canopy of tall, leafy trees. Suddenly, a black bird zoomed down from its perch, knocked Phim's hat off and grabbed a hair from Artémissa's head as it flew away. 'Ow!' she complained as Phim scrambled for his hat. They looked around expecting a possible raven ambush but, unusually, the bird was alone. Hesitantly, they carried on.

It was quite late and Arté commented on the full moon rising between the trees, wondering if it would affect her metabolism as the sun's rays did. The full moon was quite brilliant – a golden orb turning to argent as it rose in the sky. Phim was just about to comment when he saw a man coming along the path towards them.

There was something odd about him. His gait was unsteady and Phim thought he was drunk, but then the man howled and crouched down on hands and knees. He howled again – a mournful, ragged and anguished sound.

Phim was about to go to his aid, but Arté clutched his arm. He noticed that her face was stricken with panic. 'What's wrong?' he asked but his question was interrupted with another anguished moan. Phim looked back at the man. His form was changing.

Arté hissed: 'Werewolf – run!'

Chapter 6:

Were (we're) weird

Phim was frozen with fear and fascination. The man's jaw grew outwards, his nose flattened, his eyes and ears grew backwards, dark brown and black bristly fur covered his whole head and down his backbone. His muscles grew enormously. His legs and arms bent and cruel claws scratched the ground below. He doubled in size. Vicious fangs grew out of his jaws and a black tongue was slobbering drool.

The transformation was complete in only seconds. The werewolf howled at the full moon, gnashing his teeth and pawing the ground. He turned to the two onlookers. His eyes betrayed a lust for violence and murder and he galloped towards them, raking the ground with his terrible claws.

Arté didn't hesitate. 'Get on. Now!' she commanded, bending before him. Phim flung his arm around the vampire's neck and she took off like a flash of lightning, easily outdistancing the werewolf. She zigzagged back to the cottage. Ketekete screamed down like a merlin hawk as soon she got Phim's telepathic call and got to the door just as they reached it.

Safe inside, the three collapsed in a gasping heap and Phim gestured a lock command at the door and windows. He looked at his friend and his familiar. Ketekete was breathing hard. Arté breathed normally, but looked extremely concerned.

'The werewolf will come for us,' she said. 'He has seen his quarry. He will not give up until he has murdered, dismembered and eaten us.' She chuckled grimly. 'But only the good bits. He will be here in three or four minutes.'

'Luxima has … protection spells … about … aside … around the cottage,' Phim said breathlessly. 'I activated them … when we … can… come…came in. It should be … fine.'

He crossed to the sink for a drink of water. He rested his arms on the bench trying to get his breath under control. He was shocked at what he had seen: both the man's werewolf transformation and the vampire's speedy retreat. He recalled that, even though Arté photosynthesised her food from the sun's bounty, she was still a vampire! *And that was what vampire's do. Wow!*

He turned to face the others.
'Well…I have been studying spells – protection spells,' he announced. 'Maybe I can't…would…could…something this for this…'

Boom. Boom. Boom!
The door shook on its hinges.
Boom! Boom! Boom!
With a furious roar the werewolf was outside.

'The cottage will protect itself,' Phim said. 'Luxima's spells will be suffer…suffice…sufficient.'
'Okay?' said Ketekete doubtfully. 'Was that a fact or a question?'
'Werewolves.' Arté was panicking. 'Werewolves and vampires are mortal enemies. If he knows I am in here …'
They heard the werewolf smashing the furniture and plants outside.

'I think I can did…do a spell,' Phim blustered, 'something to boast… coast…boost the protection layer. Stop him.'

The shutters on the windows beside the door were rattling wildly. Suddenly four incisions scored down the shutters from top to bottom as the werewolf's claws attacked the wood. There were sparks and flashes from the spell-cast wood but the werewolf doubled his frenzied assault. He punched the weakened shutter and it splintered and fell away. Another punch and the window shattered, scattering sparks. Luxima's magic was weakening. The enchantment was no match for the werewolf's rage.

'Ketekete, I need to fix this spell. Can I …would I…could I…?'
The werewolf was fracturing the walls, demolishing the chimney…
A panicked Ketekete said: 'Sure. Take it – take it!' Phim plucked a perfect green and black tail feather.

Another jolt from the werewolf rocked the cottage.

Frantically Phim looked up the protection spell in his study book: the gesture and the words and the… Then suddenly an inspiration came to him. A memory vision. *I know what to do.*

Seraphim closed his eyes, raised his right hand like a policeman saying 'Halt!'. He clutched the feather in his left hand, brought it close to his mouth and sang through it: a passionate, wild, anguished melody. While he was singing, the chaos outside intensified with the werewolf howling, growling and screaming.
Seraphim pulled himself up to his full height and commanded: 'Erstarren Sie bei Vollmond vor Ihrer Gewalt.'[67] He pointed at the door between them and the werewolf. A host of sparks left his right hand – a chain of coherent light that passed through the main door as if it wasn't there.

Immediately – silence.

Arté and Ketekete were stunned but Phim was concerned. Again, he realised he had inserted other words in the spell.

---

[67] Freeze from your violence during the full moon.

I meant to say: Hören Sie bei diesem Vollmond von Ihrer Gewalt auf.[68] *Where did I get those other words from? My mind and my mouth are divorced. And what did the words mean? And, if the spell that I cast with Arté is anything to go by, it should be permanent. What have I done?*

Ketekete flew to the unshuttered and broken window beside the front door. She beckoned the others to come and see. In the full-moon's glow, the silent yard was a bomb site: chairs, tables and shutters were snapped and broken like kindling, plants were shredded, and the place was littered with glass. But there was no sign of the werewolf.

Phim tested the door. It was jammed. He used another gesture and the door creaked open a few millimetres, as if an elephant was leaning against it. Phim and Arté shoved the door – the vampire's strength was very useful – and they saw the reason.

The werewolf was lying against it, frozen solid.

'Huh! A werewolf popsicle,' Ketekete said, cheekily.
Arté was not so convinced. 'Have you a silver knife to stab him with to decapitate him? Or a silver bullet? Or…'
'No!' Phim was shocked. 'This is a man. We can trick…treat him man… humanely. When you were a starving vampire, did I forsake… sale…stake you? Did I cut off your head?'

Arté was abashed. 'Sorry. Sorry. It's just that vampire and werewolves… Mortal enemies. Sorry. Are you going to make him a vegetarian too?'
'Well… we will see. But I am so tired. I have to rest… Let's leave it til morning.'

They shut the door and Phim established the protection wards for the cottage, trusting the spells would keep them safe until the morning.

[68] Stop your violence at this full moon.

Thankfully, the spells were a combination of gestures and runes, rather than words, written on the floor and walls, so his difficulty with speech would not be a problem. Exhausted, the three of them lay down on their beds and fell into a deep sleep.

In the morning, Arté and Phim shifted the werewolf into the sun to thaw. Ketekete flew into the forest saying she wanted berries, but actually she didn't trust Phim's spell to contain the werewolf. As she flew, a hawk zoomed by and landed on the wrecked chimney stack.

As he thawed, the werewolf changed back to human form. Naked. This amused Arté, who was basking in the sun and half-heartedly cleaning the mess that the werewolf had made. Phim, flustered, got the man a towel and some clothes and sent Arté on her way. She stormed off in a huff to clean up the mess behind the cottage.

In truth, Phim had to admire the man's form. He was more than two metres tall and muscular. Dragons and phoenixes, lions and lambs and helix forms were tattooed around his torso and limbs. As the ice melted, the man spluttered and shook himself.

He spun around and gazed at the cottage, the forest and the wreckage strewn everywhere. Then he stared at Phim angrily. 'What's going on? Who are you? What am I doing here? Where am I?'

'It's okay,' Phim consoled the man. 'You are along…as… at Luxima Aerolaness cottage. The wizard. You had an epic…epidemic…episode. You are safe.'

The observant hawk flew off. The man dried himself and put on the clothes. 'Well? Who're you?' he said indignantly. 'Why stutter?'

'Street…site…sit down,' Phim said calmly. 'Sit down and would… want… I will explain.'

The man sat on a chair and looked at Phim defiantly. Unfortunately the chair had a broken leg – courtesy of the werewolf's rampage – and the wolfman overbalanced and ended up on the ground. He stood up quickly and with a fierce look, threw the offending chair over the cottage roof. 'Are you making fun of me?' he said angrily.

With upraised hands and open palms, Phim said: 'No! No! Things are bread…brook…broken.' His calm tone didn't match his churning insides at all. 'Sorry. Maybe you should stand and I will expo… expect…explain to you. Okay.'

The fire in the wolfman's eyes diminished perceptibly.

'My name is Seraphim but modest…mope…most people call me Phim. I am an apprentice – Luxima Aerolaness is my melody… model…mentor. I…am sometimes…the words don't …didn't…' Phim took a deep breath. 'My brawn…brain and my mouth… They are often not in sync. Sometimes the words are…' He shrugged. 'It is better when I slope…slow it down.'

Another breath. He saw that the man was more relaxed, so he continued.
'Last night…we – well, looked after you, after a fusion…fashion. With your…episode.'

The man looked at Phim closely, remembering. 'Oh no!' he said, his hand over his mouth. 'You. On the path. And the girl. Oh no,' he said softly. 'It happened again. My – "change". Someone has died? Of course. Always, somebody is dead…' He bowed his head and clasped his hands between his legs. 'Oh no, oh no,' he groaned. 'Someone's dead. Didn't want to do it. Didn't want to.'

Phim put his hand on the man's shoulder and said: 'No-one has died. It's okay. The plankton…play… The place is a mess, but – no-one died.'

'How…' the man looked up at Phim. 'How can that be? I saw you. On the path. The girl. And then the "change"… Someone dies. Always. How come?'

'Look, come here,' Phim said patiently. 'Come into the cottage.'
He ushered the confused man in to the cottage and they sat down in the dining room.

'Let's start at the beetle…big…beginning. What's your number… name? Where do you live?'

'Koan. Name is Koan,' said the man. 'I live at Silensia. Village fifteen kilometres west of Torrencia. Well – I lived there. About eight months ago. I was bushwhacked in the forest. I thought it was a wild dog. Or a lone wolf. It was huge. It savaged me. I lost consciousness. When I came to, my brothers were there. But they didn't want to talk. About the creature that had attacked me. It was quite odd. I was sick for two weeks. The villagers were betting that I wouldn't make it. But I recovered.'

Koan spoke abruptly, his sentences were short, his deep voice gruff. Phim realised that eloquence and Koan were strangers.

'Then, the "change" came suddenly. I was dizzy. My legs couldn't hold me. Then I blacked out. In the morning I was somewhere else. In the forest. Naked. With blood all over me. It was from animals: birds, sheep, goats, deer. I thought I could cope with it. But the killing went on. Every full moon.

'Then, last month, some strangers were killed. Perhaps I was responsible? I don't know. My family and the other villagers were suspicious. They ran me out of the district. They threatened to kill me. It made me so angry. I wanted to shake them and make them see sense. But, they were my family. Friends. I had to go…

'So, I have been wandering in the forest. Until I saw you two. And then I got dizzy. And… You know the rest.' Koan looked at Phim intently. 'You know? You know what I am?'

Phim nodded. 'Yes. We know what you are. But I think I can harm… hello…help.'

'Yes? But … how?' Koan angrily leapt up from his chair. 'Don't want to be this way. Want to be normal. Useful. I don't want to kill. Don't want to be angry. Don't want to be a danger to anyone…'

'Well,' Phim said, 'I think I has…have… helped you already. You see what …how my speech… I used a spell on you…last night and I suspect…actually, I think that your…'

Just then, Arté walked in through the back door. Immediately Koan's hackles rose, his shoulders tensed, his hands closed in fists and he assumed a fighting stance. He didn't transform, but his physique and readiness for violence were intimidating. With a low, guttural growl he uttered one word: 'Vampire.'

Arté said menacingly: 'Werewolf.' She flashed across the room in a heartbeat, positioning herself at the table opposite the wolfman, bristling with belligerence, her fangs flashing. In seconds her fingernails grew into cruel talons.

Phim was astonished: *I guess this is what vampires and werewolves do?*

'No!' Phim slapped the table between the two. 'No. This has to start... stall...stoop...'

His stammering seemed to goad them into action. Koan leaped across the table, arms swinging. Arté vaulted the wolfman like a fast-action high jumper. Both spun ready for the next thrust. Phim pounded the table again and yelled: ' Stop. Now!'

The combatants glared at each other. The wolfman beat his fists against his thighs. Arté was calculating and confident. Her grin was diabolical. But both paused.

'Just listen to me,' Phim said breathlessly. 'Okay. So...so...both of you changed, but you are human.' He pointed at Arté and said, 'Maybe you are none...neither...not a normal woman,' and he pointed to Koan, 'and you are not a norman...northly...normal man, but you can be human. Humanity doesn't only restrain...rested...reside in men and women.'

Phim concentrated. *This is too important. I have to get the words right. It has to be right.* He took a deep breath. He continued calmly, slowing down his words.

'To be human you only have to be humane. You can rise above your basic insects...instincts and the bigotry of your clans. You can be **more**. Not with the biased blinkers that your asset...ancestors were cursed with. See each other – clearly!'

Still in an aggressive stance, both listened to Phim.

He looked at them with a steely gaze, pointing at them as he introduced them to each other.

'Koan – Artémissa is a vegetarian vampire. She is green. She can make her football...food from the sun. That's why she is green. She will not hope...harp...harm you.'

'Artémissa – Koan wants to stop killing. He is a reluctant werewolf. He wants to chatter...charge...change his condition. You have to be pace...patch... patient with Koan. Don't provoke him. Be compassionate. Be human. Okay?'

Slowly the tension between the girl and the man lessened and they relaxed. Their eyes were still wary but they lowered their hackles and unclenched their hands.

Phim focused on the wolfman and thought about his mismanaged spell. He realised it could remove the danger of the werewolf permanently.

'Koan: I can help you tone down your aggression. Your analysis... annul...anger is at the root of your problem. I can help you relax more, renovate...remove...release the aggression. Okay? Cool it down a bit. If you want to, you can work here. Work in the grey...green...garden and the orchard, cut wood for the fire, maintain the place, hunt and catch fig...first...fish. You can be the handyman for the cottage. Actually, a handyhuman.'
Phim looked at them and they met his gaze.
He raised both of his hands, palms upward. 'Deal?' he said.

Both raised their heads fractionally, looked at each other, nodded.
'Deal,' said Arté reluctantly.
'Deal, ' said Koan gruffly.

Whew! I was going to say that they should shake hands, but that's for another day. At least they aren't fighting to the death. Yet.

Just as well, because Arté blurted out: 'Where is he going to sleep?'
'No problem,' Koan answered angrily. 'I will sleep outside. In the woodshed. I don't want to share the same air as that vam…'
Phim coughed urgently and Koan backtracked. 'I will be more comfortable there.'

'Okay, okay,' Phim said calmly. 'Maybe we can wok…work together to clean up the message…mess outside?'

Koan nodded once, and left the room by the main door, still glowering at the vampire – but not as aggressively as before. Arté frowned but she only looked darts, not daggers, at the departing wolfman. She left by the back door.

Over the next fortnight, the truce for Koan and Arté spread to their everyday life. Admittedly, the former adversaries didn't mix socially, but they tolerated and were polite to each other – in Phim's hearing at least. He was happy that he could get back his routine, and he invited Koan to his yoga, tai chi and zumba exercises, and the wolfman accepted. He introduced a meditation session before breakfast and dinner in an effort to release the aggression and anger that still resided in Koan.

Arté was interested in Phim's studies and questioned him about the spells he was working on. He was flattered. 'The one branch of magic that I don't want to explore is necromancy,' he said with obvious distaste. 'Necromancy is concerned with mastery over distant… distaste…um…death. I don't want to think about that. Dis….um… Death is death. I think we shouldn't toy with that subtract…subject. It is an absolute result.'

Obviously, Ketekete was not happy about Arté's interest in Phim's studies. She distrusted the vampire's curiosity and, telepathically, she shared her concerns with Phim but he dismissed them. The parrot was not satisfied, but she kept her opinion to herself.

But she didn't mind expressing her telepathic thoughts about Koan's presence – such thoughts as: *this feral runt, this slobber doggy, junkyard cur is dangerous and should be sent off.* Phim pooh-poohed the idea, but grinned surreptitiously at the cheeky parrot's turn of phrase.

Koan made his home in the woodshed. He was quite happy to work at the outside household chores. He fixed the outdoor furniture, the shutters, window, and the chimney. He fished and hunted and cooked his carnivore food outside so Arté didn't have to deal with the carcasses in the kitchen.

(Sometimes, when Arté was not looking, Phim and Ketekete sneaked a fillet of fish or quail breast.)

The garden became a space for the wolfman and the vampire to enjoy a sort of détente. Koan turned the compost, dug the garden and did odd jobs like mending the fences. Arté looked after the seedlings, planting them out in the beds that Koan has prepared, and weeded them. Initially when one of them arrived, the other left, but in just two weeks, they had become comfortable sharing the same space.
But not talking.

With Koan around, another bonus for the companions emerged. Smell. His almost supernatural sense of smell meant he could alert the cottage's occupants if anyone was approaching.

Ketekete was most amused, and referred to Koan as 'The Sniffilator'. Not to his face though.

One day, Koan detected a strange presence outside the cottage garden fence, and alerted the others. Arté was already in the garden on the other side, Phim came out of the cottage and Ketekete flew onto the handle of a spade beside them. 'What can you see?' she asked.

'Not see. Smell.' Koan put his nose in the air and sniffed. Ketekete, wing over her mouth, mouthed: 'The Snifflator' to Phim and Arté but suddenly Koan was off.

He ran to the far side of the garden where it joined the forest. The others followed him. He was sniffing a big silver birch tree, and suddenly he reached out and rapped his fists on the trunk as if it were a bass drum. A rangy creature popped out of the tree and sprawled on the ground before the astonished company.

'Ow, ow, ow!' the creature moaned. 'You've burst my eardrums. I can't hear you. You deafened me. Ow, ow, ow!'

Chapter 7:
'Doctor, I have a problem!'

As the shock of seeing the creature receded, Phim examined her.

He guessed it was a female given the obvious three breasts under her 'dress'. Her dress seemed to be made of layers of multi-coloured leaves from throat to mid-thigh and her arms and legs were bare. She was slender and very tall – about three metres. Her skin, if that was what it was called, was patterned with rough, golden-brownish streaks as if she had been coated with candle wax. She had brown hair that stuck out like a wire brush, and a pleasant face: hazel eyes, milk chocolate lips and tidy ears – all four of them. Phim noticed that both her hands and feet were graced with eight long digits with four knuckles, as well as thumbs and big toes.

'Who are you?' demanded Koan aggressively. 'What are you?'
The creature moaned on the ground and complained: 'I can't hear you. You deafened me.'

Phim came behind her and said pleasantly: 'What's your name?'
She turned and said conversationally: 'Oh – my name is Tasselis. And what's your name?'
'Huh,' Ketekete said under her breath. 'Deafness cured.'
Phim ignored the comment. 'I'm Seraphim, but you can call me Phim.' He introduced the three friends. 'This is Arté … Ketekete … and Koan.' Then he asked, in bewilderment: 'But…sorry…what are you?'

'I'm a dryad, of course,' Tasselis said, matter-of-factly. 'A tree spirit.'

'Um…so…' said Ketekete, 'what are you done…doing here? How can we help you?'

Tasselis sat up, folding her long legs under her. 'Ah well. I have a cough that won't go away. Ahuuurgh, ahuuurgh. I've had this cough for three weeks and it wakes me – ahuuurgh – all the time. I thought it was a whooping cough but it could be a croup or a barking cough... ahuuurgh. I get it late at night, or in the morning. Sometimes it is at lunchtime or afternoon. You can hear it now... Ahhhuuuuurgghhh, ahuuuuurgggggh!'
Tasselis spluttered and coughed alarmingly. The quartet stepped back.

Tasselis got up from the ground and towered over them.
'See – ahuuurgh. Can you help me?'
'Why do you think we can help?' Phim countered.

'I am concerned that my cough could infect the trees. Fungal rot or leaf stress disorder or something else. This is Luxima Aerolaness's cottage, right? The wizard? I want to see him about my cough.' Tasselis realised her cough had disappeared, so she summoned up a 'good one'. 'Ahuuurgh, ahuuurgh, ahuuuuurgggggh!'

'Um – unfortunately he is not in,' said Phim. 'He has golfer...gospel... gone away and......'
'So,' Arté interrupted, 'we don't know when he is coming back, so I think you should see someone else.'

'Oh?' The dryad was quite flummoxed. 'Maybe he has a sproutling? An intern?'

'Well, I am...' Phim began, but Arté interrupted again: '...pointing out the path in the forest. That leads to a road. If you go north, you will get to Torrencia. There are many healers and doctors there...'
Phim gave Arté a dirty look which she ignored.

'Okay, okay,' the dryad sighed. She turned and walked towards the path. 'I guess I will go there and … ow, ow, ow.' She stumbled and caught herself on Koan's brawny arm. 'Ah – I have sprained my foot. Or maybe it is a broken bone? A failed graft? A greenstick fracture? I think that's it…Ah, ah, oh!' and she collapsed into Koan's arms.

The wolfman was nonplussed. 'What? What should…? How…?' Ketekete sniggered.

Phim said: 'Ketekete, clash…clear the table. Koan, pink…pick Tasselis up and carry her back to the kindness…kitchen. **We** will see what **we** can do,' emphasising the pronoun and shooting another disapproving look at the vampire.

Koan laid the dryad on the table and, with a confused look, excused himself and went back to his other duties. Arté stood inside the main door, arms folded and a churlish look on her face. She was worried about the competition for Phim's attentions if another female settled in to the cottage. And Tasselis was so slender and tall…

Phim bent down to examine the dryad's foot but he could not see any problem.

'I think it's better now,' Tasselis said. 'But my elbows are playing up again. They are so achy and painful. I think it's iron chlorosis. Or arthritis. Or maybe it is the first signs of cerebral palsy. Or Parkinson's? And my back. So achy. Ow, ow, ow. Now it's in my left thigh. And knee. Do you recommend amputation? Next spring I could have grown a new one anyway… '

Ketekete, chuckling, flew out the window leaving behind a scoffing thought for Phim:

Arrogant stuck-up tree-fondling hippy. She is mental.

'Um…um…', Phim stood up and rubbed his head in puzzlement. Before he could open his mouth, Tasselis gripped his arm and gasped for breath. 'Oh, it's…it's…my…asthma…hah…hah…my…breath…ing…hah…hah…can't…breathe…'

'Calm down, Calm down,' said Phim calmly. 'Just breathe. Breathe. B r e a t h e… B r e a t h e… '

Tasselis did what she was told and her breathing returned to normal. Then she coughed again, spluttering all over the floor. 'Oh sorry. I must be developing a "flu".' Cough, splutter, splatter. 'That new one. Not the bird flu. Or porcine flu. The bovine flu. Moo, moo…' Cough, splutter. 'Or Covid flu…' Splatter. 'The next one. The Oak Leaf Fungal flu.' Cough, splutter, splatter.

Phim backed off and said placidly: 'Just sit there and rest. I have to concept…consort…confer with my nutrient… nurse…'

'Why are you talking funny?' Tasselis questioned. 'Stuttering. Or maybe you are foreign?' She rose from the table, and touched her forehead, bending down in abject self-contemplation.

'Oh! Maybe you're not talking funny. Maybe my ears are not hearing what you are saying. I have semi-dislocated deafness. Sap in my ears.' She waggled and put her fingers in her four ears, one by one. Then she rested her head in her many-fingered hands and groaned. 'They are working fine. Whoa! So, I have brain disorder. I have dementia. Alzheimers. Maybe I have schizophrenia. Or a psychotic break…'

In the mean-time, Phim backed over to where Arté was standing and whispered: 'What's her game?'

Arté whispered back: 'Nurse? Nurse!'

'Sorry, I just had to get a break from her,' he said. 'Her complaints are completely fiendish…fidgety… fictitious. I don't believe she knows anyone…anywhere…anything about her supposed illnesses. They are just random warm…wine…words to her.'

Arté turned to face away from Tasselis. 'Hypochondria. Invented conditions and symptoms. They just want to be the centre of everyone's attention. It's all about "Me! Me! Me!" '

'Aha. I see. And…you thought that when we joust…just met her,' Phim realised. 'That's why you said that she should go to Torrencia. I see, I see, I see…' Arté biting her tongue, didn't argue.

'Hypochondria?' he said, musing. 'The illnesses are not ready… relate…real. Just in her head?'
But… maybe I can help her. Maybe a spell that will make Tasselis think she is healthy. I have to get her out of here and study my books.

He headed back to the table muttering 'Okay, okay, okay.'

The dryad looked down on him and was about to pronounce on some other imaginary illness but Phim stopped her. 'Tasselis,' he said, 'I am going to helm…help you. But I need to prepare – so please go back outbid…outer…outside and join Koan in the garden. You can help him there.'
The dryad was about to respond but Phim pre-empted her.
'No. If this magic is going to word…work, I have to foamy…folk… focus completely. I have to be alone.'
Again, Tasselis was about to speak, but Phim said forcefully: 'Go! Go to Koan.'

The befuddled dryad turned and crossed to the main door. She attempted to speak to Arté but by the time she uttered her first word, the vampire had flashed out the door, as if she had never been there at all. Puzzled, Tasselis bent under the door and went in search of Koan.

She found him tending the apple trees in the orchard. 'Phim said that I could help you,' she asked desultorily. Koan took in her height and said: 'Sure. Prune these trees.' He took the secateurs and showed her how to prune branches. 'Oh,' she exclaimed in distress. 'Oh – the tree is crying out to me. It thinks you are going to kill it. Murder, murder!'

Meanwhile, Phim picked up one of Luxima's books – *Charm Your Way To Success.* He was looking for a spell that would convince the dryad that she is healthy. In just fifteen minutes managed to select, learn, devise and memorise the spell, despite all the interruptions.

Ah. The interruptions.

After Phim had ousted Tasselis from the kitchen, he had just four minutes of calm before Koan burst through the door.

'Crazy dryad,' he exploded. 'Prune apple trees – she thought I would kill them. Pick up prunings – she thought she was infected by codling moth. Gave her a wheelbarrow – she complained of a slipped disc. I gave up. Sent her to Arté. Crazy!' He turned and slammed the door as he went out.

Phim went back to his studies. Five minutes later Arté suddenly appeared at the table.

'She's insane,' she stormed. 'I was doing the laundry out the back. That beanpole asked me if she could help me. "Get the washing out of the tub," I said. She dipped her hands in the hot water and cowered in fear. "My fingers are bifurcating." She drew her hands and, sure enough, her fingers were splitting in half. The warm water had softened them She was freaking out, so I got her out into the sun. I needed some sustenance myself, so we sat down in the backyard.

'She calmed down – sort of – just muttering about curly leaf disease and bonsai training. I was basking in the sun. Then that psychotic tree sylph freaked out again. She was dancing on the spot and rubbing her hands over her face and hair and arms. "I have sunburn!" she shouted. "Sunburnt skin and hair and blotches on my body. I have melanomas and cancer and leukaemia and…" So I said: "Get out of the sun and go see Ketekete in the chicken house. She would know what to do." And I pushed her in that direction.'

Arté stormed out the back door, saying over her shoulder: 'She is certifiable. I can't deal with her.'

Five minutes later, Ketekete flew into the cottage landing, as always, on the cabinet. She sent Phim a telepathic message.

That tree hugger is demented. She came into the chook[69] house, bent her head to fit in the space and grumbled about rheumatoid arthritis and cramps. Then she asked me why my 'compatriots' build their nests in trees, tear off bark and twigs and shit all over the branches. I said that I didn't know what she meant. She huffed and puffed. I was giving some seeds and grains to the chickens and that incompetent daisy sniffer got a mouthful and proceeded to choke on it and complained that I was asphyxiating her. I left her there – she is demented. Someone should put her out of her misery that…that… pole-proportioned dendrophile[70] is to …

Phim broke into Ketekete's tirade to 'say': *Okay, okay – but I have a solution. Another spell. And I suspect you want to make it permanent…?*

Yes please. I pray to all of your eight gods, please! she thought and she offered her posterior to Phim.

---

[69] chook = chicken (Aotearoa New Zealand slang)

[70] A person (dryad?) who loves trees

He plucked another feather – a good, strong one. He brought his book with his chosen spell to the kitchen bench and selected all the components for a potion. Ketekete looked on.

He ground the ingredients with a mortar and pestle, added ginseng tea and whisky and then poured the mixture into a beaker and placed it on an iron grill above the fire. When the potion was bubbling, Phim collected the beaker and used tongs to pour the potion over an incense stick.

As he did so, he was struck by an idea which seemed, somehow, to be completely right. An inspired process. A way to combine his music and the feather together.

Seraphim suspended a small cymbal above the incense and struck it eight times with the spine of the feather. The tone of the cymbal was pure and resonating and, after the last one, faded into silence. Then he asked Ketekete to get everyone to come in, especially Tasselis.

Within moments Ketekete had gathered the grumbling others. Seraphim directed Tasselis to sit beside the table. 'Ketekete – could you go to the cabbage…cabinet. Arté and Koan – stand on either side of Tasselis.' The werewolf and the vampire flanked the dryad, and glanced at each other, privately amazed that they were okay to be so close. Tasselis was still muttering about her aches and pains.

'This will help you,' Seraphim announced confidently to the dryad. 'Breathe deeply, and dog…dolt…don't say a word.'

In the silence he lit the incense. A rainbow flame sparked and crackled then diminished to a smouldering ember. Seraphim took the incense stick in his right hand and, with the feather in his left, he wafted it around Tasselis making sure every part of the dryad was exposed to the fragrant smoke.

At the same time he sang an eight-note melody: 'Sa aitad alati'[71] at the eight termini of the body: her feet, hands, shoulders, crotch and head. The rainbow-coloured and heavy vapour smelled like summer nights under a starlit sky. Like climbing a mountain that promised a glorious view. Like hope and fulfilment.

Seraphim left the incense stick smouldering in a holder in front of Tasselis, sang the melody again and at the same time vigorously struck the cymbal with the feather. The sound increased, ringing and echoing around the room, and then slowly faded into silence.

Phim, Ketekete, Arté and Koan turned to the dryad questioningly. Tasselis's eyes were closed. She was erect and tense, holding her breath. The incense smoke seemed to enter her body by osmosis. As it cleared she exhaled, relaxed and opened her hazel eyes. A beatific smile played around her milk chocolate lips. She looked at them each intently for a few moments, and then said calmly: 'I feel good. Really good. So – how can I help you?'

Before Phim could speak, Koan brusquely interjected: 'Well – pruning the trees. That would be helpful.'
'Sure, yes,' the dryad complied. 'Could I speak to them though, and explain to them that I will give them a haircut? They will understand that.'
'Uh – sure. Sure. That's fine,' said the perplexed wolfman.
The two tall ones stooped under the door bound for the orchard. Koan was preparing for the task ahead so he didn't hear a big black and white bird flapping off the cottage's roof and disappearing into the forest.

In the kitchen, Arté and Ketekete were flabbergasted and turned to Phim in amazement. Ketekete flapped her wings in applause. 'Wow! You made that leaf licker happy alright.'

---

71 You will help always.

'She…she's…helping Koan?' Arté was stunned. 'She's not complaining about anything. She said she's fine. How did you do that? Amazing.' Her face was glowing with pride in Phim's achievement. Arté glanced at Phim from under her eyelids and the glow turned into a blush. *He's quite talented and handsome in a geeky sort of way.*

But Phim was puzzled and he accidentally spoke aloud: 'I used the wrong words again. I know the words – they were rotten…wrote… written there in the book. I relay…retract…read them. I memorised them. I meant to say "Sa oled alati terve." But I said: Sa aitad alati.[72] That's dijoint…distinct…different. What have I done?'

He flinched, realising that the other two were privy to his confession. But it didn't matter.

Ketekete didn't care. *The ends justify the means,* she thought to him, *whatever that means.*

And Arté was so delighted that the dryad was not moaning and groaning about her spurious ailments that she, also, didn't care. They waltzed out of the cottage to their various tasks.

Alone in the kitchen Phim sighed. *What have I done?*

It was two days before Phim realised what his mistaken words had done to the dryad. He was outside taking a breather from his study and noticed that Tasselis was running around like a mad thing.

Apparently Ketekete requested that Tasselis could influence the local walnut tree to drop its nuts prematurely so she could feast on them. Arté solicited her to demand the forest trees that they not grow so high so she could have more sun. And Koan demanded that the dryad

[72] Sa oled alati terve – You will be healthy always.
Sa aitad alati – You will help always.

convince some of the big trees to move closer to the woodshed so he could cut them down for firewood.

The dryad wanted to grant every request even when it went against her basic nature.

Tree for firewood? That would be abhorrent to her, but she was doing it for Koan. Why? And height restrictions for Arté? Walnut gathering for that parrot.

Phim realised what was happening. Rather than making her realise she was healthy, as he had intended, Tasselis was unquestionably compliant with every suggestion that others made, even if the request was anathema to her. Phim called the trio to him as Tasselis was frantically busy satisfying their desires.

'This has to stop,' he whispered forcefully 'She will blow a funeral… fuss… fuse. Have some companion…competition…compassion. She is **not** your slave.'

The others were ashamed of what they were doing and apologised before going back to their work. Phim walked over to Tasselis and said: 'The others want you to launch…leafy…leave this work now. I want you to rest in the sun for a while, before digit…dimmer…dinner.'

The dryad gave him a sunny, contented smile. 'As you wish,' she said sitting down beside the flower garden in the sun and closing her eyes.

The irises, tulips, roses, begonias and orchids sensed her presence and their colours and perfume expressed their contentment.

Chapter 8:

Coming...

The next day Phim asked Tasselis to treat the mossy thatch roof of the cottage, making it clear that it was for all of them in the cottage, including Luxima – not a personal favour for himself. He explained that her great height and facility with all vegetation could help the moss that protected the rain from penetrating the roof.

Tasselis thought: *It improves everyone's lives, I am uniquely qualified to do this task, and I know what the moss needs. I can be useful!*

She was amused by Phim's very tactful way of making the request and she thought about stringing him along with a doubtful expression on her face, but she realised that people didn't understand her body language very well, and it was not in her nature to deceive people, even in jest. So, she clapped her hands and said she was happy to do it.

For the next ten days, things went well. An idyllic time.

Tasselis was happy that the others didn't plague her with impossible demands. *I like it here. I can look after all the forest: trees, shrubs, bushes and plants helping them to grow magnificently. Phim is a good sort – despite his communication shortcomings. Ketekete is a bluffer – she calls me a 'dew drinker' and a 'tree bitch' but I know she likes me. Arté is a good friend – we have an understanding. Obviously. And Koan – he is gruff and rough, but he has a heart of gold. And he is … handsome, like a gnarled oak tree. Yeah – I like it here.*

Indeed, Tasselis and Arté had become the best of friends. And Tasselis spent a lot of time with Koan and the wolfman seemed to make time to do more gardening than before.

Ketekete, despite her cheeky language, liked Tasselis, now that the dryad was free of her hypochondria. She often shadowed Tasselis when she was walking in the forest dispensing her own brand of magic. Once, Ketekete saw a black bird circling, fluttering and, apparently, talking to the dryad, but it flew off when it saw her. The sunlight reflected off its wings with an iridescent brilliance as it flew into the forest and it seemed to have a white bib on its throat.
That was…a tui? the stunned parrot thought. *No, no – it can't be.*

An idyllic time. Almost.

Increasingly, Koan grew more grumpy and agitated as the month wore on and eventually he abrogated his help in the garden with Tasselis and marched off. Ketekete and Arté nervously consulted the calendar and alerted Phim that it was just two days before the full moon.
'That mongrel will be a landshark tomorrow night,' said Ketekete, under her breath.
'Yep,' Arté agreed.
'Not a problem,' Phim said breezily. 'Not a problem.'
Arté and Ketekete were not convinced.

Next day, at breakfast time, Koan roared when his toast was burnt, thumped the table because his coffee was cold, and threw the chair across the room. Tasselis was stunned, Ketekete flew up to her favourite perch and Arté flashed to the wall assuming a wary, fighting stance.

The wolfman, angrily glaring at everyone, stormed out.
'Calm down,' Phim placated. 'Just leader…leaf…leave him alone.'
'But,' Arté protested, 'it will be a full moon tonight, and that means…'
'It's solo…sorted,' Seraphim insisted. 'You'll see!'
And he went on with his studies.

Koan spent the rest of the day splitting firewood with a mad look in his eye. Tasselis made herself scarce in the garden on the other side of the cottage.

Arté was cooking and occasionally going outside to bask in the sun but she kept a close eye on the wolfman. Ketekete flew as high as she could into the forest canopy.

Koan didn't come in for supper. Everything infuriated him. Phim left him a sandwich and a tankard of ale in the woodshed.

After dinner, Phim asked Arté to go for a walk, to look at the sunset from a favourite vantage point. Arté didn't think twice. Time alone with Phim was always welcome.

The sun sank into the horizon and the reds, oranges, green and yellow colours billowed like blossom against the sky. A golden full moon was peeking over the mountains like a shy girl.

As Arté looked at the brilliant colour scape and the patterns in the clouds, Phim studied her. He thought about the emaciated, greasy-haired, hollow-eyed and pale girl he had met just five weeks ago. Now, her body had filled out remarkably. She was intelligent, confident, curious, straightforward. And green!
She was...beautiful.

He was about to say something to her but he saw Koan walking purposely behind them. Phim held Arté's arms and whispered: 'Trust me. Don't be alien…album…alarmed. Koan's coming up the path.'
Arté turned her head, her mouth twitched, her sharp incisors gleamed and her arms were tense but she didn't break free of Phim's grip.

Koan's gait was unsteady, uneven. He snarled like an animal and muttered 'Vampire!' He crouched down, his face elongated, dark bristly fur sprang up from his body….et cetera, et cetera…
The beast gathered himself for a leap towards the two spectators and…

…froze solid.

Phim and Arté came down the path and circled the frozen werewolf. One was satisfied, the other incredulous.

'What?' spluttered Arté. 'I didn't see you uttering a spell. How…?'
'Because of Ketekete's feather,' he explained. 'It makes the spell perjury…purposeful….argh!' He concentrated. 'Permanent.'

As if she was summoned, Ketekete flew down from the trees. 'Hey – Bitey McSnapperperson is frozen again. Werewolf popsicle. I thought you could do it.'
But telepathically she admitted: *Actually, I hoped you **could** do it, but I was nervous – so I got into the cheap seats above, for the show.*
Phim raised his eyebrows and gave a subtle nod.
You are an absolute chicken – no offence. But – your feather saved the day, just as the text said it would. The spell is permanent.

Tasselis came along the path from the cottage, chewing on a stick of beeswax. They turned to her. Her face was a study in amazement.
'What is that?' she asked.

'Well – it is active…acne…actually Koan,' Phim said clumsily. 'He chains…changes every full mo…'

Tasselis interrupted. 'Oh, no – I don't mean that. I know Koan is a werewolf – he told me. And what you did for him.' She pointed beyond to the forest. 'But – what is that?'

Phim and Arté looked to where she was pointing behind them and studied the forest beside the path. It was as if there was a translucent curtain between the trees and the path and someone was gently shaking it. As they watched, a hand appeared and drew the curtain aside.
A man stepped through.

He was pale, his face was handsome crowned with shaggy blonde hair.

He was just under two metres tall and he was clothed with a red flax plaited loin cloth, so they could see his hairless physique. He had a bone flute around his neck on a flax string. The man looked around at the forest, the orange moon, the stars that were appearing in the dusk.

Then he looked at them. Confidently, regally, he walked to where they stood in stunned silence. He looked them up and down – especially Arté – and, to their surprise, addressed himself to Ketekete.

'Kia ora. Tino kore. He kākā koe? Kei te aha koe i konei?' [73]

Without thinking, Ketekete answered in the same language. 'Kia ora. Āe. He kākā ahau.'

The newcomer was visibly astonished.
'Ka taea e koe te korero? Me pehea e taea ai?' he asked.

The conversation went on for a few minutes and then the stranger left them and focused on the forest, the distant mountains and the roar of the river in the valley below.

Phim turned to Ketekete and interrogated her. 'Who is that? What did he walk…woke…want? And what landfall…humph…language did you speak?'

'Sorry. I was surprised,' the parrot cringed, embarrassed. 'This is the language of my home. Aotearoa. I should have said – Luxima came to me in the forests of Aotearoa and asked me if I wanted an adventure. Well – I am always up for that. Things were a bit crowded at home, so, I came with him. We used a portal like the one this patupaiarehe came out of now.'

---

[73] Translation is below

'Patupaiarehe?'

'The faerie folk from Aotearoa. Nature spirits. They have some magic too. They can be dangerous.'

Phim was aware that the faerie was close and could be listening to every word, so he suggested, telepathically, that Ketekete should: *tell me what he said to you and your answers – word for word.*

Sure, the parrot 'said'.
The patupaiarehe said: Good health. Hey you? You are a kākā? Surely not. What are you doing here?
And I said: Yes. I am a kākā.
Him: You can speak? How can that be?
Me: A wizard made it so I could talk. I was as surprised as you are. But it's okay.
Him: Why are you not in the forests of Aotearoa? Why are you in this forsaken place?
Me: The wizard called me and asked if I wanted to help his apprentice as his familiar. He took me from Aotearoa and placed me in this place. It's not so bad.
Him: This is the wizard?
Me: No – he is the apprentice. The wizard is away at the moment. But he is coming back soon.
Him: Huh. Who is the frozen one? He looks like a land-taniwha. All those teeth and claws.
Me: He is a werewolf – and a most dangerous creature.
Him: And the tall one? She is ugly.
Me: She is a tree spirit – gentle, but ferocious when she gets riled, mostly about damage to trees and shrubs.
Him: And this green one? I've never seen a green wench. She is a beauty. I like her. Like her, like her – if you see what I mean.
Me: She can be dangerous also.
Him: Ha – I am too. I am a powerful wizard myself. And that apprentice doesn't look up to it. Hmmm – Let me look at this place. Maybe I can set my roots down. Huh – I could be Emperor, rule here…

The interchange lasted only a few moments. Phim straightened up, girded himself, and approached the man as he was gazing at the starry sky.

'Hello. My name is … Seraphim. Seraphim Starfire. And yours is…'

The man looked around, affronted. He appraised the apprentice haughtily. 'Hmmm,' he said, 'I see you can speak the common tongue. My name is Tahurangi. My home is in the Urewera, Aotearoa.' He pursed his lips and wrinkled his nose as if he had smelled something unpleasant. He jutted his chin and looked skywards. 'This place is – strange. The stars are – different.'

'Well, we have a council…custard…cottage, just over that hill. We could sit down and…'

Imperiously Tahurangi swaggered off, leaving Phim behind.
Huh, thought Phim, *apparently I am as inconsequential as a bug.*

He followed the stranger, who was eyeing up Arté with a 'come hither' look, posing his body to best advantage.
The vampire was apparently responding – her eyes lowered, legs akimbo, dropping her head and toying with her hair.

Phim pushed between them and pointed the way back to the cottage. A flash of anger crossed Tahurangi's face but before he could act on it, Ketekete flapped her wings loudly and announced: 'Sir. Let me usher you to our humble abode. We will provide refreshments and rest in a more comfortable setting.'

Tahurangi turned to the kākā. 'Meinga, meinga? E aue![74] Bilingual. And such a gracious – and overdue – offer.'

'Only if it pleases you, Lord. Come this way and I will show you the way.'

'Hmmm. You talk too much but… Lead on.'

---

74 Is that so!? Wow!

The kākā set off along the path and Tahurangi strutted behind her. He paused to look at the ice-bound Koan, poking the werewolf viciously. He appraised the statuesque form of Tasselis and the dryad seemed to bow to him as he passed.

Phim looked at Arté with a hurt expression, then turned and followed the retreating kākā and Tahurangi.
The vampire was puzzled about Phim's censorious look.
What did I do to earn that look?

But she shrugged and held hands with Tasselis as they slowly followed, leaving the ice-bound werewolf behind.

Chapter 9:

... and Going!

When Arté and Tasselis got to the cottage, Tahurangi was sitting at the head of the table, Ketekete was explaining some of the differences of the two worlds, and Phim was still in a sulk, but nevertheless, making supper for them all. Arté joined the others at the table and Tasselis sat beside the door.

'Here, the trees are mostly deciduous, not evergreen. But tall,' explained Ketekete, 'and the undergrowth in the forest is sparse. The rivers are broad and languid and, well, lazy in some places. And, you see, the stars are different. Te Ikaroa[75] is disordered, no Tautoru[76], no Matariki[77].'

'Ah, I could see that,' Tahurangi said thoughtfully. 'It is strange. This world is just a pale imitation of Aotearoa. My world has contrasts at every corner. Our eyes delight with every new vista. Volcanic mountains have forests on their lower slopes and streams from melting snow become rivers. Hot pools become geysers and mud pools and there are caves with glowworms, languid lakes and majestic mountains. My snow-capped alps border the forest like gigantic sentinels. Rivulets turn into rushing rapids, rainbow-coloured waterfalls cascade and spray the trees with sacred essence. Then the rivers gambol, tumbling and burbling against impervious rocks and pause into deep pools of liquid delight. Hanahana![78]'

---

[75] Te Ikaroa - The Milky Way

[76] Tautoru - Orion's Belt

[77] Matariki - The Pleiades

[78] Magnificent!

Most of the audience were captivated, hanging on every word.

'Ah, the rivers are marvellous.' Ketekete closed her eyes with happy memories. 'Fresh water from the heavens. I used to play in the waterfalls, swooping in…'

She opened her eyes but abruptly abandoned her reminiscing when she saw the angry look on Tahurangi's face. He shook his head at Ketekete, which she interpreted as an order to 'shut up', and continued his talk.

'Aotearoa. My forests are verdant and bustling with life. Every shade of green is there: the bright green of the moss, the dusty green of the kōwhai, the brown-green of the kauri, the dark, emerald green of the tōtara, the fresh green of the ferns.'
He paused and looked at the dryad with wide, hypnotic eyes.
'You should see the kauri, majestic trees – a dozen men linking hands can just reach around the circumference. Kahitikea – the tallest tree, rejoicing in the wetlands. And the kōwhai – hosts of golden flowers that drip honey dew that the tūī love to feast on.'

'Ah! I miss that,' Ketekete sighed. 'Flying through the forests was wonderful. I used to have …'

Tahurangi silenced the bird with a sweep of his hand. 'Te hiapai hoki.[79] I was speaking,' he said autocratically.
'Aotearoa! My forest and mountains and rivers. They run joyfully to the sea – the harbours and coves and beaches. Sun-loved beaches of golden sand. Quiet rock pools fed by the gentle waves. Outcrops of the headland, bashed and battered by the surf, the rugged rocks and the relentless waves are jubilant combatants in the everlasting war between land and ocean. The warming sun. The remote moon and the starry constellations.

[79] What a damn cheek!

'I used to lie down in a clearing and look at the stars. They were brilliant. Constellations like diamonds. Shooting stars that stitched the night sky like a quilt.'

But Ketekete interrupted again: 'When we saw Matariki in the night sky we knew that…'

Again, an impatient gesture. 'Ākene ioe i a au![80]' Tahurangi glared at the roof, not at the kākā. Apparently, the parrot was beneath contempt for the patupaiarehe. With a frustrated out-breath, he looked at his captive audience, and continued.

'The birds, the non-talking birds –' Tahurangi stared icily at Ketekete '– were marvellous in their profundity: the secretive ruru, the chortling, iridescent tūī, the darting, dashing pīwakawaka, the pompous kererū, even the giant moa and the nocturnal kīwī. Marvellous birds. And the eels – slippery but delicious eels. Ah! Te ao ataahua – Aotearoa![81]'

He sighed and stood up, stretching his arms.
Striking a pose, Phim thought.

'Well – I will see what I can make of this world. I'm tired. My bedroom is this way?'

He was indicating Phim's bedroom and he stepped towards it.
Phim was about to say something but Ketekete was too quick for him. Unfortunately.
'This is Seraphim's bedroom. We can make you a bedroom …'

---

80 You watch it or else!

81 The beautiful natural world of Aotearoa

Tahurangi turned aggressively and eyeballed the kākā. 'Whakaputa mōhio.[82] You talk too much,' he said angrily. Delicately he held his bone flute with his right hand, played a haunting six-note melody that stopped abruptly before a cadence. At the same time he sliced his left hand downward.

Then he turned again and marched into Phim's bedroom.

His audience were stunned, as if they had woken from a dream. Tasselis went out to her favourite oak tree and Arté went to her bedroom avoiding Phim's sulky looks.

Ketekete looked at Phim, mouthing words. But no sound came out. She tried, and retried and, panicked and shocked, she flew to her spot above the cabinet.

Phim pleaded with her: 'Ketekete, Ketekete. Please. Talk to me. Talk to me?' but the parrot hid her face under her wing to shield his entreaty and her embarrassment. Phim called her telepathically, but she remained silent. He realised that Tahurangi must have placed a muting spell on the kākā.

He gave up and sat down heavily, lost in thought.

My familiar. Muted. The faerie muted her. She is annoying with her quips and pranks, but I rely on her. And, I think, she relies on me. We are bonded. I have to do something. And that patupaiarehe – a muting spell! That is over the line. He had no right!

Phim thought through everything that had happened.

The words, the language, was hypnotising... But the melody of the flute and the gesture... Maybe that's where his magic is...bound up with his flute. Something... something...

He searched through Luxima's books for some clue...

82 Know-it-all!

Phim woke with a headache. He was still at the table: books and papers scattered around. He looked for Ketekete, but the parrot was nowhere to be found. Phim staggered to the kitchen for a drink of water. As he was sipping it, he turned and saw Tahurangi coming out of Arté's bedroom – naked. The faerie swanned arrogantly across to the room he had requisitioned last night, Phim's bedroom. He didn't look left or right but sneered, chuckling: 'Tarau makere.[83] That green-skinned wench – she wants me again.' He reached the door and closed it.

Opposite, another door opened and Arté came into the kitchen. She drew a robe around her body, her hair was mussed up and her eyes widened with shock when she saw Phim at the bench. She began to speak but he shook his head and ducked outside, averting his gaze.

Blindly, he followed the path to the forest thinking the worst.
No, he admonished himself. *No. She is just a friend. I have no expectations. She can do what she wants.*
But his thoughts didn't tally with his feelings.
Get it together. That's what Luxima would have me do. So – concentrate. What about Koan?

He reached the werewolf. The moon had set, the sun was three fingers rising, so the melting had just begun. He sat down, tortured by his feelings. He didn't notice Tahurangi until he saw the faerie prodding the werewolf.
'Careful!' said Phim.
'He's still frozen – he can't harm me,' said Tahurangi disdainfully.

Phim didn't say that his warning was to protect Koan from the unwanted attention of the stranger, not the other way around.
'Nifty,' Tahurangi said. 'The frozen spell removed the danger to your companions from this murderous beast. Look at its fangs and claws.

---

[83] Promiscuous woman!

The strength of its shoulders and legs. I would have done it differently. But this 'weird wolf' is still a danger, wouldn't you say?'

Phim was about to say that Koan was human ninety-six percent of the time but, apparently, it was a rhetorical question. Tahurangi was talking to himself.

And he answered himself. 'Yes. The beast should be eliminated. No danger to anyone. Especially that green skinned minx. Ah, she is a beauty… ' He chuckled revoltingly. Phim clenched his fists.

The change from werewolf to man was underway and the melting was rapid. The faerie took hold of his flute gently and blew slowly. A sinuous, twisting, undulating melody curled out of the instrument. The sound snaked around the ground in front of Koan like a vine, a creeper… and it became manifest.[84]

Before Phim could protest, the vine wrapped itself tightly around the thawed and exposed limbs of the wolfman.

Koan had recovered enough to rage at this unwarranted treatment. 'What the f…' he yelled. 'What's happening? Arrghhh! Why are my hands tied?' He was trying to stand up but fell back because of the restrictions on his legs. 'Arrrggghhh! Who's done this? Why?'

'Huh – because you are a beast,' Tahurangi answered arrogantly. 'That's all. I treat my beasts this way. Ākene ioe i a au!'[85]

'Who are you? What are you doing here? You can't do this. Untie me. Let me loose. I want to talk to Phim. He'll sort you out. Untie me!'

---

[84] The vine is almost certainly Kareao – Ripogonum scandens – Supplejack. It is a common rainforest vine endemic to New Zealand. Kareao is supple, flexuous and pliant but incredibly strong stems.

[85] You watch it or else!

'You beasts talk too much,' sneered the faerie. Just like last night, he grasped his flute, played a six-note melody and sliced his left hand downward. The wolfman was suddenly silenced.
He continued to open his mouth to yell but no sound emerged. He was completely mute.

Phim was appalled. 'Listen,' he protested, 'you can't do that. You have no rind…ring…right! He is my frame…fries…friend and a valuable …'

Tahurangi spun around and faced Phim with a furious look.
'Ko wai koe?[86] You too?' he sneered. His eyes glistened and he lifted the flute and began to blow…but suddenly, changing his mind, he stood upright, dropped the flute on its flax string and sized up the apprentice mage. 'Hah – you could be useful. I have to learn what this 'Luxima' is capable of before I… Well, never mind. But talk only when I speak to you. Or else…' He fingered his flute. 'Now, I have to get back to that green wench. Kotiro ataahua.[87]' Abruptly he turned and left Phim and Koan, taking the path back to the cottage.

Phim was flabbergasted. 'The arouser…arrangement…arrogance of that man,' he vented. 'Intolerable chair…chauvinist.'

He turned to Koan who was still on the ground and needed help to sit him upright on a fallen tree trunk. Koan was silently mouthing obscenities.

'Let me see if I can unclip…unroll…unwind this vine on your hands and feta…feeler…feet,' said Phim optimistically. But it was no good. Brute strength didn't budge it and every counter-spell that Phim could

86 Who do you think you are?

87 Beautiful girl

think of was totally ineffectual. Koan was ropeable[88] – literally and figuratively.

At least, thought Phim uncharitably, *his bonds are so tight that he can't do any damage and with the muting spell we don't have to listen to him ranting.*

Phim was so distracted by his efforts to free Koan, he didn't realise that Arté approached him and was tapping him on the shoulder. Phim jumped in shock, and then turned away from the her. 'I'm busy here,' he said rudely.

Ignoring his curtness, Arté asked: 'What happened to Koan? Why are his feet and hands wrapped with .....something? String? Rope? And why can't I hear his yelling?'

'Maybe your fast…faun…fancy blonde hunk should answer that,' Phim replied ungraciously.

'That faerie? He did this! Like Ketekete?'
The other part of Phim's reply rose up like a bubble in her brain.
'What? "Fancy blonde hunk"? Why did call him that? I don't like him. At all. He is so offensive – discourteous, arrogant and presumptuous.'

'But … I saw him leader…leaky…leaving your room. He said … well, he said that…' Phim ducked his head in embarrassment and looked away.

Arté was clearly incensed. 'He came into my room. My room. I was asleep and he climbed under the covers. Unannounced, uninvited. Naked! He reached for his flute – maybe he wanted to serenade me – but I ripped it off his neck. I said: 'Get. Out. Of. My. Room!' I think I

---

88 Able to be roped and so restrained (Aotearoa New Zealand slang)

exposed my fangs at him, because he left the room quickly. I grabbed my gown because I wanted to see where he was going. And I saw – you. And – you left. I was so embarrassed, but I couldn't find you anywhere. Then, I thought… you would be… with Koan and…'
Arté ran out of words and, dejected, she covered her face with her hands.

Phim reached out and gently pulled her hands from her face.
They looked intently at each other, seeing the truth in each other's eyes.
Sorry, sorry, thought Phim. *I should have trusted you more. I was jealous.*
Sorry, sorry, thought Arté. *The only person that could come to my bed is …*
The thought was too private to acknowledge. Yet.

Suddenly, Arté straightened up. 'Wait. I haven't told you about Tasselis. When I was looking for you and saw Tahurangi, I guessed he was coming back from you and Koan. Anyway, he didn't see me. He went up to Tasselis and told her about the golden tree. The kōwhai, he called it. He mentioned it last night. His words are…hypnotic. Even when I was hidden, they drew me in.

'Tasselis was just right there, and I could see that he was ensnaring her. He convinced her to transform herself into a kōwhai tree. His words created a picture of the tree, and they affected her. Her legs seemed to fuse together, she grew roots from her toes, she raised her arms and fingers about her shoulders and branches and twigs sprouted, the lacy leaves adorned her body and then, amazingly, golden flowers bloomed. They were upside-down cups or trumpets of the most glorious, golden yellow, hundreds and hundreds of them. They rained down as a gilded floral carpet before her feet.

'I was entranced and I had to get closer. Tahurangi saw me, and lecherously suggested that we should lie down on the golden carpet. I think he was planning to bed me there. Wishful thinking! Well – I am a vampire. In a heartbeat, I disappeared.'

As he listened to Arté's story, Phim became increasingly horrified. 'The faerie has to go. Ketekete, Koan, Tasselis – enchanted. And your inspect…insect…insult should be challenged. He even theorise… therapy…threatened me. He has to go!'

Phim paced up and down before the expectant vampire and the furious but bound wolfman. He talked himself through all the bits he would need.

'I think I can make solemn…sombre…something that would attract the faerie. Something that could enrol…envied…enmesh him. His magic is quite strong, but I think…I know…it is conversation… confirm…connected with the flute he wears. If I could use that flute… I think I could make a spell that would trace…tramp…trap him.'

He paused, looked skywards and then down as if he could see the solution around him, in the trees, or the ground. He closed his eyes, gnawed the knuckles on his left hand and tugged his ear with his other hand as he worked out in his mind what to do.

Phim resumed his pacing. 'I could make a potty…poultry…portal. I looked up "portal" last night, and I believe I could do it. And shoe… shove…shut it permanently. I have to study it though in Luxima's books. Maybe fix…fit…five or six minutes.'

He stopped pacing and looked at Arté and Koan.

'So – I have to study, request a feather from Ketekete, get the flute, practise the spell, and create a portal. Easy,' he said optimistically.

'I can help,' Arté said firmly. 'I can distract him and leave you to study.'

'How will you distract him?' Phim asked cautiously.

'He's a faerie, but still a man. And men think with another piece of their anatomy than their brain.' She looked at Phim and she could see the objection rising in him, so she hurriedly reassured him. 'You know that I despise him for bewitching my friends. Know that. Just trust me.'

Phim was not very happy with this plan, and he worried about the risk for Arté, but he realised that it was the best option. They sorted out some details and Phim sent a pleading telepathic message to Ketekete. They bid Koan a farewell, promising that they would release his bonds when they dealt with the faerie.

They ran down the path to the cottage. Phim paused and looked at Tasselis-kōwhai tree. It was magnificent – the fine filagree leaves, the radiant glow from the golden yellow flowers, the carpet below. But Phim couldn't find any trace of Tasselis in the tree at all. The dryad has disappeared into the essence of the kōwhai.
At that moment, Ketekete flew down and rested on the main branch of the kōwhai. She reached with her foot against the trunk and gently nuzzled it.

Phim caught her thoughts.
I am almost homesick when I looked at this kōwhai tree, but I am so furious that this patupaiarehe has transformed my friend.

She looked at Phim and Arté, significantly.
The three nodded to each other with an unspoken demand:
This faerie has to go!

Phim telepathically told Ketekete what he wanted her to do. The trio went quietly into the cottage and surveyed the scene. Tahurangi was studying the books on the tables, turning the pages over rapidly. When he had looked at four or five pages, he discarded the book, spinning it around on the table like a curling stone. Many tomes and volumes were piled up already on the far side of the table.

He straightened up, casually glancing at the kākā and the apprentice mage but focusing on Arté. He affected a pose – legs askew, pelvis forward, arms folded, head on a haughty and insolent angle – and sneeringly said: 'Ah! I see you want more?'

Unseen, Arté grasped Phim's hand briefly – a reassuring grip – then she walked across the room to stand opposite the faerie. 'Well,' she said coquettishly, 'I see that things are different now. I recognise an alpha male – a man who is a go-getter, a no-nonsense man. I –' and she swayed her hips suggestively, 'I appreciate that.'

She sashayed towards her bedroom but, most importantly, away from Phim and Ketekete.

'Maybe, we could discuss your … plans? More comfortably.' She reached her bedroom door, and turned, beckoning Tahurangi with a wave of her hand, and entered the room. He strutted like a rooster, enthusiastically leaping the table and benches and followed her. Phim bit his knuckle, but he knew that he had work to do.

Quickly, he gathered some ingredients from the pantry and placed them in a pot on the stove. He turned to Ketekete and the parrot flew down to him and presented her tail. Phim grasped a feather and pulled. The bird flinched, but made no sound. Then Phim sped to the table and found the books with the spells he had researched the night before. He studied them, memorising the words, gestures, symbols and mandalas that he had to use. He went back to the stove, poured the potion into a mug and set it down on the table.

He took a deep breath, thinking about the process he was about to enact. Ketekete nodded to him and flew back to the cabinet. Phim returned to the kitchen bench. Then, he hit a gong.

Immediately Arté appeared from her bedroom and sat down on the other side of the table. A flustered Tahurangi staggered out of the vampire's room, blinking rapidly at the scene before him. He focused on Arté and made for her, but the vampire eluded him and sat on the other side of the table. Tahurangi breathed angrily: 'Tarau makere![89]' but before he could move, Arté offered, with a swing of her hips: 'Maybe you should refresh yourself. Here – a fortifying drink. Maybe you need more stamina to catch me.'
She laughed prettily, and offered the mug.

He drank it all in one go, eyeballing Arté with a lusty intensity and flinging the mug away. 'Kua mau tō iro?[90]' he sneered and reached for her. Instantly she jumped back three metres. He made to follow her but his legs didn't work and he fell to the ground, unconscious. The potion had worked.

The three friends crept up to him, bending over and examining him for any sign of recovery.
Arté straightened up and kicked him in the ribs. 'Arrogant bastard!' she muttered.

'Sh, sh,' Phim whispered. 'Don't wait…walk…wake him. But – are you okay? What happened?' he asked apprehensively. He didn't really know if he wanted an answer.

'Ha,' she said, grinning. 'We played tag. He pursued me and I evaded him. Easily.'

---

89 Promiscuous woman!

90 Have you learnt your lesson?

Phim let out a relieved sigh. Ketekete nodded. They both knew how the vampire can evade people.

Phim took control of the situation. 'So…Arté – can you clip…click… clear the bench and the table. We need an unoiled…unopen… unoccupied space here. Ketekete, can you take his flap…flew…flute. I will prepare the mandala and the symbols we need.'

Arté did as she was asked while Ketekete snipped the flax string around the patupaiarehe neck and passed the flute to Phim. In a few minutes the trio stood before a cleared out room. Phim had drawn the intricate mandala on the floor with chalk and surrounded it with protective symbols. At his feet, an enigmatic arrow pointed away from them.
The spell was quite vague about this step, thought Phim.
And I need to make it permanent. Before I can utter the words, I need a sign, a signal, a…

Once again, a thought entered his mind. The perfect sign – an inspired memory. And he knew it was right.

Seraphim took the flute, placed the feather into the barrel, and blew a melody. Just three notes, repeated, in a syncopated rhythm, growing in intensity. Then, in a resonant voice, he said: 'Ko tenei tirohanga mo Aotearoa ka whakapoapoa i te patupaiarehe kia kore ai ia e whakarere.[91]'

The light dimmed and a sparkling fog began to grow from the mandala's crossing lines and angles, sweeping away from them into the rest of the room. Slowly, but with increasing pace, a scene opened, a magnificent vista of snowy mountains, a waterfall feeding a river, tall trees and ferns, birds singing – chortling and twittering and ringing. A path before them led into the forest.

---

91 This vision of Aotearoa will enchant the faerie so he will not leave it.'

Arté was amazed. Ketekete was homesick. Almost.

Seraphim whispered to Arté: 'Can you pull the faerie's ears – hard.'

'Gladly!' she murmured gleefully.
She tugged Tahurangi's ears and the faerie woke up with a start.

'Hika mā!'[92] he exclaimed as he struggled to get up.
Then he saw the scene before him.

'Tōtara. Rimu. Kauri. Awa. Tūī. Korimako. Ahhhh…Te ao ataahua[93] – Aotearoa!'

He wandered up the path, lost in the beautiful but illusory world that Seraphim had made for him.

Seraphim rubbed out the arrow with his foot, and loudly uttered the word: 'Marama.' He dropped the flute and, with the same foot, smashed it.

Abruptly the scene disappeared.

Tahurangi was gone.

---

92 For crying out loud!

93 The beautiful natural world

Chapter 10:

The enchanted mirror

With Tahurangi's disappearance his magic also dissipated. Relieved, they went outside. Ketekete whooped and chattered incessantly, so glad to have her voice back. Tasselis was restored to her tall self, but appalled that the patupaiarehe was so convincing that she gave up her mission for caring for all trees to be a rooted kōwhai, a tree she didn't even know existed. Koan came back along the path from his incarceration. He strode up to the cottage and yelled angrily: 'Where is that blonde bimbo? I'll rip him apart!'

'Calm down,' Phim said. 'He's gorge…gown…gone. His magic has… vanished.'

Koan took a deep breath as Phim's meditation training had him taught to do. Then he rushed over to Tasselis and asked her if she was feeling alright after her ordeal. Arté took the moment to hug Phim and kissed him on his cheek. 'I knew you could do it.' And hugged him again. Closely.

'And you!' Phim was wide-eyed. 'You were amour…amber…amazing. A consummate action…actress.' He looked at her soulfully. He recognised that his emotions, though unfamiliar, were powerful. And this disturbed him, though he enjoyed the feeling.

But two matters concerned him. He looked at Tasselis. He knew that it was his magic that made the dryad so biddable. She wanted to help everyone, even if it would put her in danger. *That's my fault. Tahurangi got to her so easily. I need to find a way to protect her.*

The other thing was about his misplaced words. He looked around for the parrot. She was cavorting around them, chortling and prattling on as if to make up for the enforced silence. 'Ketekete? Ketekete, come here,' he requested. The kākā paused her frolics and, puzzled, flew to him. Phim told her that he had wanted to send Aotearoa but the spell did not come out like that. 'I had "Aotearoa" in my mishap…miner… mind but, for some reason, out popped "Marama". What is "Marama"? Where did I send Tahurangi?'

Ketekete chuckled: 'Marama is the moon. You sent him to the moon.'

Immediately a ruckus erupted behind them. It sounded like a bear bellowing in a giant tuba. Ketekete, Phim and Arté quickly looked around, fearing for the worst.
It was Koan. Laughing. 'The moon. The moon!' he guffawed. 'Priceless. The moon. I will think about that with every full moon.'

So – things went back to normal. Almost.

Phim added Tasselis to the yoga, tai chi and zumba exercises he'd been doing with Koan and he introduced another element to the meditation session with the dryad in mind – positive reinforcement and self-awareness. He hoped it would protect the tree spirit from giving herself up totally when someone asked something of her.

It seemed to work. Tasselis took over the garden and supervised Arté and Koan in their weeding and donkeywork. Ketekete referred to it a 'passive serfdom' but they didn't mind.

Arté sunned herself and took more of a part in preparing the meals.

Koan was an absolute asset as a maintenance man, and Ketekete's 'sniffilator guard-dog'.

The kākā mainly pleased herself. She flew each day over the forest, ate bugs and small lizards when out of Arté's sight, and failed to restrain her cheeky comments and antics.

Phim studied hard, and practised his spells – unfortunately.

But… Phim and Arté? Arté and Phim?

After the business of the faerie, there was an awkwardness about their relationship. Arté wanted to talk about it but whenever she tried, Koan or Tasselis would interrupt her. Phim ducked his head and made an excuse to get back to his books and spell-casting.

But several times he surprised himself at the window looking at Arté sunning herself. Obviously he knew that she was getting sustenance and refreshment for herself – he was responsible for that – but he couldn't help himself about thinking how beautiful she was. Hormonal influences aside, he was impressed by her confidence and forth-rightness. His unconscious mind delivered a description of Artémissa as 'The Green Goddess'. Consciously he thought this description was twee and cutesy, but it still stuck in his mind.

Of course, he couldn't hide his feelings from the parrot. Ketekete had relaxed her suspicions of 'that draculina blood-sucker' particularly after the 'foreign faerie incident'. She recognised that Arté was a good friend – courageous and faithful. But the kākā couldn't forget the disquieting crystal ball image of Arté savagely biting Phim's neck. She couldn't reconcile that graphic scenario with the reality of the helpful, courteous, friendly vegetarian vampire.

Empathetically the kākā was aware of all the emotions that the apprentice mage was feeling, but she ignored the passions that were apparently burgeoning in Phim's heart. Basically, when Phim was thinking about his relationship with Arté, Ketekete filled her mind with: *Rhubarb, rhubarb, rhubarb...*

A fortnight passed. Then, one morning, just before lunch, Koan let out a guttural yell. 'Come! Come!' he commanded.
[Ketekete referred to his yell as 'barking' – but not to his face.]

Tasselis came over from the garden, Arté put on a wrap after her sunbathing, Ketekete settled on an outdoor chair beside Koan and Phim, dizzy from studying and failed spells, came out of the cottage. Koan was sniffing and pointing at the path from the forest from where a figure was emerging.

A woman.

She wore a stylish red velvet hat, adorned with peacock feathers and a deep red velvet evening gown split to the hip on one side. It had a plunging neckline that exposed her bosom. Her honey-blonde locks cascaded down in tight ringlets and, as she approached, she twirled around showing a shapely leg ending in black stilettos. She swung her ringlets and the backless dress was exposed to its best advantage. Her perfume reached them – a mixture of vanilla and cinnamon with a hint of musk and patchouli.

Koan and Phim stared. Ketekete and Tasselis were bemused and Arté was dismayed. What a woman!

Phim was about to say something – anything – to this apparition. His mouth opened and closed like a goldfish but uttered no sound. The woman pre-empted him.
'Greetings Seraphim!' she said in a honeyed, mellow voice – a voice that promised reassurance and spoke of compassionate control.

'My name is Felicia Breedlove and I am a very good friend of Luxima Aerolaness. He sent me to see how you were. I see you are well – but apparently … speechless?'

Then Felicia fixed each one with her steely blue eyes and greeted them all in turn, her left hand playing with the feathers in her hat.

'Greetings Ketekete. Your feathers are preened and glossy. Yes – best to be attractive when you deliver your helpful but harmful hints and intelligent but snide snarks.

'Artémissa – you're glowing with health. Your new lifestyle certainly agrees with you. Your pallid colleagues in the city are green with envy – although they have more vitality in the wee small hours.

'Greetings Tasselis. Your garden is a wonder and I can see why you are always tending it. The other trees in the forest are missing you though, but I guess your work here is more … important. Never mind.

'Koan – a fine figure of a man. I see you have been working out, maintaining…things? Maintaining is…hard, but you are a … hard man.' She nodded suggestively, and tossed her hair.

'Shall we go in?' Felicia strolled into the cottage leaving the five friends astonished. They looked at each other, then rushed to the door.

Actually, four of them rushed. Arté shook her head. *Something is…not quite right…* She looked around. The forest was eerily quiet and she couldn't hear the river so well. She watched a big black bird with a purple and red head flying towards the cottage but everytime it approached within twenty metres of the cottage, its wings flew up and it stopped like a insect pinned to a board. *A crucifixion.* It was flying from branch to branch, but it could never get any closer.
Something is…off.

Bewildered, Arté walked slowly to the door.

She went into the cottage and saw the others in a perfect tableau. They formed a V-shape with Tasselis and Ketekete on the left, Phim and Koan on the right, and Felicia at the apex. Tasselis and Koan were on the floor, Ketekete and Phim on benches. Motionless, they gazed at Felicia Breedlove.
The symmetry was propitious. And quite unsettling.

Felicia sat on the edge of a chair, legs crossed with the split in her blue silk gown showing the shapeliness of her leg from thigh to her black patent leather boots. She was playing with her hair with her right hand, winding the ringlets around her fingers. With her left hand she played with the pheasant feathers on her blue beret. Arté thought this provocative gesture made her look like a Madam.
But…something…something…

Felicia suddenly addressed her.
'Ah. Come in, come in,' she said. 'Now we are all here. Artémissa – sit down in the middle. Just below me.'

She caught a wary look in Felicia's eye, so Arté complied, hesitantly.

'I was just talking about my old friend Luxima,' the woman declared. 'We have been friends for a long, long time. He is very sorry that he is not here with you, but he is working on a project that will astound you. In a little while, when he comes back here, to this cottage, he will reveal it to you. He is very busy at the moment and he wanted me to visit you and…'

Felicia went on and on. Tasselis, Ketekete, Phim and Koan were drinking in every word, but Arté vacillated. She wanted to hear what Felicia was saying because it seemed to be important, but a niggle in her brain was fighting to be recognised.

Something….something…is off. This is somehow…false. She is… She is…

Then she got it. *Hypnosis! She is hypnotising us.*

She clenched her jaw and looked at Felicia noting the same flash of wariness in the woman's eye. Instinctively Arté unfocused her eyes and relaxed her jaw, faking a semi-somnolent state. Without pausing Felicia studied the vampire for a few seconds and, apparently reassured that everything was going to plan, went on with her spiel.

Arté maintained her vague, disassociated manner, but inwardly she was pondering Felicia's scheme.
Why is she hypnotising us? I have to figure it out….

She thought back to when Koan 'barked' and Felicia appeared.
She was walking out of the forest… But…she was not dressed for a hike. She was…well, a femme fatale. Her red velvet evening gown, split from hem to navel, her low cut… Red? What?

Without drawing attention Arté did a double-take at Felicia in the armchair.

It's blue. No…no… it was red before. But now it is blue. What? And … um…stilettos then, but …now boots. And the feathers … were peacock feathers. Now they are pheasant feathers!

A sudden realisation made her almost shout out and point an accusing finger but a flash of semi-awareness from Felicia's eyes warned her. She immediately resumed her trance and was pleased to see that Felicia's wariness was waning.

That's it – she is a witch. She has cast an illusory spell or something like that. But …what is her magical method. She is not using incantations. Could her perfume be an enchantment? No…not good enough.

It would affect us all differently. Her body… Well – some of us were affected more than the others. But what about gestures… Ah! The feathers. The stroking feathers on her left hand. That's it! Stroking the feathers produces a hypnotising effect. But…what is her end game? Why are we all here? What is she doing to us?

Just then, Felicia rose from her seat and tidied up her black satin evening gown, pushed her hair back, and fondled the raven's feathers on her black Chloé wide brim hat and declared: 'Well! Everything is fine. Just fine.

'Tasselis – go to the garden and pick me a salad. And just root yourself beside the rapunzel. Root yourself…

'Ketekete – fly to the pantry and eat all the nuts and seeds you can find there. Just feed and feed…you want to…

'Koan – get the axe from the woodshed. Can you sharpen it nicely? Sharpen it… and come back here….

'Artémissa – go to your room and bed yourself down in the trunk there… And sleep… Just sleep…

'Seraphim – come with me to your room. I have something to show you. Come…come…'

All the friends rose and followed their hypnotic instruction. Tasselis and Koan went out the main door, Ketekete to the pantry, Phim followed Felicia to his bedroom. Arté stepped into her bedroom but once Felicia had entered Phim's room she shot back to the table.

Tasselis rooting in the rapunzel? Ketekete eating? Koan sharpening the axe? That's what they usually do – but Felicia is egging them on excessively. Her directions have a clinical element. Obviously it is Phim she wants. What is doing with him? I must wake him up. If we are fight this witch, Phim is the only choice. He is the magic user. I have to warn him, but how? He is hypnotised. I have to do something to stop her.

Arté idly shuffled the books and pamphlets on the table as she mulled over a way to stop the witch. One of the books fell on the floor and, as she retrieved it she noticed the title burned on the cover: *The Dark Arts of Necromancy.*

When Phim talked about the use of magic he would always say that he would never, never cast a spell that involved Necromancy. Oh well, I have to get something else…

Just then, she dropped the book again, on the table this time, and the book fell open. Her eyes were immediately drawn to the spell on the page: *The Mirror of Destruction.*

Destruction! That is a bit extreme, but…Felicia is up to no good. She knows us somehow. How? But – 'Mirror of Destruction'? Phim would be appalled with this spell. But he is in thrall to her. They all are. How can I get to them? To him? How I can make him see?

Then she had an idea. She carefully tore a corner and ripped the remainder of page out of the book. She placed it in a book entitled *Enchantments for Everyday Use.* She hid the book behind her back and flashed to Phim's room. The door was ajar.

Felicia was massaging Phim's neck and shoulders and whispering in his ear. She was barefoot and bareback – only a pair of lacy black panties and a red fascinator adorned her body. On her head, the black beret sported three golden rooster tail feathers. Arté was relieved that Phim seemed to be clothed.

'Sorry,' she interrupted. 'I need Phim for a moment.'
The vampire gripped Phim's arms and in a heartbeat they were outside. Even so, Arté saw that Felicia's face momentarily went from shock at the interruption to rage.

Arté flashed around the other side of the cottage behind some bushes, carrying the hapless Phim.

'Where is Felicia? he kept asking.
'Stop it! She is using you.'
'Where is Felicia?'
'She is a witch! She means to harm you!'
"Where is Felicia?'
In desperation Arté kissed him – hard.
His eyes widened in surprise.
'What? What did you…?'
She kissed him again, more tenderly. And he responded. Sort of.
Arté searched his face. His eyes cleared and he shook his head.
'What happened? What is going on?' he said in confusion.

'I can't explain now. She will come back for you. Listen! Felicia is a witch. She hypnotised you – all of us. She wants something from you. You have to destr…um…confront her.'

'Felicia? She is a … nice lady. She was… She was…' Phim's head hurt. He rubbed his forehead.

'Can you remember? Her dress, her clothing, her boots changed colour. Yeah? Remember?'
Arté saw comprehension on his face. 'And she knows things about us – me, Koan, Tasselis. How can she know? Luxima has not seen us. I don't believe she is your wizard's friend.'

Phim shook his head and took a deep breath. 'Oh…I see. Yes – you're right. I…um… She wants to me to revolt…revert…reveal… something…. reveal… I can't remember… You think she is not a friend of Luxima's?'

Arté shook her head vigorously. 'You have to fight....um...confront her with some sort of spell... I know you can do it. I found a book on the table. Maybe it would be helpful.'
'*Enchantments for Everyday Use*. I'm not sure that would....'
'I see this spell. It could be useful?'

Phim saw it was a spell that had been ripped out of its book – a certain style of yellowed parchment. 'Huh. *The Mirror of Dest...* – the pack... pale...page is torn. "Dest..."? What should it...'

Arté spoke quickly, realising that the material of the page didn't match the others in the book. She passed the torn spell to Phim and dropped the book on the ground. 'I think..."Destiny". Surely it is "The Mirror of Destiny." This could reveal Felicia's real intentions? But we have to be quick!'

'I guess. I have a milk...mirage...mirror in my bedroom.' He read the instructions for the spell. 'And the instructions are quite signal... simple. Okay. Can you distract her – so I can prefer...prevent... prepare?'

'Not a problem.' Arté smiled grimly and bowed. 'Don't you know I am a great actress?' She took Phim in her arms and, in a heartbeat, she had carried him like a doll to the main door.
She saw Felicia looking outside, around the far corner, so she pushed Phim into the cottage and faced the witch.

Felicia turned. 'Ah! You're here. And **here**.' Arté ignored the emphasis and, shrugging, faked nonchalance. The witch grimaced and said: 'Where's Seraphim?'

'Oh – I returned him. He is in his bedroom. I just wanted to talk with him. We all have our chores.' Arté sighed, faux fetchingly. She wanted to give Phim enough time to get what he needed for the spell.

'For example, Koan is the handyman – he maintains all the cottage and outside furniture, and cutting firewood. And he helps in the garden. And Tasselis cares for the trees and shrubs. I help her too. Then I prepare supper and dinners for…'

'Yes, yes, yes,' the witch interrupted testily. She stroked the three rooster feathers with her left hand and, with her mellifluous voice, said: 'And what did he say?'

'Sorry?"

'When you got Seraphim from my clutc… my massage. What did he say?'

'Um…he wanted to know…um…what I was planning to make for dinner. I wanted to see…um…his preference…'

Felicia was not fooled. 'Ah! I knew it. Somehow you resisted.'

Her voice was sharp as a saw blade and she stopped her feather-stroking. She walked along the cottage's wall, eyes like stilettos, staring at Arté. The vampire retreated into the cottage and she glimpsed Phim darting into his bedroom. *Hopefully he has what he needs,* she thought desperately.

Ketekete was still stuffing herself with nuts and seeds by the kitchen window. She jumped when she saw Arté and flapped with alarm. A stoppered pottery jar with an intricate pattern of vine leaves fell off the window sill into the garden and smashed. But it didn't deter the kāka. Wide-eyed she continued her feast as if such treats were going out of existence.

Felicia entered the cottage still ruthlessly watching the vampire. Arté had almost flashed out the back door when the witch clapped her hands. Immediately, Artémissa and Ketekete were immobile. Riveted. Frozen.

'Too slow!' the witch chortled. 'You thought you could fool me? I don't know how you resisted me, but I have caught you now.

'Seraphim will get me all the power I need. Then I will deal with Luxima. That wizened wizard will be no match for me.'
Felicia strutted around the vampire, hissing and spitting.

'Huh! When I get my hands on what I want from Seraphim, I am going to make you suffer. You're a sorry excuse for a monster. If you were a proper, blood-soaked nosferatu maybe you could best me. But, no! You are a pathetic, green mutant. A worm. Wait till Koan comes back with his sharpened axe. I am going to make him chop the dratted dryad up, and that' – she glanced at the frozen kākā – 'fat and insolent bird. Then I will make him execute that miserable, failed apprentice mage on the dining table.'

Felicia came close to the vampire and whispered in her ear.
'I will make sure that you can see and hear all of that. See your precious mage cut to pieces. And then, my wolfman will dissect you. Dismember you. Eviscerate you.'

'Then, I will cook you, all of you, and feed you to my Koan – my pet werewolf. My virile, lusty, werewolf. I will be triumphant!' With a gruesome pirouette, she cackled and spun round and round the vampire.
Out of the corner of her eye, Arté saw that Phim was eavesdropping. His shocked face said it all. He stole back to his room as the witch finished her ghastly dance.

When Felicia got back to Phim's bedroom, he was sitting on the bed, faking a calm and suggestive appearance. But, in his mind, he was compartmentalising like a filing cabinet. In one drawer, the horror of the witch's plans; in another, his consequential panic; in yet another were the logical steps of the process he had decided to follow.

Suddenly, another drawer opened in his mind. An idea was deposited as what he must do with the feather and the music he had to sing to make the spell permanent. He didn't question it. He knew it was right.

'Where were we up to,' the witch murmured in his ear, straddling him on the bed, stroking the bird of paradise plumage on her fascinator, 'before that wicked vampire disturbed us? Hmmm? That's funny. She is a vampire and I am a vamp! Ha, ha, ha. Felicia Breedlove – Luxima's friend. And your confidante. Your…concubine, if you like?

'Well…I think you were just going to tell me,' she wheedled. 'Tell your concubine. There need be no secrets between us? Hmmm? Tell me about your power. Your fantastic power to transform everything around you until it suits your purpose. How can you access it?'

'Yes…I was just going to tend…talc…tell you. Just as well we are in my rose…roost…room…um…because it is in this rose…roost… room.'

'Here? In this room? Where…?' Felicia turned this way and that. 'Where is it?'

'There,' Seraphim pointed at the wall to the mirror beside his wardrobe.

It was a big mirror – as tall as Phim himself – with a fancy, gilt, baroque mounting, curling around the mirror. A dragon sprawled across the top of the mirror, a serpentine tail curling around its body, jaws open, with piercing eyes that gazed at the admirer below it.

A moment of anxiety. Phim gulped. He glanced at Felicia, but she was approaching the mirror, examining in with hungry eyes. *Whew…she didn't see my panic. Breathe. Calm… You can do this. Arté – and my friends – are depending on me.*

The witch turned quickly, avarice just barely hidden behind her look. 'So – how do you do it?' she cajoled, almost mewing. 'Surely you could tell me…your friend. Maybe, your lover? You don't need to have any secrets from me. What do you do?'

'Well…when I have an important spun…spelt…spell I use the mirror and I have an innovate…incident…incantation, and then I do what the milk…mirage…mirror tells me.'

'Ah! I see. Or…I think I see. Maybe you could show me.' She sensuously stroked the feathers on her hat. 'Just to see you in action. Action man. I like to see a man in action, hmmm?'

'Oh…oh…sure. I can do that.' Phim got off the bed and slowly approached the wardrobe. 'Well…I get this dish, here, and I light this fauna…fearful…feather – just so…' Seraphim clicked his fingers on his left hand and mouthed a word. A flame sprang to life in the fingers of his right hand – a little trick that he had perfected two weeks ago.
He lit Ketekete's tail feather, waited for it to catch properly and dropped it on the dish. 'Then I sing a song, and an incident… incantation and look into the mingle…minuet…mirror and…that's it really. The mirror refresh…reflects what I should do or say.'

'Do it! Do it! I want to see,' the witch asked desperately, ambition burning in her face.

'Well…okay.' He raised the dish and sang an ancient modal melody with syncopated rhythms. The feather's ashes swirled up like incense spiralling, twirling, entwining between him, the witch and the mirror. Then Seraphim spoke, confidently and resonantly: 'La verità sarà rivelata in questo specchio e sarà manifesta'[94]. He swung the mirror to face Felicia.

---

94 The truth will be revealed in this mirror and be manifest.

The mirror's surface was cloudy and bubbly like a saucepan of custard. The incense smoke circled Felicia's whole body and, unconsciously, the witch breathed it in. At the same time, the image in the mirror cleared.

Seraphim expected that the spell would make the mirror reveal Felicia's destiny and, with this knowledge, he could hopefully change her mind. *Or befriend him. Or be a concu…*
[He was still under the witch's influence.]

But he didn't expect this.

Felicia Breedlove looked at the mirror. There, in the mirror's image, she was a youthful vamp. In reality, she had begun to age. Wrinkles ravaged her face and neck. Her ringleted hair had faded to grey, thinned and fallen out entirely. Her eyes sunk into their sockets, her face was blotchy and her lips grew thin and dry. Warts and hairy moles grew on her nose and face. Her ears drooped. Her body shrunk, her breasts withered, her limbs folded themselves up into arthritic poses. She fell to the floor moaning, drooling, and coughing.

Phim was shocked. 'What happened? What is gorgon…going on?'

Felicia could barely speak, but the image in the enchanted mirror replied.

'The form of the real Felicia was an illusion. You thought she was, maybe, thirty years old? Actually Felicia is four hundred and thirty-nine years old. Luxima Aerolaness and she are mortal enemies. She'd descried what you had done: the vampire, the werewolf, the dryad – even that foreign faerie. She didn't know how you could do it. You're just an apprentice. You have something else – something that was unexpected.
'She thought she could get that power somehow and totally vanquish Luxima. But – you have bested her. She used all her magic to get you –

and the others – to obey her but… she is exhausted. She can't even get her hands to perform the spells. She can't voice her incantations. She …is…done…'

The image in the mirror faded.

The real Felicia, writhed on the floor like a slug. Faintly she whispered: 'I… I am…dying…'
She coughed. She convulsed. Her breathing became erratic, her pulse weak. She closed her eyes.

'I'm sorry,' Phim whispered. 'I didn't know this wooden…womb… would happen to you. But I had to save the others.'

In a grotesque laugh, she choked on her phlegm and mouthed something. Phim bent down to catch her words.
'The others?' she whispered. 'No. It was that vampire. She fought me. Resisted.'
Suddenly she opened her eyes and looked at Phim with a mixture of frustration and admiration.
'I couldn't…compete. She…loves you…'

She breathed her last, and her shrunken body contracted like a deflated balloon. Suddenly, a flash from the corpse blinded Phim's eyes and he immediately closed them.
After a few moments he opened them with difficulty, focused and looked back at the remains. He saw a mound of ash.

With her death, Felicia's magic dissipated. Phim was aware that the others rushed in to the bedroom, but they hung around the door. In the breeze they ushered in, the ash dispersed into the cracks in the wooden flooring. Felicia was … gone.

Arté came to him, and took his arm. 'That's okay,' she consoled. 'She was going to do terrible things to us.' She took his arm and lead him to the main room. They sat down at the table, Arté's arm around Phim's shoulders. Ketekete, Koan and Tasselis followed and stood around, helplessly. Koan had his sharpened axe, Tasselis had a basket of salad greens, and Ketekete was trying not to vomit up the results of her feasting.

They knew that Felicia had hoodwinked them and they were embarrassed and humiliated. They were silent for a long time, thinking about their abject susceptibility.

Phim glanced at the parrot.
'Sorry,' he apologised. 'I took another tail felter…feather from you so the speed…spiffle…spell would be comfortable…complement… complete. Sorry!'
The kākā, coughed to clear her throat and said: 'Shirley, Shirley.'[95] But Phim heard her telepathic thought: *Um…sorry, I didn't notice.*

Phim thought about the last thing that Felicia said.
And the kiss! It woke me up from my stupor. Arté. The Green Goddess. She is…marvellous.

Phim straightened up and looked at the others. Especially at Arté. His thoughts were scattered, but she gazed at him, then rested her head on his shoulder and took his hand in hers.
My thoughts were nebulous, but the reality of her presence was tangible in the clasp of her hand. Thank you.

Arté looked out the window. The trees were lit by the afternoon sun. She saw a big black bird with a purple and red head fly from the top-

95 'Shirley' was a punning joke between them. Shirley – Surely.

most tree and sail off through the forest. An idle thought crossed her mind: *I know that bird…*

She unclasped her hand and stood up. 'I will make a cup of tea for everyone, okay?' and she moved to the stove.

'And I will make some snacks,' Tasselis supported her. 'Some salads, avocado, crackers and fruit chutney.' Ketekete burped and looked even more green, if that was even possible.

Thinking about life and death, Phim toyed with the books on the table, idly flipping one book, or another. One caught his eye. It was open, and he could see that the pages were a certain style of yellowed parchment. He reached for it and discovered a page had been ripped out. A little tag was left in the book.

Arté turned from the stove, flashed across to the table and stuck out her hand: 'Don't…'

But it was too late.

Phim got the slip of parchment out of his pocket, the slip that Arté had given him, and placed it in the book. He looked at the incantation on the slip of parchment. In his mind he realised that he had mucked up the words again. The parchment's script required him to say the words:

La verità sarà rivelata in questo specchio e sarà distrutta.[96]

He didn't say that.

Why? Why do I mistake the words? What possesses me? I don't know. I. Don't. Know. But….what is the translation of the words… 'distrutta'… that is 'destroyed'. Wait. What spell is this?

---

[96] The truth will be revealed in this mirror and it will be destroyed.

He looked at the slip of paper. The spell was headed: *The Mirror of Dest…* He smoothed out the slip and placed in the book with the remaining tag and read: *The Mirror of Dest…ruction.*

He looked at Arté in shock. 'You! You said the speed…spend…spell was *The Mirror of Destiny*? Not *Destruction*!'
Shock turned to anger.
'You want to despite…detail…destroy another being? You want me to destroy another little…listen…living being?'

She was about to say something but no words emerged from her throat.

At the same time, he looked at the title of the book: *The Dark Arts of Necromancy*. He was appalled.

He dropped the book as if it were an iron frying pan on the fire.

'You know that I didn't want antique…anxious…anything to do with needle…necklace…necromancy. You knew! You butter…berserk… betrayed me! I killed Felicia. I killed Felicia. I am a murderer!'

He stormed out of the house.

Chapter 11:

A dark, dusty dungeon

Well – Phim thought he was storming out of the house.
He stomped over the threshold of the main door and with his next step he appeared at his bedroom door.

Everyone looked startled. Arté was the first to react. She went to Phim to beg him for forgiveness, but Phim was so furious he turned and stormed out through his bedroom door.

And appeared at the back door.

The friends looked stunned and glanced at each other. Again, Phim spun round and walked through the back doorway … and appeared at Arté's bedroom door. Everyone looked baffled. Phim slowly stepped through the vampire's bedroom doorway … and sauntered out through the main door looking confused.

"What gives?' Koan said loudly, voicing the question on everyone's minds. Tasselis bent her head and stepped out through the back doorway and, at the same time, Ketekete flew out through Phim's bedroom doorway. The parrot flew out through Arté's doorway and collided with the bookshelf opposite. The dryad banged her head on Phim's door. There was a chorus of 'Owwww!' from the two venturers.

Koan decided on positive action. 'Ha! I'll get us outta here.' Koan charged at the window and swung his axe. The axe struck the wall and bounced back like a rubber ball, hitting him on his forehead. Thankfully it wasn't the cutting edge, but even so Koan fell down dazed. Tasselis helped him up and rubbed the injury with her many fingers.

A piercing whistle surprised everyone. The kettle was ready for the tea and Arté poured the hot water into the teapot with a mixture of rose petals, rosemary and hawthorn. She looked at the fire noticing that the flames were purple with green highlights and the smoke was royal blue. She backed away to the table not sure if the fire was dangerous. She poured the tea into the mugs on the table – but the tea tumbled out in cubes. The vampire examined the cups and pronounced: 'It's … frozen?'

Tasselis fetched the snack tray: crackers with onion relish, salad, cheese and a selection of sliced fruit: apples, pears, and bananas. The dryad put the tray on the table and instantly the food went back into its original packaged and unpeeled condition: the crackers stacked up in a container in the middle, the salad in one corner, a hefty blob of relish on another, a block of cheese in another corner and all the fruit, uncut and in their skins in the fourth corner. Tasselis lifted the tray in her arm and all the snacks again became ready to eat. She set it down again and instantly its contents reverted to the unprepared version.

They stared at the tray speechless. Flabbergasted.

'Okay, okay,' said Phim at last. 'Let's sit done…down and figure this thing out.'

Phim sat down at the table. Tasselis sat on the floor and tended to Koan's wounded head. Arté was not sure where she should sit – beside Phim? Or opposite him? Or hide away from his still angry stares. She vacillated and rapidly, as vampires do, flashed down in all three positions and eventually sat at the foot of the table. Ketekete sat on the table opposite Phim.

Well – the kākā intended to sit on the table but her tail feathers got in the way. She glanced at them, and suddenly she was spinning around and wiped several books, two cups and a candle stand off the table. Her magnificent green and black tail feathers had been replaced by a male peacock's plumage, two metres long. The feathers spread out in a glorious rainbow fan like the fronds of a tree fern: bright blue, green, purple, yellow and red. But where the 'eyes' in the train would be, were a set of orange lips, with a magenta tongue poking out in a 'Nyah nyah nah nyah nyah!' gesture.

Phim called to Ketekete but the parrot was more concerned at her suddenly unruly tail.

Ketekete – calm down. Calm. Down. he said telepathically to the kākā.

It worked. She stayed still, looking at Phim.

Just calm down. We will figure it out. Sit there, on the back of this chair. Okay?

Ketekete roosted on the chair's top rail, but because the plumage's weight had changed her balance-point, she was forever adjusting her body, nervously and ungraciously.

'Obviously,' Phim said, 'something is going on. It seems to be quite bendy…been…benign. The doors. The flask…flames. The tea. The snooks…snacks. They seem to be prams… pranks.' He nodded at the wolfman. 'Sorry about your injury, but I think the violets…violence was created by you, not on you. And Ketekete – the feathers are quite miscast…mishmash…mischievous, not mangy…mallet…malicious. But it looks – and smells – like magic. Any thoughts?'

'Maybe,' the dryad speculated, 'Felicia Breedlove? Maybe she left some magic behind like an echo?'

'Hmmm,' the apprentice mage considered. 'I don't thaw…think so. When she died, all her magic disco…dismount…disappeared. She said that she used all her magic to create her illegal…illumine…illusion and fool us.' He briefly nodded at Arté and admitted: 'And she was quite ruthless.'

'Indeed,' Arté asserted hotly. 'She was wicked, and she got what she deserved…' She bit her lip as Phim cast another disapproving look at her.

Oblivious of the tension between Arté and Phim, Koan spoke up. 'Maybe it is a joke? Maybe Luxima is playing a trick on us.'

'Well – that's fair comment,' thought Phim, looking up at the ceiling.

'Nah!' blurted out Ketekete. 'He would not do that. All the while I spent with him, he would not waste his magic on a prank, more's the pity. But – what about the patupaiarehe? He was more of a trickster than Luxima.'

'The foreign faerie,' considered Phim, 'Tahurangi? Just like Felicia, when he went thought…though…through the portal, his magic disable…disarray…disappeared. No – I think it's not from her…him. So – another magazine…magic user then? What d'you think?'

Arté's had an idea. Remembering some of the magic books she had seen on the table when she was discussing Phim's, studies she recalled one about summoning creatures. But she did not want to say out loud in case Phim would reject it on principle. She looked at the books on the table and casually picked the one she remembered and showed Ketekete the title.
With her quick and intelligent eye the kāka realised what Arté was doing. She nodded slowly at the vampire.

'Um…he-hum,' the kākā casually said, 'as you say, this magic is quite benign.' She almost overbalanced again and she glanced at the irksome plumage. 'You have done so much for us. I am sure, with your vast repertoire of spells, you could work out who this person is. Maybe… a..um…' – she peeked at the title of the book that Arté was holding up – 'maybe a conversation…' – frantically Arté pointed at the title again and Ketekete furtively re-read it. 'Con-jur-at-ion spell?' She carefully enunciated the word. 'Maybe you could do one of those?'

'Huh. Yeah. Yeah. That's possible,' Phim mused. 'I was reading about it somewhere…somewhere…' He searched the books on the table for the title he had seen before.

Arté sent the book she was holding, skimming across the table to Phim's waiting hand. He looked at her, and Arté knew he knew. She dropped her head and fixed her gaze on a spot on the table, not sure if she could bear his look. Admiration or contempt – both would be intolerable at this moment.

Phim studied the book: *Conjuration for Dummies*. He opened it and read, tugging his right ear with his thumb and forefinger. The others went about their business. Or as much as they could, given they were trapped in this room.

Tasselis continued tending Koan's head. Koan chomped on an apple from the dryad's snack plate that was magically restored after one bite. He thought it was quite cool – a never-diminishing apple – but then he realised the apple had disappeared from his throat before it reached his stomach.

Ketekete was still getting used to her tail feathers, fanning them in and out. [Actually, she was quite impressed.]

And Arté cradled her face in her hands and sighed. *How can I make it up to him? We were getting on so well. I think he was…maybe…having feelings for me too. What should I do…?*

It didn't take too long for Phim to formulate a plan. He leapt out of his seat, grabbing a piece of chalk from the table. He drew an eight-pointed star on the floor. Inside each point he drew intricate designs,

but the outside of the star was clearly defined. He lit three candles then he got his friends and placed them around the star's points: Koan and Ketekete on the left and right of him, then two candles, then Arté and Tasselis each side of them, and the last candle opposite him. Arté looked for a sign that Phim had forgiven her, but he was totally focused on his task. When Phim placed the kākā on her star point, he telepathically said to her: *Can I please….* and she interrupted him with: *Shirley*[97] with a birdy grin.
Phim left with a peacock feather in his hand.

Again, inspiration came out of nowhere – the music and the feather and right thing to do. Seraphim took his place. He breathed deeply, then holding the feather with both hands, he drew a figure-eight above the star, singing a stanza from the devotions to the Divine Octet. Then he stopped and intoned: 'Laqad astad eia taka, 'ayuha al musta khdim al sihri, wa'atlub mink madha tafeal huna?'[98]

He continued tracing the figure-eight with the feather and added another stanza from the devotions while thinking*: Yay! I performed this spell perfectly. No mucked-up words.*

Suddenly, a bright blue, green, purple, yellow and red vapour fell from the feather landing on the floor inside the clear space within the star outline. Sparks shot out from the feather in all directions. Slowly, all of the colour ran out of the feather onto the ground, leaving a black and white frond. At the same time, the many-hued vapour coalesced in a mass on the ground like a ball of colourful jelly. The colours merged and the cloudy jelly spun around like a mini-tornado, ten centimetres tall. As it spun it seemed to solidify. The five friends gazed at this vision but they could not make out the whole picture. The spinning form slowed down – slow, s l o w , s l o w and stopped.

---

97 'Shirley' was a punning joke between them. Shirley – Surely.

98 I summoned you, magic user, and demand what are you doing here?

A little man stared at Phim. His skin was the colour of ripe tomatoes. He had a purple fez balanced on the back of his silver-haired head. He wore a green, yellow, red and purple vest and his gathered trousers reached to mid-calf. He wore yellow pointed slippers and, bizarrely, he was standing on a skateboard.

He appeared ill at ease. He blinked rapidly and a nervous tic jerked his head down to his shoulders. His fingers were doing a frantic dance – interlacing themselves forwards and backwards, fidgeting, and rapidly tapping them on his palm. His legs had the same idea – crossing his left leg behind his right knee and then reversing them – a feat of incredible balance on a skateboard.

'Well! You got me,' he said, giggling nervously. 'Ha! Ha! Ha! Hope you don't mind about the pranks. Tricks. Japes. Knavery, waggery, tomfoolery. Well, well, well. Three holes in the ground! You could have done worse. I could have done worse. Maybe I should have but I just wanted to have fun. Such fun, fun, fun! I thought you should stay inside – you lot should not be inflicted on the rest of the world. Ha, ha, ha! By the way, commiserations. No, no, no – congratulations. About the witch. The wicked witch. The wily, wicked witch. The wanton, wily, wicked witch! Ha! Ha! Ha! I detected some magical activity not to do with Luxima and you. I guess it was the witch. She was a bad business though. I have seen her before. Met her. Curse her. Anyway, I couldn't do anything until someone released me.'

All the time he was tapping his fingers and standing on one leg and then the other, fidgeting.

'That was a lucky escape. Not sure how it happened. I was in my urn for ages and suddenly I was in the garden. Then, I could see Felicia was dead – her magic disappeared. Evaporated. Dissipated. Good riddance, by the way, great riddance – and, given my years of captivity, I thought I should have fun. So! I pranked you! That was fun. Funny. Such fun,

fun, fun! Ha! Ha! Ha! Well – I'll see you later…' and the little man planted his left foot down, crouched down and began to skateboard away.

'Wait!' Phim shouted. The little man stopped mid-action.

Phim gulped and went on in a normal, calm voice. 'I have sunburn… summery…summoned you. You can't escape the summoning cipher… circlet…circle. You can't go anywhere.' He cleared his throat as the diminutive man glared at him. 'I want to what…when…know are… you are…' Phim took a deep breath, concentrated and said carefully: 'Who and what are you? And what are you going to do next?'

'Ah! Sorry. I didn't introduce myself. It's a long time since I met somebody. A person. Or pseudo-mage.' The little man giggled and spun around on his skateboard. 'Or a werewolf. Or a vampire or a dryad. Or …' The man paused and looked at Ketekete – her green plumage, her intelligent eyes paired with a fierce beak, her talons, and her ridiculous peacock's feathers. 'Wow! I like your plumage. Did I do that? I did well, I think, better than I expected. But what are you? Some sort of parrot but what…'

Phim butted in: 'Who and what are you?'

'Impatient. You moderns are impatient and moody. Keep your hair on! Keep cool. Don't panic and keep your shirt on.'

Phim raised his left hand with a pointing finger and the little manikin realised this could be a threatening gesture.

'Okay, okay, okay. As I said, it has been a long, long time before I met other people. I think it is two centuries…actually, two hundred and thirty-one years, eight months, five days and…' – the man looked at his non-existent watch – 'ten hours and forty-eight minutes since I have talked to anyone…' Without warning he blew up like a gas balloon that almost reached the roof. Furious, he snarled at Phim: 'And you want to know my name!'

The others shrank back, but Phim stood his ground and said, calmly: 'You are still in the summery…summoning circle. And yes – I would like to now…new… know your name. And when…what are you are.'

The man shrank back to a Phim-sized body and said, with a care-free expression: 'You're a cool customer. Not so articulate though. How can other people understand you? If I was going to do…'

Another left-hand-with-a-pointing-finger gesture and the colourful man recanted. 'Hah! Yes, yes, yes.' He sighed as if he had been caught out play-acting, and his fidgeting intensified. Then he said, rapidly: 'Well my name is Ruhaniyyat al-Hailahlah al-Musredeeninah. Ah ha! Can you try it? Huh? You can try it? Can you? Can you?'

The man held up his hands palm upward, bent his legs and cocked his ear to see if the apprentice mage would attempt it. But Phim was not going to fall for that trick. He pursed his lips and stared intensely at the man.

Ruhaniyyat al-Hailahlah al-Musredeeninah relented: 'Okay. Okay. You don't need to try it. It's quite a mouthful, I guess. Ha! Ha! Ha! Such fun. Okay – you can call me "Ru". That will I answer to. Too. Two. Toot.' Ru placed his clenched and gleefully imitated a trumpet. 'Tooot-ta-Tooooot! Tooot-ta-Tooooot!'

He looked about the room and innocently asked for a drink. 'I am quite parched. My urn was dry as a dustbowl. It was a dusty dustbowl in my urn.' Ru looked around the room and hit on Tasselis. 'You are handy. With your many fingers – digitally dexterous – magnificent metacarpals. I see there some ice-tea on the table. Could you get me a drink? I have not had a drink for two hundred and thirty-one years, eight months and….'

'Stay there!' Phim shouted at Tasselis as he could see that she was about to move away. 'If you go, the summoning statue…stark…star will not hold him. He will escape.'
Tasselis froze.

Phim focused on Ru. 'Don't try that agile…agent…again. And don't chance…change the subject.' He carefully enunciated his request again. 'What. Are. You?'
'Ah! You're good. Very good. Luxima has trained you well, I see. I detected your magic – in my urn. My dusty urn. My dark, dusty dungeon. Ahahahah…' His eyes filled with tears and he bent down on his skateboard, huddled and wretched, his hands over his face. Arté was going to comfort him, but an abrupt gesture from Phim stopped her. The intuitive message between them was: 'Don't break the summoning star.' Arté nodded, looked at her feet and thought forlornly: *Intuition? If you see that I got the message, why can't you see that I am so, so, sorry about Felicia?*

Parting his fingers, Ru was looking to see if anyone would touch him. He gave up, jumped to his feet in an acrobatic somersault and looked at Phim, apparently surrendering to his request. 'Wow! With Luxima's tutelage you have come a long way. A long, long way. Where is Luxima anyway? I would like to see him again. It was long, long ago…'

Arté had to pipe up. 'Luxima? See him again? You mean that you met Luxima two centuries ago…'

'Artémissa!' Phim held up his hand and shushed the vampire. She looked down and blushed – a lime colour suffused her cheeks. Phim drew Ru's attention back to him and he commanded: 'Ru! I summoned you. You have to tart…tear…tell me. What. Are. You?'

The man looked at his feet, the tic jerking his head this way and that. The yellow slippers were shuffling back and forth on the skateboard. He laced his fingers back and forth and mumbled something into his chest.

'I can't hear you!' Phim said forcefully.

Ru drew himself up and spat his answer. 'I am a djinn. Okay? A jinnee. A shaitan, an eblis! A genie.' He plonked himself down in a lotus position on his skateboard, spun himself around three-sixty degrees and blew a raspberry[99] to everyone. He came back to face Phim.

Tasselis spoke. 'So – you pranked us all. Can you un-prank us now?'

He turned to the dryad. 'Sure. Now you know what I am, it's not so much fun anymore.' A crafty look came over his face. 'But,' he said casually, 'my magic can't be performed until I get out. I can't un-prank you until you remove the summoning circle.' He leapt up, danced on the skateboard and looked at them all, waggled his hands around his ears, stuck out his magenta tongue and crooned childishly: 'Nyah nyah nah nyah nyah!'

The 'eyes' on Ketekete's peacock's tail – the orange lips, with the magenta tongue poking out – made sense now. It was a cartoon of the genie.

Phim sighed and looked at everyone around the circle. He tugged his right ear with his hand. 'Well…anyone?'

'I have a question,' said Ketekete immediately. 'What you said before, Phim.' She stared at the djinn until he looked at her. 'What are you going to do next?'

---

[99] 'blew a raspberry' – razzing or making a Bronx cheer. To make a noise similar to flatulence that may signify derision, real or feigned.

The djinn laughed uproariously, slapping his thighs, then collapsing into giggles. At last he answered: 'Don't know. Maybe – when I get out of the summoning circle – I will un-prank you. Or I may prank – **harder!**'
He said the last word viciously, and was delighted when the parrot flinched. 'Or maybe I will do what djinns do … well, you know.'

Ru paced around the circle looking at each one in turn.

'I can make the cottage and everyone in it become two dimensional, fold you up and post you to the Caliph. Ha! Ha! Ha! Is the Caliph in this place? He used to be here? Never mind…' He shook his body like a go-go dancer, spun around and flicked his hands rhythmically as if he was counting to a hundred. 'I could take you to the fiery pits of hell. Some of my colleagues would enjoy tormenting you. Or shrink you and place you in a thorny nest, float down the river to the Watthorford Falls. Such fun! Or maybe I will kill everyone with a 'E' in their name. Ha de ha! That would be three of the five of you. Or four? 'Phim' or 'Seraphim'? Poor Luxima. So sad, too bad. Ha! Ha! Ha! '

His reply collapsed into giggles again, and he fidgeted with his hands, lacing them up and down alternatively and danced with his feet on the skateboard.

Braving Phim's possible censure, Arté asked her question again. 'Did you meet Luxima two centuries ago?'

The djinn turned to face Arté and laughed. 'Ah! The vegetable vampire. The salad sucker. I do like your green tinge – much better than the ghostly, pale members of your erstwhile tribe. No… I lied. Hah de ha. Sometimes, I lie. Lie like a rug. Ha, ha, ha! Luxima recovered…no, that's the wrong word…he requisitioned my urn from Felicia when he won one of his many cursed battles with her. Won, one, faz, vici, toa! Twenty years ago now. Hah! But…sadly, I have never met him.

Luxima. I sensed him. And now I can sense this apprentice. The pseudo-mage Seraphim. I sensed them all. My urn was sealed for… well…two hundred and thirty-one years, eight months, five days, ten hours and forty-eight minutes. The last person who sealed me in there was – Ta duh! You guessed it. Felicia Breedlove. Felicia Breed-hate! I hated her, loathed her. Curse her. Whoop! You have cursed her already. To death. Ha, ha, ha, ha, ha,….'

Ru descended into manic laughter.

Koan spoke a stentorian voice. 'Who rescued you. From your urn,' he said. The djinn turned around to his questioner.

'Ah! The were-runt! Breaking things is your forté, hmm? The urn. The broken urn? Not your style though. You didn't break it…But, that is a problem. My urn was a pottery vessel, stoppered up. I sensed it had a grape vine pattern on it. Vine? Wine. Vino! I could do with a spot of pinot noir just now… Maybe you have some here?' Weaving his hands together in a pleading basket Ru turned about on his skateboard, juggling his feet in a dazzling tap dance.

'It was a warm, breezy day. I liked the breeze. On the window. I sensed the breeze. I sensed the magic users. I sensed that Felicia. Felicia Breedhate. After twenty years she was returning. I sensed her evil force. Curse her! It was building, and building, and building, and building, and building…'

Koan exaggeratedly cleared his throat which was enough to re-start the story from the jiggling, distracted djinn. 'Then – I was free. My urn smashed in the garden. It was intoxicating! After a while, when I had my bearings… You know that I have a compass in my head. I know where East is, all the time. It makes me…'
'Your broken urn?' Koan questioned menacingly.

'Well...I sensed that Felicia was dead and – well – ya de ya de ya. You know the rest... It was not a magic user I know. If it were a magic user I would have felt it. Who was my rescuer? I can't say. More's the pity – for all of you – hee hee hee – because I can't do what djinns do! Hee, hee, hee...'

Arté shot a look at Ketekete and the parrot ducked her head. [Pun intended.]

'Well,' Ru continued on, 'that's enough I think. Time to go. See you later...or maybe never. Or soon – very soon. Maybe I have plans for all of you. And a final ending, if you know what I mean. Ha, ha, ha, ha ...' The manic laughter echoed around the room as Ru swept his skateboard in a circle from Koan to Ketekete.

The spinning skateboard struck the parrot, reeling her around. Her feather train knocked the candle beside her and the flames ignited the plumage. Ketekete leapt out of the circle with a squeal and immediately Arté flashed to her bedroom and returned a blanket to quell the flames.

At the same time, Ru recovered his skateboard and sped across the broken summoning circle on the opposite side, a feral grin on his face.

Chapter 12:
ADADHD

It took about one and half seconds.

Phim was completely calm. He looked at the flames and saw that Arté, with her vampire speed and good sense, had contained the fire. Ketekete was unharmed, so he directed his attention to the fleeing djinn. In an instant, he remembered the lunchtime debacle with Luxima. He connected the memories from his mentor's tutelage and his own study. Without hesitation he put his left hand on his sternum, pointed with his right hand in a formation of crossed and uncrossed fingers and said, with full authority and conviction: 'Gelo.'

The fleeing djinn was frozen in mid-carve.[100]

Tasselis and Koan were stupefied. 'What's going on?' they chorused and looked at each other in amazement, and then amusement.
They turned to Phim.

Phim let out his breath.
Whew! What a situation. This djinn is…too much.
He turned to the others. 'Is everything offal…oil…okay? Any injuries?'

Arté ducked her head again and mumbled. She was nervous that the broken summoning circle was her fault.
But Ketekete answered Phim, telepathically.
Sorry about that. I broke the star. But…my kōtore[101] was scorched. Sorry. But Arté was amazing. She knew what to do. I have not been a good friend to her – you know that – but she saved me when the situation could not be more dire. I owe her. And you should cut her a bit of slack, okay.

---

[100] Carve: a manoeuvre in which the skate-boarder makes a long, curving arc.

[101] bottom, buttocks

But – she betrayed me about Felicia…

Yes – she betrayed your trust but she had a reason. Mitigating circumstances. Felicia enchanted you. All of us. Felicia would have butchered us. Arté is a true friend – she saved us. She saved you.

In slow motion, Ketekete turned to Phim with a superior look: *And you love her.*

Phim looked at his feet, threw Ketekete a 'I-know-you-know' look, cast a brief but apologetic look at Arté, checked out Koan and Tasselis, and peered at the frozen genie.

'I don't know,' he admitted, 'how long this fracture…freckle…freeze will last so…' He shrugged and raised his hands.

'Well, we have to get rid of that delusional djinn,' said Ketekete, unhelpfully. 'He is more demented than a crazy cat lady.'
'Maybe we should take the djinn outside?' suggested the dryad.
'But the doors are still interlocking,' countered Arté. 'We can't get out of this room.'
'Back in his urn?' proposed Koan.
'But.' Phim said, 'Ru said his urn was smart…smell…smashed. Outside. In the gang…garden. His magic is ancient – I'm not sure I can cower…courtly…counter it. And I don't know how to travel… trap him in another contour…container in time.'

Ketekete shot a look at Arté. The vampire frowned knowingly at the kākā as if to say: 'You have to admit it, not me.' Again, the parrot ducked her head. [And also again, pun intended.]

'Well,' Koan said adamantly, 'this djinn is mental.'
'Absolutely!' chorused Tasselis and Ketekete.

'I'm not so sure,' mused Arté. 'He was incarcerated for a long time. That would be tough for anyone. But something about his... distraction. His fidgeting. His agitation. Oh! I know...'
She flashed over to the table, took out a book and thumbed through rapidly.

'Here, here. This is a passage from *Create Order From Chaos,*' she said as she returned to the others, and read:

> You may see this person as forgetful, having difficulty listening to others, spacing out, fidgety, feeling restless, impatient, with a low tolerance for frustration, talking excessively, rushing through tasks. These are classic symptoms of Attention Deficit Hyperactivity Disorder, or ADHD. When someone is living with ADHD, their symptoms are a result of their mental health condition rather than a choice.
> People with ADHD have trouble taking responsibility for performing day-to-day tasks. To others, they may come across as insensitive, uncaring or irresponsible, which can damage their relationships.

She looked at all of them as if her discovery would make everything okay. But – Ketekete was burnt, Koan had a sore head, the snacks and drinks were still 'pranked', the room was a prison, and Phim had no idea of a solution.

The kākā had to pipe up. 'That's why he gabbled so much. Race-car brain. Looney tunes. Out to lunch.'

'No. That's not fair,' Arté said. 'Just saying – Attention Deficit Hyperactivity Disorder. ADHD.' She dropped the book on the table. 'It is a shame. He can't help it,' she mumbled. 'Someone should cure him. '

'Actually, ADADHD,' Ketekete quipped again. 'Another Djinn's Attention Deficit Hyperactivity Disorder! Could be a song title.' She improvised a dreadful jingle: 'ADADHD, what's the matter with me!'

Arté thought: *Just like someone we know,* but she didn't voice that unhelpful comment.

But Phim did – telepathically.
Just like someone we know.

Who?

You!

Awww...just saying it like it is.

Not helpful – we have to find a solution before the djinn unfreezes. So...shut it!

Phim acknowledged the vampire. 'That's considerate and collect... compost...compassionate,' he conceded, and Arté glowed. 'But,' he added, 'I'm not sure how to day...dean...deal with Ru in the meantime. He was unfriendly. Throne...thread...threatening. He could harm us...'

With the summoning circle broken, they snuffed out the candles and sat down again, Tasselis and Koan on the floor against the wall, Arté and Phim on the benches and Ketekete balanced her peacock's tail, now successfully, on the top of the chair.

Arté had an idea, but she wanted to encourage Ketekete to own up to it.

'Um ... not sure about this,' she said cautiously. 'Ru mentioned, twice, that – "you know what djinns do". What do djinns "do"?'

Tasselis leapt up waving her arms in the air. 'Djinns reward their rescuers! They gift three wishes.'
Arté looked at Ketekete. Significantly. Intensely.
Ketekete hopped from one foot to the other. Uncomfortably. 'Um…I hate to tell you this…but…'
'Out with it,' said Phim.

'I knocked Ru's urn out of the kitchen window,' she confessed. 'I didn't know… I was looking for seeds and nuts and… Felicia fooled me but …' The kāka hung her head in shame. If she had arms and knees she would have knelt and cradled her arms in supplication. 'Sorry! I set Ru free…'

'Ah! You didn't free him,' said Arté triumphantly. 'You rescued him. Hooray! You are due three wishes because' – and the vampire imitated Ru's whining voice – ' "that what djinns do".'

The kākā brightened. 'What! Can I wish for …anything? An endless supply of nuts and seeds and…'

Ketekete, Phim said telepathically. *You have to use it to our advantage. All five of us – okay?*

Oh okay. But seeds and nuts would be helpful for your cottage's budget and I…

No. We have to consider all of us. For example, the first wish could – should – be to undo the things that Ru did to us – including your ridiculous plumage. We should talk normally so everyone can see your commitment. But I will give you a prompt…if that's okay?

Of course. We are bonded. That's what it means – I guess.

Phim addressed the others. 'Well, I think – with Ketekete's help – we can get out of this miss…message…mess. I am going to release the deejay… djinn and make him "do what djinn's do" – grunt…grant three wishes to Ketekete. Maybe you should be out of the wake…way – out of the way. Ru could be voluntary…violets…volatile – with his magic restored.'

Arté, Ketekete, Koan and Tasselis moved to the back wall. Phim looked around at them all, drew a big breath, and faced the frozen djinn. He approached him and tapped him on the shoulder. Immediately, the djinn fell down, turned around and looked with astonishment at the apprentice mage. He was gesturing with his hand but Phim pre-empted him. 'I know who reserve…recalled…rescued you from the ear…urn.'

Ru looked startled and, amazingly, was speechless.

'Ketekete knocked the putt…pottery vessel off the window silk…sill, and it smart…smush…smashed in the garden. And…' Phim grew more erect, jutted his chin at the djinn and said with a steely stare, 'you knew that, didn't you.'

'Well, maybe…it was debatable…' fussed the djinn, sitting up on the floor. 'Maybe I saw something like, a bum, sporting green and black… tights or bloomers, that was, maybe, around the vicinity of the window above… It could be an accident though, an act of the gods. I mean, there are eight gods, so take your pick. You know that there are freak accidents every day. I know an Ent who has been struck by lightning six times. At the same spot! His name was Carerel, and it addled his brain. He wanted to be a bar-be-cue chef – can you imagine that…'

'Didn't. You.' Seraphim said forcefully.
'Yes,' Ru said in a small voice.
'And you have to "do what djinns do!"' copying Ru's voice exactly. 'Don't. You.'
'Yes,' Ru said in a smaller voice.

'Ketekete repeat…ripened…rescued you. You have to grunt…grant her three wishes. Over to you, Ketekete.'
Phim grabbed another chair and ushered in the parrot to sit on the top rail, looking down on the djinn. Ru stood up and looked resentfully at the bird.

'Well, my first wish is…' Ketekete began.

'No, no, no!' protested the djinn. 'I can grant wishes for a person, not for a bird. That's ridiculous!' He laced his hands and hopped from one leg to the other, fidgeting. 'That's like giving a butcher's shop to a dog, or giving a cat control over an estate or… Actually, I saw a cat who was willed everything by his old owner and…'

'Ru! This bird is articulate,' Arté put her spoke in, 'and, it appears, more intelligent than you! "Do what djinns do!" '

Phim glanced at her, a small grin of approval. But when he turned to the djinn, he was all business.
'Do it!' said Phim emphatically.

The djinn cowered. His hands were clasped and legs bent. Ketekete hurried her speech in case the djinn made some other objection.
'Well, my first wish is…' Ketekete began…

Phim telepathically sent out: *Undo all the things that the djinn has done to us this day…*

'…un-prank all the things you have done this day.'

The djinn waved his hand casually. Immediately, Ketekete's tail was restored to her welcome green and black tail feathers – and all the ones that Phim had removed in the last few weeks were back. Tasselis looked at the snack table and all the fruit was diced and sliced and the crackers were ready to eat with their onion relish, salad and cheese. Koan, his bruise gone, rushed out the back door, and appeared – in the back door!

'My second wish is…' Ketekete waited for Phim's telepathic message.

Phim was thinking about Arté and felt bad about his tiff with her. He still felt betrayed, but he realised that Arté was under duress. He had been enamoured with Felicia because of her flirty magic – not infatuated, not in love, but simply enchanted. Arté took an extreme risk to get him away from the witch. And he thought about what Felicia had said before she died. *Arté kissed me,* he thought, *and it felt …good. Right. She is a good friend to me. What can I do for her?*

An inspiration came to him – about Arté's compassion for the djinn, the ADHD diagnosis. Arté was right. Someone should cure Ru. He aimed his telepathic thought at Ketekete and…

'…that your ADHD will disappear,' said Ketekete, 'and you will function as a …judicious djinn. Intelligent and thoughtful. And moral. Compassionate. And don't hurt people. Or creatures.'

Um… that was not what I said, Phim thought to Ketekete.

But…basically, it is. Sort of, Ketekete replied to Phim. *I thought you were suggesting wishes, not dictating them?*

'Hmmm…that is a multi-layered wish,' said Ru, 'but I'll grant it. This time. I don't know what ADHD is, but it seems to be bad…' The djinn jumped from foot to foot, angling his lower leg behind the other knee, just like a Celtic dancer. 'I don't like multi-layered wishes. One time, a fellow djinn had a three-wish situation and the fellow got a multi-layered wish for all three wishes.' He flapped his head this way and that. 'Actually, he had to give the man a ten-wish commitment. You don't realise what a wish take out of us, especially when it is a… '

At the same time, the genie waved his arm. Immediately he stopped speaking, sat up straight, laced his fingers in a prayer position, looked at Ketekete, bowed and in a calm and placid demeanour said: 'That is your second wish. And your third…?'

The five friends were stunned by the change in the djinn.
Gone were his fidgeting, his manic looks, his excessive talking and far-flung fantasies.

The djinn appeared puzzled at the astonishment of the others. He frowned at Ketekete and requested: 'The third wish?'

Phim was rattled. *What should be the third wish? The genie's urn was in Luxima's cottage, and he got it from Felicia.. A trophy? Or a prize? Spoils of war? Maybe Luxima had a task that only a genie could perform? I should give the djinn back to Luxima – wherever he is. He can decide what to do for Ru…*

Phim transmitted the thought: *Ketekete, can you say 'You are free to go to Luxima Aerolaness to see what he wants you for…' or something like that. Okay?*

Ketekete said importantly: 'My third wish is you are free…'

'Thank you!' said the djinn.

He waved his hand and disappeared.

Chapter 13:

Double, double, toil and trouble

Phim chuckled. 'That rascal. We said, "do what djinns do!" and that's was…want…what they diddle…doodle…do. They wriggle and sunk…snuck…sneak and adapt the meaning of the wicket…winky… wishes until they get to their own advantage. He's gone. Hopefully, he won't come back.'

'At least his pranks are gone,' commented Tasselis, munching some crackers and cheese. She passed the platter to Koan and he took a big bite of the fruit.

'And, I think, his ADHD is gone too,' said Arté, sitting down at the table. 'That was well done, Ketekete.'

'That was all Phim,' admitted the parrot. 'We were partners.'

Arté glanced shyly at Phim, hoping that he would imagine that they were partners too, but he wasn't looking. He was rubbing his eyes and massaging his forehead and, taking a big breath, he said: 'What a dice…dab…day! Felicia and Ru. You can do was…want…what you want, but I'm knitted…knocked…knackered. I have to sleep, so…see you in the moron…month…argghh…morning.' He wearily waved to them all and went to his bedroom.

The next morning, before breakfast, he woke up Arté. 'We need to talk,' he said soberly. 'Can we work…warm…walk in the forest?'
Arté dressed herself quickly and went to the kitchen.

Phim was already at the main door, dressed in long sleeves, trousers and a big hat. He indicated that she should follow him.

It was a beautiful morning. The sun had just risen, coating the dew on the cobwebs and foliage with sparkling diamonds. The trees seemed to breathe with an invigorated energy and the air was charged with possibility. Arté gloried in the sun's rays, and she reached out for Phim's hand, but he went ahead and hooked his hands under his armpits. The vampire followed him at arms length, waiting for the guillotine to fall.

At last Phim spoke. 'I have trespass…treated…treasured this lacey… lass…last few weeks. Getting to need…new…know all of you. And espresso…essay…especially…you.' He paused and gave Arté a soulful look, then continued on the path. Arté skipped to catch up.

'Ketekete, bless her, spud…spot…spoke to me about your actives… actions want…went…when that white…witch was her…here… I know you were defeat…defending us…me… And you used that special…spell to defend…defeat her. But…you used me to be the instant…instruct… instrument…'

He stopped and looked at Arté. 'Sorry…I can't say…that…what I want…mean… Clear. Ly.'

He closed his eyes and clasped his hands in front of his nose in a prayer pose. He concentrated and focused his thoughts. He opened his hands and when he spoke, his passion and pain seemed to stream out from of him.

'You knew I didn't want to work with necklace…necromancy. You knew that. But you gave me that species…special…spell. It saved us… but I killed her. I killed her. I can forgive you – of course. You saved us. Me. And you medic…arrgh…mean so much to me. But you've betrayed me. And I can't forget. I…I…'

He faltered, and grabbed his forehead with his left hand, massaging it frantically. 'I have to stay…stoop…step back. Just the way it was before. I can't ...I can't do... This. Just...forgiving you, but knock... not forgetting.'

Phim placed his hand on hers, and gave her another longing gaze, then he rushed off into the forest, leaving a destitute and grieving vampire behind. Green tears ran down Arté's cheeks.

She wanted to remonstrate with him. She wanted to say that Phim didn't kill her – it was the truth of what she **was**. That the mirror revealed the truth about Felicia to herself. That's what killed her. That Felicia was planning to kill them all anyway – except Koan, her pet werewolf.

But Phim was gone. Arté could easily chase him, make him see sense – but it wasn't the right time.

Arté was strong. Resilient. Courageous. But she fell to her haunches and sobbed.

The next two weeks were quite different. The established routines continued – especially for Koan and Tasselis. They were fine. More than fine. They seemed to have an easy relationship reminiscent of an old-married-couple.

The relationship between Phim and Arté was superficially cordial but volcanic fissures were building. Ketekete was well aware of the volatile emotions between them. The kākā believed Arté was genuinely in love with Phim and distraught that she could not speak to him.
But, empathetically bonded, Ketekete knew that Phim struggling with conflicting emotions about love and duty, passion and integrity, building up in him.

The parrot was preparing for an eruption. And one day, it seemed that the lava was boiling over.

Arté was preparing lunch for the five of them: salad with tomatoes, cheese, olives, relish and flat breads. Phim* came from the forest. Suddenly, he* shouted at Arté.

'Again, this rubbish! Why can't you make something decent rather than this slop. Maybe Koan would be a better chef. I'm sick of this vegetarian offal!'

He* stalked to the back door and disappeared.

Arté was distressed and eventually angry. She completed her lunch preparations and rang the gong. Koan and Tasselis came in from the garden, Ketekete flew back from the thatched roof, and Phim came in through the main door. Arté marched up to him and said coldly: 'Enjoy this offal.' She pushed past him using her pointy elbow to punch him in his stomach and stormed out, thinking: *I don't like this slop anyway. It's no use to me. Give me sunshine any day.*

'Ow!' said Phim, bruised and mystified. He turned and looked at her but, of course, she was gone.

Offal? What gives…? he shrugged. *Moody.*

After lunch, Tasselis and Koan went, hand in hand, back to the garden and began preparing the beds for the next crop of veges: leeks, broad beans, spinach, cabbage and broccoli. They were hard at work but Koan, 'the sniffilator', detected something. He sensed that there was someone behind the rosemary bush. When he approached he realised it was Phim*. 'What d'you want,' he asked brusquely.

Phim* jumped out, crouched in a "tah-dah" pose and sang, in a juvenile falsetto voice: 'Tasselis and Koan, Sitting in a tree. K-I-S-S-I-N-G!' Then, with a lascivious leer he* said: 'Well – I don't think they were kissing, they were …' Phim* mimed a raunchy, pelvic thrust motion.

Koan knew full well what Phim* was implying. The relationship between the wolfman and the dryad was at a critical stage. More than friends, but... So Koan's angry reaction was justified. He made his huge hands into fists and...

But Phim's meditation lessons had affected the wolfman's responses. Rather than a quick vault to sort out that vicious tormentor, he turned, grabbed a bucket of compost, and raced to the garden gateway. Tasselis was in the way, so Koan pushed past her. She was bewildered. *Why is Koan so angry? What did I do?*

The wolfman reached the rosemary bush but Phim* had gone leaving only his scent. Koan followed the scent along the path to the forest, but lost it. Then, he spied him, on his haunches examining a toadstool. Furious, Koan stood behind Phim and emptied the whole bucket of compost over his head. 'Just don't!' the fuming wolfman said. 'Don't!'
Koan stalked off back to the garden.

Phim was shocked. He blinked, stood up and scraped off most of the rotting vegetables and other detritus. *What? Why 'don't'? Why the compost? Why?* He went to the river to wash off the compost which was drying on his skin.

Ketekete was foraging for grubs and insects in the forest. The total vegetarian diet didn't entirely suit the kākā, but she didn't want to upset Arté, now that they were friends.
After she had had her fill, she flew back to the cottage and lighted on the table.

Phim* was studying Luxima's books. As usual.
Not so usual was the response that Ketekete got when she arrived.

'What are you doing here?' said Phim* in high dudgeon. 'You are spying on me!' He* stopped tugging on his* left ear, slammed the books closed and leapt up from his* seat.
'Ah, I see. You're getting the information for yourself and that vegetating vampire you are always flirting with! Ha! The putrefying poultry and the greeny witch-bitch. You can go to hell. Get out! Get out!' Phim* took a mug from the table and biffed it at the parrot, just missing her head. It shattered on the kitchen floor spilling dregs of tea.

What's going on? Why are you doing this? Ketekete tried to telepathically talk to Phim* but, apparently, he* had blocked her. She got no response from him* at all.

When Phim* grabbed another mug, the kākā decided that retreat was better than confrontation, so she flew out the window. The mug sailed out of the window and smashed on a post, just beside where Tasselis was weeding.

Tasselis leapt up and, baffled, looked around. Phim* appeared in the main door. He* looked at her and gave a nasty, mocking laugh. 'What?' he* said rudely. 'Carry on with your menial work, why don't you? That can't be hard for you. You're ugly as a weedy shrub yourself. An ugly shrub with no upbringing at all. You belong with your plants. Weeding, digging, making mud. Rooting in the ground. You should root yourself, if you see what I mean. Ha, ha, ha!'

The innuendo was not lost on the dryad. Incensed, she threw down her tools and stalked off.

Arté witnessed this troubling scene as she had come around from the back yard and saw Phim*'s insults. Now she flashed to the main door and confronted him. 'Take it back,' she said, furiously. 'Tasselis is a gentle, helpful soul. Apologise. Now!'

Phim* laughed at the vampire, the same nasty, mocking laugh. 'And?' he* sneered. 'You and what army. It's the truth. She's useless, fussing about her plants and trees. They are salad stuff and firewood fodder – that's all.'

He* moved closer to Arté and whispered, 'And what about you? A vegetarian vampire who can't realise her own bloody destiny. You could sublimely vanquish your enemies. – make them beg for mercy then rip them to shreds. Instead, you're a vampire who befriended a tree hugger, treats a werewolf as a colleague, and is pining about a certain mage who has nothing but contempt for you. Loser. Betrayer! Huh! You're pathetic.' And he* turned and went back into the cottage.

Arté was devastated. She hung her head on her chest and sank down on her haunches. Her depression overwhelmed her and she struggled to think.

But something. a voice inside her, told her to wake up. The voice was strong and insistent, saying: 'You are better than that!'

She rose to her full height and thought assertively: *He's wrong. I am proud of what I have become. I don't need that bloodthirsty destiny. I am my own person. And, actually, Phim was responsible. If he doesn't like it, stuff him. He's not the boss of me.*

She breathed deeply, and marched into the cottage, confrontation etched to every fibre of her being. When she reached the kitchen she heard Phim's bedroom door slam. But, looking to her right, she saw Phim coming in through the back door. 'I don't need you,' she shouted. 'You're not the boss of me! I am what I am, and that's okay. I'm not a loser. You made me this way and I am glad. Ecstatic!' She stuck out her chin and glared at the apprentice mage.

Phim said with an uncertain smile: 'Sure. It's good – isn't it?' He was confused.

Tasselis stormed into the room and leant on a chair beside the table, glowering at Phim. 'Fine! You don't need to see me anymore. I love my plants and trees and that is more important. I will live in the shed with Koan, and don't you dare make fun of me again.' Her passion was demonstrated when her grip of the chair back tightened and the rung shattered. She stormed out.

'What's happening?' Phim asked Arté. He was perplexed. The vampire looked daggers at him, pushed past him – again – and went to her room, slamming the door.

Telepathically he called Ketekete: *Come here. Come here. Please.*

The parrot flew resignedly and perched on the windowsill, not the table. *That's unusual,* Phim thought to himself, but he was more concerned about the haranguing had from Arté and Tasselis. *Everyone is mad at me? Why?*

You should asked yourself! the bird thought self-righteously.

What? I don't understand. Is it something I said?

Why are you blocking me. Sometimes your telepathy is, well, absent. You're obstructing us. You don't want me to be a partner now? But we are bonded. What gives?

Phim was staring at the floor, puzzled about what the kākā was saying to him. He couldn't figure it out. He turned and saw the smashed mug on the floor in a pool of spilt tea. *Huh! I expect it was Koan,* he thought distractedly. *He is so clumsy sometimes. Someone should clean up this mess.*

He looked briefly at the kākā, with the nonchalant air of an infant who has not read the room. *Could you do it?* he thought offhandedly. *I have to study.*

Sure – the books are the most important thing, Ketekete fumed. *Nothing should be in the way of your study. Not chores, not friendship. not partnership. Well – nothing doin'.*
And she flew out the window.

Three days.
The silences and altercations went for three days.
Phim* went on insulting, belittling, and not communicating with his friends. The four friends were incensed and furious, and the relationship with Phim suffered badly. In fact, it was abysmal. It was compounded because, five minutes after the conflict or insult, Phim pleaded that he didn't recall – or mean – the words he was apparently saying and his seemingly half-hearted and confused apologies didn't make up for the intended slight.

As incensed as they all were, it was worse for Koan. He was on a knife edge. He appreciated what Phim had done for him – the way he made sure he would not kill anyone when his change occurred – but the moon was waxing, and his aggressive behaviour was starting to peak again.

On the day of the full moon Koan was at the river, hoping to isolate himself. He didn't want to harm anyone, especially his friends, but the werewolf inside him had no compunction about offending social expectations.

In the evening Phim* followed him to the river. He* posed provocatively in front of the wolfman, moving his* hips from side to side and gesturing aggressively. A murderous rage rose up in Koan but he just managed to contain it. Phim's calming and meditative sessions had that effect. Through gritted teeth he asked: 'Why are you doing this? Is this a test? Nah! You shouldn't … uggg … test me. Rrruuuggh.'

But instead, Phim* insulted him again. 'What a pathetic little man,' he* sneered. 'Little mind, little mojo. Mini-macho. Swim into the freezing river? Blue balls and shrivelled dick. Whoo hoo! Little, little man. You should be slaughtering your rivals and bedding their wives and daughters. What a pathetic, little man. Wolfman? You should be Wuss-man!'

Just then, the rising moon appeared on the horizon and Koan howled. He became a werewolf, looked at the apprentice mage* and charged, claws raking the ground, intending to rip him* limb from limb. He almost reached him* and caught sight of the panicked look in Phim*'s eyes – before he froze. Solid.

Wiping the sweat from his* brow, Phim* admitted: 'Whew! At least that spell worked.'

Circling around the frozen werewolf, Phim* continued to insult him – something about his absent father's heritage and his mother's occupation. He* grinned at the werewolf triumphantly, looking intensely into the monster's eyes. 'Well, I am going to see that you never murder anyone again – especially me! I am going to the woodshed to get the axe and smash you into a million pieces. So long, wolfman. See you…never!'
The apprentice mage* turned and ran down the path to the cottage.

Unbeknownst, Arté had followed and heard the shameful act of Phim*'s derogatory remarks and his* plan to kill Koan. She approached the werewolf and said to his frozen face: 'I will get you out of this. Be strong.'
Then she flashed like a bolt of lightning, easily outpacing Phim*.

She went into the cottage and saw Phim absorbed in his books. She was puzzled, and didn't make a sound as she approached him but, suddenly, she was distracted by something outside the window. She tiptoed to the window – and saw Phim* marching to the woodshed to fetch the axe.

Bewildered, Arté stumbled. Phim looked around from the table, distracted. 'What'?' He composed himself. 'Um…is there anything you need right now?' He pulled his ear with his right hand. His face was filled with tension but Arté saw, in his eyes, the glimmer of longing.

'No. Nothing,' Arté said. She didn't know how to act. *I have to figure this out before…*
'I was…um…looking for Koan. Where is he?'

'I think he was going to steady…station…stay away for his ….um… change. Somewhere remodel…remark…remote. Y'know. Full moon. Frozen.'

'Oh, I see. Okay – keep studying. I will get someone else to help me.' And she left by the main door. But her head was humming!
There are two Phims? What..? How…? Same stature, same clothes, same everything. The way both say things, do things – their trousers, shirt and hat in the sunlight, their habit of ruffling their hair before eating, their habit of pulling on their earlobes when they are thinking…
Wait! I think… I think… Yes!
That's it. Phim always tugged his right earlobe with his right hand. Always, the right earlobe. But, I remember now, when this Phim was the unpleasant, insulting, obnoxious person, he* tugged his left ear! They are not completely the same!*

Arté, infused by righteous determination, sat up straight, balled her hands into fists, and fixed her eyes on the forest.

There are two Phims! And obviously, the evil one is planning to murder Koan. I can't let that happen.

She flashed down the path into the forest, beating Phim* by a good margin. She hid the frozen werewolf in a thicket of trees – vampire strength coming to her aid.

Then she ambushed Phim* on the path and plucked the axe out of his hands as if it was a matchstick.
'We are not letting you hurt our friend,' she commanded, and in a heartbeat, she vanished.

She took the axe back to the cottage and placed it before Phim on the table.

The apprentice mage wearily looked up at the expectant vampire. The last three days had taken their toll on his normally sunny and optimistic disposition. 'What now?' he said, depressed and fatalistic. 'Is Koan going awake…awash…away from us?'

In his distraction (interrupting his studying) and nervousness (it seemed that Arté was always angry at him) he tugged on his earlobe. The right one.

Thank goodness! she thought and without any preamble she said: 'There are two Phim's.'

Chapter 14:
Fire burn, and cauldron bubble

'What d'you mean "two Phim's"?' he said warily.

'I was just checking if you were the right Phim. You recall that I was asking about Koan. And you said he was isolating himself. The other Phim* is rude and obnoxious and demeaning and…'

'The other one?' Phim was puzzled.

'Okay, okay,' Arté reasoned. 'There are two Phims. One is you – the other one is…out there. The other Phim* is objectionable! He* says mean, belittling, rude, vulgar and upsetting remarks to us. Our friends. But he is the spitting image of you. He has the same face, same voice, same stance, same mannerisms. We thought it was you – but I saw him out the window in the woodshed. Just now. And I saw you, at the same time, studying your books. At the same time! There is another "you" out there!'

'What was he done…doing in the woodsman…wood-chuck…woodshed?' Phim asked.
'He was getting an axe to murder Koan,' Arté said casually, 'but that's not the reason…'
'What!' screeched Phim and leapt up. 'We have to say…shave…save him! Where is he now? We had to get Koon…Koan to say…safety and…'

'Already done!' The vampire waved her hand dismissively. 'He is in no danger. He is frozen and I have hidden him from the evil Phim*. What we have to do is figure how this …thing… is imitating you. And what he* wants? I think…I feel, that he* is up to no good. His* insults and insinuations are getting worse.'

She realised another difference from Phim and Phim*. The evil Phim* didn't have the same communication difficulties.
And Phim's communication difficulties are getting worse. But – that is another problem…

'Ah,' Phim pondered as he sat down again. 'That's why all of you have been diminished…dispersed…disgruntled and ironing…ironwork… irritable with me.' Then another thought occurred to him. 'Ah! That's why Ketekete was uplift…upset by me. Somehow the other Phim* was bluebird…blotting…blocking our bonding thoughts. Or maybe he* couldn't do it?'

He quickly looked at Arté. 'Do you mind …?'
'Of course! She could be helpful?'

Phim called Ketekete telepathically: *Come here. Come here. Emergency meeting. Danger.* In an afterthought he 'said': *Please.*

The parrot flew in and perched on the windowsill cautiously. 'What'd'you want now,' she said crossly with a dirty look at Phim.

Arté interrupted. 'Ketekete, there are two Phims.'
Surprised, the parrot looked at the vampire and straightened up. 'Two Phims? What?'
'I saw them. I saw this Phim at the table – the nice one – and the evil one outside. They look the same. Completely.'
'When I always survey…surprise…summon you, am I …nice?' said Phim, carefully.
'Well – I guess so? I can't remember. I was always upset at you. Because you blocked me.'

'I've never bluebird…blotting…blocked you!' the apprentice mage declared forcefully.

The parrot flew onto the kitchen bench. 'I was sending my thoughts to you all the time, even when you hurled the mug at me. Or when you said to Arté and me that "the putrefying poultry and the greeny witch-bitch can go to hell." '
Phim rose horrified. 'I note…nether…never said that!' He looked at Arté and Ketekete with an abject apology in his eyes.

I see, I see! Ketekete thought telepathically to Phim.
You apologised to Arté before me. Spoon ears. You forgot about your familiar. Your partner.

Oh – sorry! She only told me moments ago. But she is… Well – she is my…

Ah ha! thought Ketekete. *Just kidding. I know! I know you love her. That's why I say rhubarb rhubarb rhubarb in my mind. And that's why I was upset about you – he* – was talking so much trash to her.*

Phim blushed.

Arté noticed and secretly understood why.
'You are communicating again?'

'Yes' Phim in a small voice and he cast his eyes down to avoid looking at Arté.

He tugged on his right earlobe. 'So…this other "me". How similar to me as he*?'

'Completely! But not in attitude,' Ketekete and Arte confirmed together, but the vampire continued: 'But…one thing.'
She turned to the kākā. 'When Phim is thinking, what did he always do? His mannerisms?'
'He always tugged on his earlobe.'

'Which side?'

'Right one. Always the right one.'

'Aha!' Arté leaped in triumph. 'When he* was thinking, the evil Phim* tugged his left earlobe! Maybe he* is left-handed? That's why I know this is you. The real, darling Phim.' She reached her hand across the table and clasped his with a meaningful look. Phim squeezed her hand back.

Ketekete blinked and shook her head slightly. Under her breath she whispered: 'Kī konā koe mate kanehe ai?[102]'
She coughed politely, and the lovebirds were startled out of their mutual admiration back to the crux of the question: what is this other Phim* doing here?

'Phim, why have you not met him?' Ketekete asked, 'that dirtbag comes into the cottage and around the grounds and harangues us, insults us. How?'

'Ah, I think I know,' Arté answered. 'He slips out the door just before you come in. He seems to know where you are. I thought that you were doing a matter-transference spell – going out one door and appearing at another. Just like Ru.' Arté raised her eyebrows and covered her mouth with her hands. Her eyes grew wide. 'Maybe it is the djinn. Has he come back?'

'Maybe…' Phim was thoughtful. 'But it doesn't fern…felt…feel right. He could harm us, but he was not inning…innocent…insulting. He would never chalk…call you the "putrefying poultry and the greeny witch-bitch". Or attic…attain…attack Koan with an axle…axe. He would use djinn-magic. No … it dose…doesn't feel right.'

102 Are you lovesick or what?

'Ah!' Arté realised something. 'Sorry to do this, but the other Phim*… um…' She screwed up her face and said apologetically: 'The evil Phim's speech is not – well – compromised. He doesn't stumble over the words as you do.' She clapped her hands and half-grinned. 'That's a good thing! Another difference!'

Phim didn't mind, because he leapt out of his chair – again – and said exultantly: 'Doppelgänger! Doppelgängers have the apple…abundant… ability to purpose…perp…perf-fect-ly copy the form of any hundred… humanoid creat-tive…creat-ture. Argh!'

He gave up on his speech and rifled through the books on the table. He picked one, and showed it to Arté, indicating that she should take it and read from it.

> Doppelgängers can even copy their thoughts and mannerisms too, as long as the host is still alive. They often work as assassins or spies. Sometimes, they simply take over a wealthy organisation or even a kingdom without anyone noticing. In their natural form, doppelgängers are horrific to look upon. They are monsters and have to be destroyed…

Arté looked hard and long at Phim and thought: *destroyed.*

At last she spoke. 'I know. I know. Destroyed. You are thinking about Felicia. But – the evil Phim is a vile creation. A monster. He is destroying the bond among us – our friendship. And I know that he was set on murdering – destroying – Koan. And after that?'

Phim looked soberly at Arté and Ketekete. 'I know,' he said, in a small voice. Suddenly, he stood up. 'I will reset…rescue…res-search tonight' he said urgently.

He looked at Arté. 'You should…showed…sure he can't be help…here if **I'm** here?'

'Yes. I know so.' The vampire answered unequivocally.

'And…Koan is sage…safe?'

Arté confirmed.

'And Ketekete, can you fled…fledged…fly to Tasselis. She – we – all sure…showed…should be in the this roster…rooster… - room. Argh!!'

'I get it!' Arté said jubilantly. 'If you are here, the doppelgänger can't be here. So, we should all be here with you.'

The kākā nodded enthusiastically. 'That shagrag[103] will not know what hit him!' and she flew out the window.

Phim sat down at the table and focused on the books.

Ketekete came into the cottage perched on Tasselis's shoulders. The parrot had briefly explained to the dryad the urgency of being in the cottage, but she looked askance at the apprentice mage. She had not forgotten her argument with him* but Arté explained it more carefully.

Arté made supper for them all and they settled down for a long evening. One by one they fell asleep in the comfort of the main room.

Except Phim. He spent all night researching every book, tome, volume and pamphlet that dealt with doppelgängers and, despite the different incantations, gestures, runes, symbols, and sigils, they followed the same process. An Evocation spell. Phim closed his eyes and steeled himself for what he had to do.

Just before dawn, he went to the pantry and got a large potato. He carved it up and made a doll, dressed with a scrap of his tunic and trousers material. He cut off a lock of his hair and fixed it on the doll's head.

---

[103] a ragged or contemptible person (or thing)

Then he woke up Ketekete and instructed, telepathically, what she should do. And, politely, asked for another tail feather. The parrot gladly acceded. Phim got his gear together in a backpack, woke up Arté with a kiss, waved goodbye to Tasselis and left the cottage.

Two minutes later Phim* came in from the forest. He* clapped his hands lustily. 'C'mon! C'mon! Wakey, wakey you snivelling worms. Back to work. And you – ' he* looked fixedly at Arté – 'make the fire. That bastard Koan is still missing. Maybe you know about that, greeny? Ah – you'll keep.'

Arté shrugged and made for the fire place.

But Ketekete drew herself up to her full height and spoke up.
'You can't talk like that to our friend. Apologise now!' Her wings fluttered menacingly.

'You're threatening me? I should hex you. Maybe I should make you think you're a chicken. We could use the eggs. Ha, ha, ha!' Phim* sneered and laughed nastily.

Ketekete flew up, dodged around the flailing arms of the apprentice mage* and grabbed a lock of his* hair, roots and all, and made off with it, out the window. Phim* launched another mug at the window. It was not well aimed and it smashed on the lintel. 'Ow! Ow! Ow! Bother that bird! I'll get her later,' Phim* complained loudly.
He looked around to Arté who was laughing quietly behind her hand, and he ordered her to clean up the mess.

She went around the table to the window and Phim* slapped her on her rump, leering lasciviously at her. She cleared away the broken mug as he* went to the kitchen bench and made a breakfast feast of fruit salad – sliced pears, apples, nashi, kiwifruit, and various seeds and nuts.

'There,' he* said softly, 'sweet dreams for you all.' He* put the bowl in the middle of the table.

Suddenly, Phim* stood bolt upright. He* was about to leave the room but his* legs and arms refused to move. They were stuck to his* body. A panicked look came over his* face as Ketekete marched into the room, followed by Seraphim. The potato doll was in his left hand and a lock of Phim*'s hair bound the doll's arms and legs. Before Phim* could do anything Seraphim gagged the mouth of the doll with his right hand.

He approached the doppelgänger, drew himself up to his full height just as an inspired thought for the instructions for the spell – the feather, the music – lodged in his mind and he knew it was absolutely right. According to the inspired instruction, Seraphim laid down the doll and the feather. He gestured with his joined hands, muttered an incantation and a scarlet light like a knife edge or a laser split the feather in two. Seraphim held the two halves together in each of his hands.

He approached Phim* until he was just a breath away, and sang a plaintive melody through the feathers. The penultimate phrase was a melody that rose higher and higher. Seraphim placed the right half-feather in his breast pocket. The last phrase was the inverse: it dropped further and further into the earth.

Seraphim picked up the doll again and placed the left half-feather on its clothing, under the binding lock of hair.
He intoned: Această imitație falsă a mea, copia mea în formă și manierisme, te voi distruge și nu te vei mai deranja.[104]
Then, with a flourish, he threw the doll into the fire.

---

[104] This fake imitation of me, my copy in form and mannerisms, I will destroy you and you will not bother us any more.

The fire flared up into deep crimson and indigo purple flames. A flash of sparkling red light and sparks almost blinded them all and a thunderous roar knocked everything off the table.

Phim, Ketekete, Arté and Tasselis blinked at the fire. The doll was consumed and the flames had gone out. They turned at the same time to see what had happened to the doppelgänger. Its form was hideous to look at, the head and shoulders were bubbling like a vile porridge, the eyes, nose and mouth were floating in the brown sludge of the skin, the arms and legs were melting and the torso seemed like a deflated ball its clothes. In thirty seconds, the whole thing collapsed. A glow of red in the middle of the mess, grew and incandescent flames burst out of it. In ten seconds, the whole thing was gone leaving only a foul odour and a stain on the floor.

The four friends gaped at the scene stunned.

Suddenly Koan burst through the door. 'What happened? What happ…' He looked at Phim and rage overtook him. 'You wanted to murder me. I'll…' He stepped towards Phim and was flattened by an oak branch that came up under his chin.

Actually, it was Tasselis arm. She cradled the stunned wolfman in her arms and led him outside, saying to the others: 'I will catch him up about everything.'

'I didn't… I shouldn't have… I described…destroyed him… !' Phim sat at the table. 'Yes … he was a money…monitor…monster but…' He buried his face in his hands.
Arté gripped his shoulders. She didn't say anything – she knew what he was feeling.

Phim sighed. 'I am…fairy…faint. So hunter…hundred…hungry. I haven't eager…eaten for a while…' and he tucked into the fruit salad, seeds and nuts on the table.

In his mind he telepathically communicated with Ketekete: *My speech is rubbish. Thank goodness I can talk to you. That was close. Thank you for the hair. It made all the difference. It trapped him. Otherwise he would have run away.*

Not a problem. That's what partners are for.

Actually, I still mucked up the words again. I practised the spells over and over and still I mucked them up.

What did you mean to say?

I wanted to say: Această imitație falsă a mea, copia mea în formă și manierisme, pleacă în pace și nu mai deranjează. It means: 'This fake imitation of me, my copy in form and mannerisms, depart in peace and bother no more.' I didn't mean to destroy him.

Arté sat down beside Phim and held his hand. 'Well done. You are a wonder. I know you wanted to preserve life, but that thing – it was an evil monster.'

'Yes, okay,' he said tentatively, 'but my works… worried…words where munip…man…munched…Argh!'

'Okay, okay,' Arté soothed him. 'It was a brute. Corrupting our friendship and love for each other. The doppelgänger was vile. It didn't deserve to live.' Arté couldn't help herself: 'Just like Felicia.'
'Yes,' Phim conceded. 'Yes… but she could realise…recognise…re-form. Okay – she didn't and the trust…true…truth found her out. But …she …re-form…Oh! Ohhh! Ahhhh!'

Phim dropped to the floor. He was convulsing. His skin was chilly and his face was a terrible shade of grey. Arté lifted him up to a seated position. The pupils in his eyes were dilated.

Ketekete flapped around on the table. *What's wrong? What's wrong?* she thought to him, but he was not answering.

Arté had a sudden thought. She looked at his hands. The right hand was normal. The left hand was white with black veins across the surface. She lifted his left sleeve and the black veins were slowly creeping up his arm. Arté thought about Phim*, slicing and preparing the dish for the table and saying: 'sweet dreams for you all.' Poison. Poison! He* intended poison Arté and Ketekete, but Phim got the fruit salad first.

The black veins were at the shoulder. With no hesitation, Arté exposed her sharp incisors and bit the vein at the shoulder. She sucked the poison out, spitting it on the floor where it smoked and smouldered.

Ketekete was aghast, but not by Arté's actions. It was the vision she witnessed: Arté biting Phim's neck. Not for his blood, but to save him.

Phim stopped convulsing. His eyes returned to normal, his face, hands and arms returned to their normal colour. He looked at Arté. She looked at him. The distractions that had been obscuring their emotions were stripped away. He sat up, gazed at her and said with a heartfelt, tender passion: 'I love you!'

'And I love you!' Arté burst out. She reached to hug him. 'Love… you…love…you…' as she collapsed convulsing on the floor, her skin a ghostly shade of olive. Her eyes dilated and rolled up into her head. She was cold, and her limbs were tense, her hands in fists. Phim cradled her in his arms. 'No, no!' he cried in anguish.

At that moment, Tasselis and Koan burst through the main door, panic stricken. Together they cried: 'Dragon! Dragon!'

A terrible roar rose up around them. Ketekete looked up and saw a darkness descending on the cottage and a hurricane wind battered the forest. She ducked her head under her wing. The thatched roof ignited and the hurricane-wind blew all the ashes away from the room below. Tasselis and Koan cowered on the floor. Ketekete hesitantly peered up at the opening where the roof once was. A dragon was hovering above: its horned head with diamond-like intelligent eyes, its mouth like a trapdoor with razor-sharp fangs, limbs and talons reaching out to the building below, its red and orange hide had triangular crenelations above its spine with a serpents tail behind purple and red diaphanous wings. A fearsome sight.

Phim! Phim! Ketekete screamed telepathically at her partner. *A dragon! Save us. You have to save us.*
But Phim was focused on his lovely Arté and didn't hear the chaos around them.

The dragon looked up and roared again.
A spout of flame lit up the sky.

Then it turned and looked at the scene below.

And spoke.

Chapter 15:
Rescue, Revelation…

'Well, well, well. What have we got here? Hmmm?'

The voice seemed familiar to Ketekete.
Phim turned and looked in amazement.

As the dragon descended it seemed to shrink. The wings and tail disappeared like mist in the sunshine. The red and orange hide coalesced into some sort of material. The limbs decompressed. One had a staff and a blue crystal in its claw. The jaw dwindled, a nose emerged and the horns melted into fiery red hair and beard. But the same diamond-like intelligent eyes drew you in like a hypnotising whirlpool.

Luxima Aerolaness stepped from the table onto the floor. Immediately he focused on Arté. 'What's going on? She's convulsing.' He touched her skin: 'And cold? What's happened?'

Phim shook himself out of his stupor and said: 'Poison. She shuttle… shurt-le…sucker…Argh!' he cursed with frustration. Ketekete took up the commentary.
'She sucked the poison out of Phim's shoulder, and spat it on the floor, but it seems to have poisoned her too. It was from this fruit salad.' Ketekete indicated the dish on the table.

Luxima sniffed the salad, and bent down, touched and sniffed the discarded poison on the floor. He got three ingredients from the pantry, mixed them with some wine in a small bowl.
He went to Phim and said: 'Get her to take sips of this mixture. Now!'

Phim held the bowl to her lips. 'C'mon Arté. Sip that…there..this. For me. For us.'

At the same time, Luxima closed his eyes, held his left arm out to the side with the blue crystal at the top of his staff winking in the sunlight and incanted a sentence, repeatedly.

The vampire sipped the liquid from the bowl. Gradually her convulsing ceased, her limbs relaxed, her colour became a healthy green again. She took a deep breath and opened her eyes. Seeing Phim's anxious gaze she hugged him as if they were long lost lovers reunited after a long separation. In a way, they were.

Ketekete said sotto voce: 'Tikina he ruma[105].'

At last they rose, joined hands and faced the wizard.

Luxima took a deep breath. He looked at Phim up and down. 'Well – you have been on a journey! And your friends too.' He eyeballed Arté and then turned and looked at Koan and Tasselis who were standing by the main door, gobsmacked. Then he looked at Ketekete, and spoke to Phim: 'And you're familiar with your familiar?'
'Partners!' Phim and Ketekete spoke at the same time.

'But…' Phim carried on. 'But where have you bent…being…been. It has bent…been moon…moths…months. What…why…when….'

'I thought I might cramp your style,' the wizard said breezily. 'I had faith in you. And, I see it was justified. You have grown much more than I ever expected. But…let's sit down and relax, hmmm?'
'It is a bit al fresco,' said Ketekete saucily.

---

105 Get a room.

'Of course!' Luxima gestured with his staff and crystal and said a few words. Rafters sprang out of the walls, thatch magically appeared and below, insulated panels covered the ceiling. The five friends were astounded.

Koan said it all for them: 'What…?'
'I do that periodically. The dragon thing. I often need to renew my thatch.'

'About that,' said the dryad. 'You are a dragon? Or a wizard? Or…'
'What's the difference?' Luxima said breezily. 'I can be anything I want. But "wizard" is usual when I deal with humans. I changed to a dragon because I knew something was going on there and I didn't know if my boy could cope with it. Although, I see you did. But, I was glad I could help with this …um…vegetarian vampire.'

'How dough…does…did…. Argh!' Phim balled his hands into fists with frustration. 'My brain has the ripe…ripeno…rite…right words by his…mine…my moon…mouse…moth..mouth refer…ref…refuses to said…saw…say them…and I…I…I…'
Phim doubled up, fell to his knees and collapsed.

Arté dropped down beside him, holding him up. Luxima bent down with concern etched on his face. 'Gather him up. Get him onto his bed,' he cried. Arté picked Phim up like a doll and in a heartbeat he was lying on his bed. Luxima sat at the foot of the bed. Arté was stroking Phim's hair and whispering: 'Okay. Okay. We got you. It will be okay.'

Ketekete, Koan and Tasselis were stationed about the bedroom door. Ketekete spoke to the wizard. 'His words are getting worse. Before he mucked up words every five minutes. Now, it is almost every sentence. Every phrase. He mucked up the words in his spells, but…well, that…'

'Okay, okay,' the wizard interrupted. 'Let me think.' Luxima shifted his feet into a balanced stance. 'I should have done this before. I thought it was a – well, verbal glitch. An adolescent thing he would grow out of. No. No. Something else…'

He gripped his arms together with the staff between them. He intoned a sentence under his breath, and then, supporting his right hand with his left, he touched Phim's body with the blue crystal on the top of his staff eight times: each ankle, each hip, each shoulder, mouth and forehead. At each spot the blue crystal lit up the room with a brilliance. No! One spot had the opposite effect. When he touched the crystal on Phim's forehead, the light dimmed and grew grey.

Luxima went to the other side of Phim's head, opposite Arté. He detached the blue crystal from the staff and delicately pointed with it to several places on Phim's skull. Again, the crystal shone with a brilliant light until it dimmed to grey in one place, just above his left ear. Phim whimpered, and his breathing became shallow. Arté pressed her head to Phim's, kissed him on his forehead and continued her mantra: 'It will be okay. We got you.'

The wizard rose and said to himself, out loud, so everyone heard his diagnosis: 'There is a tumour in his brain. It has been affecting his speech – all the misplaced, misremembered words. He has a form of aphasia. The tumour is pressing on his brain.' Luxima pummelled his right hand into his left palm. 'Ah – I missed it. I should have done…'

Rapidly he left the bedroom, scattering the onlookers, and crossed to his cabinet on the far wall. A whispered word and a gesture with his staff and the cabinet doors flew open. He rummaged inside and produced a red crystal, faceted at one end and tapering to a point at the other: a crystal dagger or a stiletto – a thing of beauty and danger. With a flick of his staff the cabinet door closed firmly as the wizard went to the table and sorted through his books. He found the one he wanted, read it quickly muttering to himself, and went back to Phim's room, scattering the onlookers again.

He knelt down beside Phim and brushed his hair away. Phim's breathing was still shallow and his wrinkled brow betrayed elements of pain. 'Arté, can you hold his head still,' he said gently. 'This could hurt.' The vampire looked at Luxima with alarm, and then nodded. She moved around and held his head in a loving but vice-like grip. 'Shhhh… We're here now. This is all going to be okay.'

Luxima rose again, pulled himself up to his full height and breathed deeply. He closed his eyes and raised the red crystal with his two hands above his head. With a whispered incantation he brought the crystal dagger down to the grey area on Seraphim's skull, point first. It didn't break the skin but hovered a hair's breadth from it. Perspiration broke out on Phim's forehead and he groaned. A distressed Arté looked at Luxima for reassurance, but the wizard was completely focused on the crystal.

A dirty grey fluid mass was emerging from Phim's skull attracted to the crystal's pointed end. When it reached the point it seemed to be consumed – the red crystal glowed and the fluid turned to gas that writhed around the point of the blade. By the time it reached Luxima's hands it floated off like a morning mist. All the while the wizard muttered his incantation.

At last the tumour was gone, and Phim relaxed into a deep slumber, breathing normally. Arté laid her head on his chest and sighed with relief. Luxima opened his eyes and rested a kindly gaze on the two lovers. Koan and Tasselis, holding hands, were heartened by the outcome. Ketekete marched along the floor and climbed up onto the foot of the bed. If she could sigh, she would have sighed too. 'Well,' she said jokingly, 'someone wants all the attention!'

Leaving the sleeping Phim in Arté care, the others went back to the dining room.

Phim woke thirty minutes later. He breathed deeply and let it out with a whoosh! Arté, who was dozing on his chest, fell off the bed. Phim sat up quickly. 'Where's Luxima? Where has he been all this time? And a dragon? What's the deal with a dragon? And why am I in bed? And why are you on the floor Arté? Can I help you up?'

Arté was astonished. Phim's words were fine. No stuttering, no misspoken words. She laid back down on the floor and laughed and laughed.

At last Arté explained what had happened, and they went out to the main room. Tasselis and Koan were sitting comfortably on the floor. Very comfortably. Ketekete was tucking into a snack of seeds and nuts. And Luxima was tidying his books, tomes, volumes and pamphlets.

They all looked at Phim and Arté.
The two lovers seemed to be encircled in an orange, yellow and red halo.

Phim gazed at Luxima steadily. He had so many questions for his mentor, but it boiled down to one word: 'Why?'

Luxima sat down and invited the two of them to do the same.

'Why did I go away for so long? Why did I leave you? Why did I leave you to do your own thing? Why did I leave you to face danger and death?' He shrugged. 'I knew you would find a way. I trusted that you would find your way.'

'Why?' said Phim again, and Luxima knew it was another question entirely.

'I trust my staff and the blue crystal. When I saw you first at the monastery, the blue crystal gave me an image of your potential. It has always done that, despite your bungling efforts in the last two years. Unfortunately it is an imperfect communication. I didn't realise that your chaotic language was a medical condition. I thought it was youthful exuberance and you would grow out of it. But, my crystal is never wrong. I realised that I was in the way, that I should give you a chance for your own magical expression. So I left.'

'Why?' said Phim. Again, Luxima knew it was another question. He decided to prevaricate. He hopped up and gestured to the door.

'Come outside,' he entreated. 'Come, come, come….'

Phim was getting his floppy hat from the door, but the wizard placed his hand on the coatrack and said: 'No. Don't do that. Come outside…'

Phim was puzzled, but complied. The others followed. They sat in the sunlit garden on the outdoor chairs. Luxima stared at Phim. 'Your eyes are quite black with red and orange highlights. See?' He turned to Arté and Ketekete. Koan and Tasselis looked on.

'When I first met you, your hair was a rusty red. When I left you, it was a dusky carmine. Now…' Phim drew a lock of his hair and looked at it closely. Not tucked up in his floppy hat but in the sunlight. His hair was a brilliant shade of crimson with gold and orange highlights.

'And – aha!' the wizard continued, playfully. 'What is happening to your forehead, cheeks and neck – hmmm.'

Phim couldn't see, but the amazement of the others piqued his curiosity. 'What? What?' he said, anxiously.

There was a look of wonder on Arté's face. 'Your freckles?' she said, dazed. 'They are all sorts of metallic colours: gold, silver, crimson, aquamarine… They are – glorious.'

'And his shadow?' Luxima directed them to look. Phim was amazed to see that his shadow had a rainbow halo around it.

'When I met you at the monastery, I was amazed at your facility with music – singing, composing, arranging. You were quite remarkable. Have you developed your singing and composing in your spell-casting?'

'Well – I guess I have,' Phim admitted. 'It seemed to be the way to bond with Ketekete. And, the spells… Especially when I have to work important spells…' He faltered. He was recalling the way inspiration came to him when he had to make permanent changes, and the phrases and music he created with Ketekete's feathers…

Luxima had his arms outstretched with a gesture of supplication. 'Why?' he said. 'Why did I go away? Why did I trust you to find your way without me here? Why did I think you would be better without me directing your education? Why? Why? Why? The answer to all these questions is genetics.'

'What…?' Phim was astounded. 'You knew my mother? Or my father?'

'No, no, no,' he said rubbing his forehead. 'Genetics. Your race.'

Luxima drew a deep breath, spread his arms and hands and struck a "tah-dah" pose.

'You are an Aasimar!'

Chapter 16:

... and Recognition

The five friends' puzzlement echoed around them like a rubber ball in a squash court.

Phim eventually voiced the question in everyone's minds:
'What is an Aasimar?'

'Ah. I wasn't sure when I found you, but when you reached puberty' – the wizard used his fingers to list all the characteristics – 'One – your eyes are dark with brilliant highlights; Two – your hair is starkly coloured with highlights; Three – in the sun, your freckles have a metallic sheen; Four – your shadow has a halo; Five – you have a facility with singing and music; and Six – ah – I hope...'

Luxima placed his hands on Seraphim's shoulders, stared intently at him and in a low but forceful voice said: 'Answer me. Do you have visions or feelings that inspire or direct you when you are under pressure? For important spells?'

Phim gulped. 'Yes, yes,' he admitted, in a small voice. 'When I made a permanent spell, using Ketekete's feathers, I had a feeling – a vision I guess – of how to make the spell work, how to make it right. Something comes over me and directs my spell-casting.'

'Yes, yes!' Luxima cried. 'Typical Aasimar.' The wizard whooped, danced and spun, arms outstretched and faced towards the sky. The others was astonished.

Eventually, Luxima caught his breath and calmed down. Then he spoke again. 'As an Aasimar, you have an angelic guide – a deva. It can help

you, particularly for the important, permanent, spells. When you are under pressure.'
'But,' Phim said. 'I mucked up the words in my spells. I didn't say them right. I didn't say what I meant to say!'
'But, the outcome was good?' questioned the wizard. 'Yes?'
Phim nodded uncertainly, but the others nodded enthusiastically.

Luxima closed his eyes and breathed deeply. 'Your deva made sure your spells would be the best desired outcome. That's why your words were, as you say, "mucked up". Your deva made sure that you enabled a vegetarian vampire to get nourishment from the sun. You made a werewolf stop killing. You cured a hypochondriac dryad and a djinn from ADHD. You protected your friends from a foreign faerie, a witch and a doppelgänger. Your deva inspired you to make your musical incantations and the words you actually used. You should applaud your deva.'

Phim furrowed his brow. 'Hey! How do you know all this?' he asked suspiciously. 'How do you know about what I – we – were doing in the two and half months you were gone?'

'Ah – snapped,' Luxima chuckled. 'I left you on your own. I didn't say that I was not keeping an eye on you. And your friends. Maybe, some of the birds were overly-friendly? Maybe an owl, or a raven, or a,' – he nodded to Ketekete – 'a tūī?' He bent to whisper to the kākā: 'I'd love to be a tūī. They are so much fun.'

The wizard looked at the five friends and spread his arms welcomingly. 'Come on. Come back into the cottage. There are things I should tell you.'

When they were seated in the lounge or around the table, he focused his attention on Phim. 'I was keeping an eye on you and your friends outside, but in the cottage I have some – well, informers?' He pointed to the wooden dragon on top of the cabinet. The crystal eyes blinked. Luxima continued: 'Sure – I was looking out for you, but I didn't want to interfere. I wanted your Aasimar nature to come out. To blossom. I was almost going to step in with Felicia. She was a wicked, conniving witch – but you handled her well. Actually, better than me.'

'I didn't mean to kill her,' Phim pleaded.
'No, no, no.' The wizard asserted. 'You didn't kill her. You showed her the truth and it undid her. She was responsible, not you.'
'And what about the doppelgänger? I thought I was just making a spell to protect from him, but he was destroyed.'
'Yes, yes.That's why I came as a dragon, to help you. But you did what had to be done, with your deva's help. A doppelgänger is evil, the antithesis of your nature. It had to be destroyed.'

Luxima stepped over to the two youngsters and embraced them. 'I am so glad that I was here to help with Arté's poison, and your aphasia. Seraphim and Artémissa – you are a good team!'

Phim glanced at the wizard. 'Well? Am I your apprentice or have I graduated to be a mage?'

'Ah – that's the thing. Hmmm.' Luxima sat down again, his chin in his hand. He took a moment of contemplation and said, tangentially: 'Do you know the difference between a magician, a wizard and a sorcerer?'

The five friends shook their heads.

Luxima used another tack. He questioned Phim as if it was a final test. 'You know this world has eight deities. I know you know that from your time at the monastery, yes?'

Phim nodded, absentmindedly. It was his youthful catechism.

'Each of the deities has a connection to the eight realms of magic. Think about what you have done.' The wizard held up his left fist. 'Seraphim: what did you do with Arté when you sought to see the future for her. And incidentally, yours.'

'I used palm reading. And Phrenology. and Tarot Cards. And eventually I used a crystal ball. And that was accurate.' Phim looked sideways at Arté and nudged his elbow at her, fondly. 'She bit my shoulder to get the poison out.'

'1 - Divination.' Luxima raised the index finger on his left hand. 'Seeing things far off or in the future. And what did you do when you discovered that Arté was not nourished by your cooking?'

'I used a spell that was – well, it was meant to be a spell that Arté would be safe in the sun, rather than die, as vampires do. But I mucked up the words, and she is green now. The sunlight feeds her. I didn't mean to…'

'Doesn't matter. Your deva made sure of that.' Luxima had two fingers up. '2 - Transformation: turning one thing into something else. By the way, it is brilliant. Photosynthesis! I would never have thought of that solution. Bravo.' Luxima nodded to the vegetarian vampire. 'And green suits you.' Arté blushed, a deep ocean-green.

Again, the wizard focused on Seraphim.
'And, when you were threatened by a ravening, vicious, raging werewolf…' Luxima bent to the side, located Koan and apologised to him: 'Sorry – just making a point.' He continued: 'How did you protect your friends – Ketekete, Arté and yourself. And, incidentally, my cottage. What did you do?'

'I froze him, when the full moon rose. But, again I didn't mean…'

'Doesn't matter. It was inspired. I know that Koan appreciates what you have done for him. And – 3 - Abjuration. Protection magic.' Three fingers were raised.
'Tasselis was a different story. Hypochondriac and miserable.' He nodded to the dryad, snuggling up to Koan. 'You remember that?'
Tasselis beamed: 'I sure do!'
He turned and again, focused on Seraphim. 'What did you do?'

'I used a spell that made her realise that she was okay, she was healthy. But I bungled the words again and…'

'Nada! Doesn't matter. And a "Thank you" for your deva.' He displayed four fingers. '4 - Enchantment – dealing with charms. Now…Tahurangi, the foreign faerie. Sorry – ' The wizard nodded to Ketekete. 'I may have left my trace back there in Aotearoa when I recruited you.'
He focused on Seraphim. 'So – how did you get rid of him?'

'Well – Arté helped. She was a brilliant actress.'
'But what spells did you use?' The wizard was intent.
'Well – I used a charm to knock him out, and then a portal to send him back.'
'Yes, yes – Enchantment and Abjuration – but what did you do to make him think he was going home?'

'I made an illusion so he thought…'

Luxima raised one finger on his right hand. 'Aha! 5 - Illusion. Summon images and sounds to confuse your enemies. Perfect for him – he was an upstart. And what about Felicia Breedlove, that wicked but charming witch. I almost intervened. We have some…history.'

'I saw you!' Arté burst out. 'You were a black bird with a purple and red head. You were trying to reach us but something held you back. A force field or something.'
'Yes, well, I could have surmounted it – eventually – but, Seraphim, I saw you had a solution, of sorts.'

'Yes – Arté was immune to her wiles and she gave me, a sort of spell, that I never meant to use, but, it worked, I guess, …'

'Yep!' Luxima nodded enthusiastically. 'I knew it was a spell that you were … reluctant to use. But, as I said, your deva protected you. The words you actually used, deva inspired, were about truth, not destruction. The words you said transformed that spell into something that Felicia was actually responsible for.'

'How do you know…' Seraphim began and the realisation dawned. 'Ah – the mirror, the dragon, was another informant?'

The wizard nodded, bent down to the apprentice mage and in a low voice, said: 'And Felicia did say something to you…' Luxima rolled his eyes and indicated with his bushy eyebrows in the direction of the vampire. 'Love is the conqueror of us all, hmmm?'

Phim and Arté looked at each other and the vampire grasped his hand – tightly. This time, Phim blushed.
The wizard raised another finger on his right hand.
'6 - Necromancy: Mastery over death. Or truth? What about the jinnee. The shaita. The eblis. The djinn. The genie. What about Ru?'

'Again, Arté was instrumental in his affliction. The ADHD.'
'Actually ADADHD,' Ketekete chortled. 'Another Djinn's Attention Deficit Hyperactivity Disorder.' Luxima stared disapprovingly at the parrot. She shut up.

'But,' Luxima continued, 'before that, how did you know what you were dealing with? How did you know who was playing tricks on you?'

'Um, I used a – um –– "contact" spell, or a "request" spell to reveal what was going on.'

A third finger on his right hand was raised. '7 - Conjuration. Deals with summoning. And, we know what happened with the doppelgänger. Seriously Seraphim, it was a monster, and you had to do what you did. It was hard, I know.'

Seraphim looked at his shoes, took a deep breath and held it. Then he breathed out slowly. Luxima waited until Seraphim lifted his head and stared at him. Then he raised a fourth finger on his right hand and said: '8 - Evocation. Concerned with destruction. Righteous destruction!'

'You see what you have done. Eight deities – eight realms of magic. Divination, Transformation, Abjuration, Enchantment, Illusion, Necromancy, Conjuration, Evocation. You have mastered them all!

'I have never seen a magician who could master three or four realms of magic – most of them can use only two or three. Most of the wizards can cope with four or five. But eight is exceptional!

Luxima looked at Seraphim closely.
'What is the difference between a magician, a wizard and a sorcerer?

'Magicians usually have a wide range of magical abilities and can cast spells, summon creatures, and manipulate the elements. But only a few of the realms of magic are available to them.

'Wizards, like me, have a more scholarly or educated approach to magic. We study and learn magic through books and formal education.

Wizardry is the control of natural, ambient, magical forces that exist in the world. A wizard grows in power by learning more about magic and how to control it.'

Luxima rose from his seat, fixing Seraphim's eye with an intense stare.

'A sorcerer is also a magic user, but their power typically comes from within themselves. Sorcerers are born with an innate ability to tap into and control magic. Unlike wizardry, sorcery is the magic inherent in a person. It represents how strong they are and not how much they know about magic.

'Seraphim: you are an Aasimar – and you are just coming into your prime. In time, you will understand more about an angelic guide – your deva. As a wizard, I can help you direct your magic in the right direction, but you will surpass me. You will build on what I show you, improve it, and you will teach me. That's okay. I welcome it.'

Koan, Tasselis, Ketekete and Artémissa gathered around the wizard, gazing at Phim.

He rose too, and he seemed to have a gentle golden glow around his body.

Luxima bowed to him and said with deep reverence: 'You are not a mage at all. I name you – Sorcerer Seraphim Starfire!'

James Stephens

James was born in Aotearoa New Zealand. He was a teacher, actor, musician and music director, a journalist and event manager – as well as a husband, father and grandfather. He was a voracious reader, a fluent writer and confident speaker.

In 2015, he suffered a hemiparesis, a middle cerebral artery territory infarct. In a word, a stroke.
He collapsed, paralysed on his right side, and couldn't speak or write. The hospital intervention was rapid and his limbs were free but his speech was absent. He had/has aphasia.

Aphasia is the loss of a previously held ability to articulate ideas or comprehend spoken or written language, resulting from damage to the brain caused by injury or disease – in this case, a stroke.

With expert therapists in speech, music and eurhythmy he has re-invented himself. He has a positive and optimistic outlook, electing to view his stroke as a 'stroke of luck'.
But his speech is still – suspect.

"My aphasia forced me to look at my life differently. My expected biography has changed. Now, I am an author – apparently."

email: james.stephens.dms@gmail.com
facebook: https://bit.ly/3bH6kZr

The Suspect Speaker Series - Reviews

The Suspect Speaker series is very unique and emotional, and the books are aphasia friendly! In each book author James Stephens presents a series of stories describing events with aphasia.

Most importantly, each story has three levels of reading to accommodate readers with aphasia: an easy level, an intermediate level, and a more advanced level. A perfect way to tell his stories and reach all people with aphasia. Highly recommended for readers with aphasia and their supporters and care partners.

Darlene Williamson, MA, CCC-SLP,
President National Aphasia Association-USA)

You have captured so many aspects of aphasia – feelings and symptoms – and the different journeys and experiences that people have, in such a rich and compelling way and from different perspectives.

Professor Suzanne C Purdy,
The University of Auckland

His stories are both moving and funny. They are also encouraging and uplifting. AphasiaNZ highly recommends Stephens's book to anyone with experience of aphasia.

AphasiaNZ

Very often, we hear what the protagonist is thinking, and wince at what happens when they try to get it out. It's a helpful device, but it's also Stephens's truth, and the truth for thousands of other New Zealanders hit by strokes or tumours, injuries or primary progressive aphasia.

Catherine Woulfe
Books editor | Spinoff

Stephens's writing will serve to be an inspirational therapeutic tool for many others living with Aphasia and their whānau/families. Thank you for sharing insights into what it is truly like to live with this hidden disability.

Naomi Bondi, NZSLTA
New Zealand Speech Language Teachers Association

The stories draw the reader in to moments of real life with compassion, keen observation, and empathy. I would highly recommend them to anyone looking for short stories that are straightforward to read and highly engaging, and to those with lived experience of communication difficulties and changes. I would also highly recommend this book to those in health and social services who work with those with aphasia and other communication difficulties as these stories provide a fantastic insight into the experiences of someone with aphasia.

Robyn Gibson, NZSLTA
New Zealand Speech Language Teachers Association

www.ingramcontent.com/pod-product-compliance
Lightning Source LLC
Chambersburg PA
CBHW020641120726
47906CB00001B/78

* 9 7 8 1 0 6 7 0 7 4 7 2 2 *